Continuing
Mandarin
Chinese

*The Complete Language Course
for Intermediate Learners*

CORNELIUS C. KUBLER, Ph.D

TUTTLE Publishing

Tokyo | Rutland, Vermont | Singapore

Published by Tuttle Publishing, an imprint of
Periplus Editions (HK) Ltd.

www.tuttlepublishing.com

Copyright © 2020 Cornelius C. Kubler
All photos © Cornelius C. Kubler except for:
Front cover: © Rawpixel.com/Shutterstock.com;
© G-Stock Studio/Shutterstock.com

Library of Congress Cataloging-in-Publication Data is
in process

ISBN 978-0-8048-5138-1

Distributed by

North America, Latin America & Europe
Tuttle Publishing
364 Innovation Drive
North Clarendon
VT 05759-9436 U.S.A.
Tel: 1 (802) 773-8930
Fax: 1 (802) 773-6993
info@tuttlepublishing.com
www.tuttlepublishing.com

Asia Pacific
Berkeley Books Pte. Ltd.
3 Kallang Sector #04-01
Singapore 349278
Tel: (65) 6741-2178
Fax: (65) 6741-2179
inquiries@periplus.com.sg
www.periplus.com

25 24 23 22 21 20
10 9 8 7 6 5 4 3 2 1

Printed in Singapore   2007TP

THE TUTTLE STORY
"Books to Span the East and West"

Our core mission at Tuttle Publishing is to create books which bring people together one page at a time. Tuttle was founded in 1832 in the small New England town of Rutland, Vermont (USA). Our fundamental values remain as strong today as they were then—to publish best-in-class books informing the English-speaking world about the countries and peoples of Asia. The world has become a smaller place today and Asia's economic, cultural and political influence has expanded, yet the need for meaningful dialogue and information about this diverse region has never been greater. Since 1948, Tuttle has been a leader in publishing books on the cultures, arts, cuisines, languages and literatures of Asia. Our authors and photographers have won numerous awards and Tuttle has published thousands of books on subjects ranging from martial arts to paper crafts. We welcome you to explore the wealth of information available on Asia at **www.tuttlepublishing.com**.

Free Bonus Material may also be Downloaded.

How to Download the Bonus Material of this Book.

1. You must have an internet connection.
2. Type the URL below into to your web browser.

   https://www.tuttlepublishing.com/
   continuing-mandarin-chinese-textbook

For support email us at
info@tuttlepublishing.com.

Contents

Preface 4

LESSON 1   **Getting Around Taipei** 5

LESSON 2   **Asking Directions to a Friend's House** 15

LESSON 3   **Shopping** 27

LESSON 4   **Buying Vegetables and Fruits** 38

LESSON 5   **At the Market** 48

LESSON 6   **Purchasing Shoes and Clothing** 58

LESSON 7   **Ordering a Meal in a Restaurant** 70

LESSON 8   **Arranging a Banquet** 80

LESSON 9   **Peking Duck** 90

LESSON 10   **More Peking Duck and Making Dumplings** 100

LESSON 11   **Eating with a Colleague in a Restaurant** 112

LESSON 12   **A Dinner Party at Home** 123

LESSON 13   **On the Telephone** 136

LESSON 14   **Calling About an Ad for an Apartment** 147

LESSON 15   **Visiting a Friend at Home** 158

LESSON 16   **Calling on Someone to Request a Favor** 168

LESSON 17   **Visiting a Sick Classmate** 180

LESSON 18   **A Farewell Call on a Favorite Teacher** 191

LESSON 19   **Hobbies** 202

LESSON 20   **Going to the Movies** 212

LESSON 21   **Talking About Sports** 222

LESSON 22   **Soccer and an Excursion to the Great Wall** 234

LESSON 23   **Emergencies (I)** 245

LESSON 24   **Emergencies (II)** 257

Chinese-English Vocabulary 269

Preface

This book, which is a concise, streamlined, combined version of the author's *Intermediate Mandarin Chinese: Speaking & Listening* and *Intermediate Mandarin Chinese: Reading & Writing* (Tuttle Publishing 2013, 2015), will help learners bring their Mandarin Chinese proficiency from the elementary to the intermediate level. It assumes mastery of the material in *Elementary Mandarin Chinese* and *Elementary Mandarin Chinese Workbook* (both Tuttle Publishing 2019) or a similar beginning-level textbook.

This book was designed for an intermediate level course in Mandarin Chinese that meets three hours a week for one academic year. In addition to time in class, students will need to prepare approximately two to three hours for each class hour. This textbook should be used with the accompanying *Continuing Mandarin Chinese Workbook* (Tuttle Publishing 2020), which is available separately, and with the accompanying audio files, which can be downloaded directly from the Tuttle Publishing website.

In a college or university environment, it is recommended that this textbook be taught at the rate of approximately one lesson per week. Each lesson is divided into two parts, so Part One could be taken up on the first class day each week and Part Two on the second day, with the third day being used for review, testing, and supplemental activities. Since it would take 24 weeks to go through the materials at this rate but most institutions schedule 25-35 weeks of instruction per academic year, this would still leave some time for other activities, or else allow for a somewhat slower rate of progress through the materials, if desired. The exact schedule and rate of progress will, of course, need to be determined based on local conditions.

Each part of each lesson in this book includes a conversation, lists of new and supplementary vocabulary, notes on the conversation, and a section specifically on reading (which in turn consists of new characters and words, sentences, conversations, narratives, and notes). Since Pinyin is included everywhere except in the reading exercises, the book is usable even by learners who wish to focus on speaking and listening.

I wish to acknowledge here the following, who have been particularly helpful in the preparation and publication of these materials: Nancy Goh, Jerling G. Kubler, Qunhu Li, Eric Oey, Amory Shih, Yang Wang, and Jun Yang.

Cornelius C. Kubler
Department of Asian Studies, Williams College and
Institute for Advanced Studies, Shaanxi Normal University

LESSON 1
Getting Around Taipei

PART ONE

Conservation

Situation: Sandra Russell, an American graduate student in Taipei, hails a taxi for herself and a friend.

1. RUSSELL: 麻烦到重庆南路的台湾银行，谢谢。
   Máfan dào Chóngqìng Nán Lùde Táiwān Yínháng, xièxie.
   Please go to the Bank of Taiwan on Chongqing South Road, thanks.

2. DRIVER: 你的国语说得不错哦！在哪里学的？
   Nǐde Guóyǔ shuōde bú cuò ó! Zài náli xuéde?
   You speak Mandarin really well! Where did you learn it?

3. RUSSELL: 我在美国、大陆跟台湾都学过。
   Wǒ zài Měiguo, dàlù gēn Táiwān dōu xuéguo.
   I studied it in America, mainland China, and Taiwan.

4. DRIVER: 你来台湾多久了？
   Nǐ lái Táiwān duō jiǔ le?
   How long have you been in Taiwan?

5. RUSSELL: 来了三个多月了。哎哟！你开得太快了，吓死人了！可不可以开慢一点？

Láile sān'ge duō yuè le. Āiyò! Nǐ kāide tài kuàile, xiàsǐ rén le! Kě bu kéyi kāi màn yìdiǎn?

I've been here for more than three months. Whew! You're driving too fast, that was terrifying! Could you slow down a bit?

6. DRIVER: 没问题，放心啦。前面就到了。

Méi wèntí, fàngxīn la. Qiánmiàn jiù dàole.

No problem, relax. It's up ahead.

7. RUSSELL: 多少钱？

Duōshǎo qián?

How much is it?

8. DRIVER: 九十五块。

Jiǔshiwǔkuài.

95 NT.

9. RUSSELL: 一百块，不用找了。

Yìbǎikuài, bú yòng zhǎole.

Here's 100 NT, keep the change.

10. DRIVER: 谢谢。

Xièxie.

Thanks.

New Vocabulary

重庆	**Chóngqìng**	Chongqing (city in Sichuan)
重庆南路	**Chóngqìng Nán Lù**	Chongqing South Road
银行	**yínháng**	bank
台湾银行	**Táiwān Yínháng**	Bank of Taiwan
国语	**Guóyǔ**	Mandarin (language)
哦	**ó**	(indicates interest or excitement)
大陆	**dàlù**	mainland
了	**le**	(indicates action continuing up to the present)
吓	**xià**	frighten
吓死	**xiàsǐ**	frighten to death
慢	**màn**	be slow
问题	**wèntí**	problem
没问题	**méi wèntí**	there is no problem, "no problem"
放心	**fàngxīn**	be at ease, relax
啦	**la**	(combined form of le and a)

Supplementary Vocabulary

要緊	yàojǐn	be important
不要緊	bú yàojǐn	be unimportant; "never mind"
坐	zuò	sit in/on; take; by (car, train, boat, airplane)
計程車	jìchéngchē	taxi
解決	jiějué	solve

Notes on the Conversation

Imperatives consisting of Verb + Stative Verb + yidian(r)

In utterance 5, look at **Kāi màn yidian** "Drive more slowly." This is a common way to tell someone how to do something. More examples: **Kāi kuài yidianr** "Drive a little faster," **Zǒu màn yidianr** "Walk more slowly," **Shuō qīngchu yidian** "Speak more clearly."

....

Le to indicate time continuing up through the present

Look at the question **Nǐ lái Táiwān duō jiǔ le?** "How long have you been in Taiwan?" and the answer **Wǒ láile sān'ge duō yuè le** "I've been here for more than 3 months." A **le** at the end of a sentence containing a time expression indicates that the action of the verb has been continuing for a period of time up to and including the present. Examples: **Wǒ xué Rìyǔ xuéle liùge yuè le** "I've been studying Japanese for 6 months," **Lǎo Liú chīfàn chīle sān'ge zhōngtóu le!** "Old Liu has been eating for 3 hours!," **Xiǎo Wáng jiéhūn liǎngnián duō le** "Little Wang has been married for more than 2 years." Be careful to distinguish sentences that have only a verb **-le** from those that have both a verb **-le** and a **le** at the end of the sentence. Contrast: **Tā zài nèijiā màoyì gōngsī gōngzuòle wǔnián** "She worked at that trading company for 5 years" vs. **Tā zài nèijiā màoyì gōngsī gōngzuòle wǔnián le** "She's been working at that trading company for 5 years."

....

Accented Mandarin

The driver in the conversation doesn't speak standard Mandarin; his Mandarin is accented through influence from his native language, Taiwanese. Speakers from many parts of mainland China and Taiwan use non-standard pronunciation. Common features of non-standard Mandarin include: (1) **zh-**, **ch-**, and **sh-** may lose the **h** to become **z-**, **c-**, and **s-** so that **zhū** "pig" sounds like **zū** "rent" and **shān** "mountain" sounds like **sān** "three;" (2) **-ing** and **-eng** may lose the final **g** to become **-in** and **-en** so that **xìn** "letter" and **xìng** "surname" sound the same; and (3) the distinction between **l-** and **n-** may be lost so that **lán** "blue" and **nán** "difficult" sound the same. Tones may also differ from standard Mandarin and there may be less use of final **-r**. Even when these distinctions are lost, context usually makes the meaning clear. As your Chinese language experience increases, you'll gradually get used to common accented Mandarin pronunciations.

....

Reading

New Characters and Words[1]

289.	快	**kuài**	be fast, quick; soon, quickly
290.	慢	**màn**	be slow
	慢走	**màn zǒu**	"take care"
291.	题	**tí**	topic; problem
	问题	**wèntí**	question; problem
	没问题	**méi wèntí**	"no problem"
292.	放	**fàng**	put; let go, set free
	放心	**fàngxīn**	relax
293.	解	**jiě**	loosen
294.	决	**jué**	decide (can't be used alone)
	解决	**jiějué**	solve, resolve
	决定	**juédìng**	decide, determine; decision

A. SENTENCES

一、高老师，我能问您一个问题吗？

二、我觉得我们一定要快一点儿解决这个问题。

三、你的同屋没什么问题，你可以放心了。

四、解放前我表哥是一位小学老师，解放后他换了工作。

五、刚刚是谁开的门？请你快一点儿关上门，好不好？

六、校长，请您放心，这个问题很快就会解决的。

七、这么多的问题，你太慢了，快一点儿，我忙死了！

八、这家公司的东西贵死了，我们快去别家吧！

九、小何很喜欢中国，所以决定以后要到中国去住。

十、王大海气死了，他有很多问题，朋友也不给他解决。

B. CONVERSATIONS

一、

方先生：老林，你决定什么时候去成都了吗？

林先生：我还没决定，但是我大概下个月去。

方先生：你去四川一定得小心一点儿！

林先生：放心，不会有问题的。

---

1. The character numbers in this volume continue on from *Elementary Mandarin Chinese*, which introduced characters number 1-288.

二、

边美生：金金，你能给我解决一个问题吗？
王金金：那我得先知道是什么样儿的问题，对不对？
边美生：我表妹明天晚上要从上海来。她叫我去机场等她，但是我明
天有事。你能不能到机场去等她呢？
王金金：没问题，你放心好了，我一定去。她明天几点到？
边美生：六点三刻。
王金金：那么，我就六点半到机场等她吧。
边美生：金金，真谢谢你了！
王金金：没事儿。

C. NARRATIVES

我姐姐快要三十岁了，我也已经二十五岁了。时间实在过得太快了！还记得小的时候，我觉得三十岁一定很老，但是现在觉得三十岁不一定那么老。其实，有很多事我还不太清楚，也有很多问题我还没解决。不过我已经长大了，要决定的事，还是早一点决定吧。

Notes

A5.　关上门 "close the door"

A6.　这个问题很快就会解决的 "This problem will be solved soon." The pattern 会⋯⋯的 means "be likely to" or "will" and expresses the writer's conviction that something will most likely be a certain way.

A8.　别家 here stands for 别家公司 "another company."

A10.　气死 qìsǐ "become extremely angry"

B1.　不会有问题的 "There won't be (any) problems."

C1.　时间实在过得太快了 "Time really passes too quickly."

C2.　要决定的事，还是早一点决定吧 literally, "The matters that should be decided, on reflection it would be better to decide them a little earlier." A more idiomatic translation might be "I'd better decide the things that need to be decided as soon as possible." Note that 要 here means "need to," "should."

Bank of Taiwan headquarters on Chongqing South Road in Taipei

PART TWO

Conversation 🎧

Situation: Elizabeth Brill, an American who is teaching English for a year at a language school in Taiwan, wants to find out which bus to take to get to Muzha, a suburb of Taipei.

1. BRILL: *(asks a passerby)*

请问，到木栅去要坐几号？

Qǐng wèn, dào Mùzhà qù yào zuò jǐhào?

Excuse me, what number bus do you take to get to Muzha?

2. PASSERBY: 哎呀，我好久没坐公车了，不晓得。你到对面的统一去问问看。要不然，你也可以坐捷运去木栅。

Āiyà, wǒ hǎo jiǔ méi zuò gōngchē le, bù xiǎode. Nǐ dào duìmiànde Tǒngyī qù wèn-wen kàn. Yàoburán, nǐ yě kéyi zuò jiéyùn qù Mùzhà.

Gosh, I haven't taken a bus for a long time, I don't know. Go to the 7-Eleven across the street and ask. Or you could also take the MRT to Muzha.

3. BRILL: *(asks the clerk at a 7-Eleven)*

请问，到木栅去要坐几号？

Qǐng wèn, dào Mùzhà qù yào zuò jǐhào?

Excuse me, what number bus do you take to get to Muzha?

4. CLERK: 二三六或是二三七都可以到。

Èr-sān-liù huòshi èr-sān-qī dōu kéyi dào.

You can get there on 236 or 237.

5. BRILL: 大概多久一班？

Dàgài duō jiǔ yìbān?

About how often is there a bus?

6. CLERK: 二三七比较久。二三六好像五分钟一班，很快的啦。

Èr-sān-qī bǐjiào jiǔ. Èr-sān-liù hǎoxiàng wǔfēn zhōng yìbān, hěn kuàide la.

237 takes longer. For 236, I think there's a bus every five minutes, it won't be long.

7. BRILL: 谢谢。我顺便买一张三百块的储值票。

Xièxie. Wǒ shùnbiàn mǎi yìzhāng sānbǎikuàide chúzhípiào.

Thanks. While I'm at it, I'll buy a stored-value ticket for 300 NT.

8. CLERK: 哦，不好意思。三百块的卖完了。只剩下六百块的而已。

Ò, bù hǎo yìsi. Sānbǎikuàide màiwánle. Zhǐ shèngxia liùbǎikuàide éryǐ.

Oh, I'm sorry. The 300 NT ones are sold out. Only the 600 NT ones are left.

9. BRILL: 那我买一张六百块的吧。

Nà wǒ mǎi yìzhāng liùbǎikuàide ba.

Then I guess I'll buy a 600 NT one.

10. CLERK: 好。一共六百块。谢谢。

Hǎo. Yígòng liùbǎikuài. Xièxie.

All right. That's 600 NT in all. Thanks.

New Vocabulary

木栅	**Mùzhà**	Muzha (suburb of Taipei)
好	**hǎo**	very
公车	**gōngchē**	public bus
晓得	**xiǎode**	know
对面	**duìmiàn**	across
统一	**Tǒngyī**	7-Eleven® (name of store)
要不然	**yàoburán**	otherwise, or
捷运	**jiéyùn**	mass rapid transit, MRT
或是	**huòshi**	or
顺便	**shùnbiàn**	conveniently, in passing
储值票	**chúzhípiào**	stored-value ticket
不好意思	**bù hǎo yìsi**	be embarrassing, be embarrassed
完	**wán**	finish
卖完	**màiwán**	finish selling, be sold out
剩下	**shèngxia**	be left over

Supplementary Vocabulary

或	**huò**	or
地铁	**dìtiě**	subway
见	**jiàn**	see

奇怪	qíguài	be strange
梦	mèng	dream
做梦	zuòmèng	have a dream

Notes on the Conversation

Negative time spent

Take the sentence **Wǒ hǎo jiǔ méi zuò gōngchē le** "I haven't taken a bus for a long time." We learned previously that "time spent" expressions that tell for how long something happened come AFTER the verb. In this lesson we learn that "negative time spent" expressions that tell for how long something *hasn't* happened come BEFORE the verb. Contrast these pairs of sentences: **Wǒ xuéle sānnián le** "I've been studying it for three years" vs. **Wǒ sānnián méi xuéle** "I haven't studied it for three years"; and **Tā gōngzuòle sān'ge yuè** "She worked for three months" vs. **Tā sān'ge yuè méi gōngzuò le** "She hasn't worked for three months."

....

Number of times within a period of time

In lines 5-6, look at the question **Duō jiǔ yìbān?** "How often is there a bus?" and the response **Wǔfēn zhōng yìbān** "One every five minutes." To express the number of times something happens during a certain period of time, mention first the period of time you're talking about and then the number of times during that period. If there is a verb, it occurs in the middle. The pattern is: Period of Time + (Verb) + Number of Times. More examples: **yìnián qù sāncì** "go three times a year," **yíge yuè lái liǎngcì** "come twice a month."

....

The verb ending -wán to indicate completion or depletion

The verb construction **màiwán**, composed of the verb **mài** and the ending **wán**, means "sell with the result that everything is depleted" or "sell out." In English we often say we've finished something without specifying what it is, as in "I'm finished!"; but in Chinese, the action which has been finished is mentioned, so you'd have to say **Wǒ chīwánle wǔfàn** or **Wǒ kànwánle shū**. Some more examples with **-wán**: **Wǒ shuōwánle** "I've finished speaking," **Tā yǐjīng chīwánle** "She's already finished eating," **Wǒmen dōu zuòwánle** "We've finished doing all of it."

....

Reading

New Characters and Words

295.	久	jiǔ	be long (of time)
	好久	hǎo jiǔ	for a very long time
	多久	duō jiǔ	for how long?
296.	完	wán	finish, complete
	卖完	màiwán	finish selling, be sold out

	吃完	**chīwán**	finish eating
	说完话	**shuōwán huà**	finish talking
297.	或	**huò**	or
	或是	**huòshi**	or
298.	者	**-zhě**	person who does something
	记者	**jìzhě**	reporter, journalist
	作者	**zuòzhě**	author, writer
	或者	**huòzhě**	or
299.	再	**zài**	again, further, more
300.	见	**jiàn**	see
	再见	**zàijiàn**	"goodbye"
	好久不见	**hǎo jiǔ bú jiàn**	"long time no see"
	明天见	**míngtiān jiàn**	"see you tomorrow"

A. SENTENCES

一、我弟弟很久没说日本话了，大概已经忘了很多了。

二、老张那个人说一是一，说二是二，你别再问了。

三、我和我的小学六年级同学说了再见以后，就很久没再见到他们了。

四、原来你说还有很多公车票，怎么现在都卖完了？

五、你大概已经忘了我了吧？我们已经好久没见了。

六、你从公司给我打电话或者找一个公共电话给我打都可以。

七、饭也吃完了，东西也买完了，我们可以回家了。

八、你要是需要换钱的话，可以去机场或者比较大的饭店换。

九、这个地方天天下大雨或是毛毛雨，我们已经好久没见到太阳了。

十、我们等王大海已经等了好久了，但是他还没吃完晚饭，叫我们再
等他一会儿。

B. CONVERSATIONS

一、

老师：我叫你写的字你都写完了吗？

学生：都写完了。

老师：这个字写错了，请你再写一次。

二、

张老师：老李，好久不见了！

李老师：是，好久不见！

People waiting at a bus stop on Heping East Road in Taipei

张老师： 你准备什么时候去香港？

李老师： 我下个星期六或者星期天就要走了。

张老师： 你要去多久呢？

李老师： 还不知道，因为去了香港以后，还要去广州。

张老师： 是吗？ 时间不早了，我得先走了。明天见！

李老师： 再见！

C. NARRATIVES

一、小学五年级的时候，我有一个同学住在我们家对面。他是美国
人，但是中国话说得比中国人还好！小学六年级的时候，他和他
家人回美国去了，听说他们现在住在美国的西岸。我已经好久没
见到他了。不知道他最近怎么样，也不知道什么时候会再见到他。

二、我有一个朋友姓温，名字叫温安然。他现在是记者，住在我们家
对面，不过我很久没见到他了。老温是我以前上大学时候的同
屋，很喜欢买东西。有一次，他买了一个大钟。我问他："你为什
么要买那个钟？你家里不是已经有好几个钟了吗？"老温说他很需
要那个钟，别人家里都没有，买了以后只有他一个人有，所以一
定要买。还有一次，老温买了一个很贵的汽车。我问他："你为什
么要买那么贵的汽车？你真的需要吗？"老温说因为别人都有这样
的车，所以他不能不买。我真不知道说什么好。

Notes

A2.   说一是一，说二是二 literally, "Say one and it's one, say two and it's two" or, in idiomatic English, "Mean what you say" or "Stand by your word."

A3.   In this sentence, notice that the two 再见 have very different meanings. The first occurs in 说再见 "Say goodbye." The second occurs in 很久没再见到他们 "(I) didn't see them again for a long time."

B1.   You've learned 叫 in the sense of "be called" or "call." 叫 can also mean "tell (someone to do something)." Therefore, 我叫你写的字 means "the characters that I told you to write."

C1.   比中国人还好 means "even better than Chinese people."

C2.   你家里不是已经有好几个钟了吗？ "Don't you already have quite a few clocks at your home?" This is a rhetorical question, in other words, the speaker believes that the person he or she is speaking to does have a lot of clocks at their home. 好几个 means "quite a few," "several," or "a lot of."

Asking Directions to a Friend's House

PART ONE

Conversation 🎧 LISTEN

Situation: Mark Donnelly has been invited to the Taipei home of his friend Zhou Zengmo. He has been riding back and forth on his motorcycle but can't find the street, so he calls Zhou to ask for directions.

1. ZHOU: 喂？
   Wéi?
   Hello?

2. DONNELLY: 老周啊，我是小董。我跟你说啊，我转来转去怎么找也找不到你说的那条巷子。
   Lǎo Zhōu a, wǒ shi Xiǎo Dǒng. Wǒ gēn nǐ shuō a, wǒ zhuànlái zhuànqù zěmme zhǎo yě zhǎobudào nǐ shuōde nèitiáo xiàngzi.
   Old Zhou, it's me, Mark. Listen, I've been driving back and forth and no matter how hard I try, I just can't find that lane you mentioned.

3. ZHOU: 你现在在哪里啊？
   Nǐ xiànzài zài náli a?
   Where are you now?

4. DONNELLY: 我在你说的那个小庙门口打公用电话给你。

Wǒ zài nǐ shuōde nèige xiǎo miào ménkǒu dǎ gōngyòng diànhuà gěi nǐ.

I'm calling you from a public phone at the entrance to that little temple you mentioned.

5. ZHOU: 好，我告诉你，你继续往邮局那边走，差不多两百公尺就会看到一家家具店。店不太大，你稍微注意一下，不要错过。从那条巷子转进来，左手边第二栋三楼就是我们家。

Hǎo, wǒ gàosu nǐ, nǐ jìxù wàng yóujú nèibian zǒu, chàbuduō liǎngbǎigōngchǐ jiù huì kàndào yìjiā jiājù diàn. Diàn bú tài dà, nǐ shāowēi zhùyì yixia, búyào cuòguo. Cóng nèitiáo xiàngzi zhuǎnjìnlái zuǒshǒubiān dì'èrdòng sānlóu jiù shi wǒmen jiā.

O.K., I'll tell you, you continue going over toward the post office; after about 200 meters you'll see a furniture store. The store isn't very large, pay some attention, don't miss it. Turning in from that lane, the second building on the left-hand side, third floor, is our home.

6. DONNELLY: 好，知道了。一会儿见。

Hǎo, zhīdaole. Yìhuǐr jiàn.

O.K., I know now. See you in a little while.

New Vocabulary 🎧

周	**Zhōu**	Zhou (surname)
啊	**a**	(pause filler)
跟…说	**gēn…shuō**	tell (someone something)
转	**zhuàn**	turn, go around
转来	**zhuànlái**	come turning around
转去	**zhuànqù**	go turning around
…来…去	**…-lái…-qù…**	…all over the place
巷子	**xiàngzi**	lane
庙	**miào**	temple, shrine
公用	**gōngyòng**	public
公用电话	**gōngyòng diànhuà**	public telephone
告诉	**gàosu**	tell
邮局	**yóujú**	post office
公尺	**gōngchǐ**	meter
看到	**kàndào**	see
家具	**jiājù**	furniture
店	**diàn**	shop, store
家具店	**jiājù diàn**	furniture store
稍微	**shāowēi**	somewhat, slightly

注意	**zhùyì**	pay attention to
错过	**cuòguo**	miss
转进来	**zhuǎnjìnlái**	turn in
手	**shǒu**	hand
左手	**zuǒshǒu**	left hand
左手边	**zuǒshǒubiān**	left-hand side
栋	**dòng**	(measure for buildings)
一会儿见	**yìhuǐr jiàn**	"see you in a little while"

Supplementary Vocabulary

房子	**fángzi**	house
右手	**yòushǒu**	right hand
右手边	**yòushǒubiān**	right-hand side
公用厕所	**gōngyòng cèsuǒ**	public toilet
跟···讲	**gēn...jiǎng**	tell (someone something)

Notes on the Conversation

Verb-lái verb-qù

The very common and useful pattern Verb-**lái** Verb-**qù** expresses the sense of "do something back and forth," "do something here and there," "do something all over the place," or "do something again and again." Examples: **zhǎolái zhǎoqù** "look all over," **zǒulái zǒuqù** "walk back and forth," **kànlái kànqù** "look at over and over again," **xiǎnglái xiǎngqù** "rack one's brains," **bānlái bānqù** "move all over the place."

....

Zěmme (Verb) yě + negative verb "no matter..."

This pattern means "no matter (how hard one tries or what one does), one doesn't or didn't or can't or couldn't (do something)." The first occurrence of the verb is optional, but the second occurrence of the verb (the negative verb) is mandatory. Examples: **Wǒ zěmme zhǎo yě zhǎobudào** "No matter how hard I searched, I couldn't find it," **Wǒ zěmme yě mǎibudào** "No matter what I did, I wasn't able to buy one," **Wǒ zěmme yě shuìbuzháo** "No matter how hard I tried, I just couldn't fall asleep," **Tā zěmme xué yě xuébuhuì** "No matter how hard she tried, she just couldn't learn it."

....

Metric system

The official system of measurement in both mainland China and Taiwan is the metric system. The key terms are: **gōngfēn** "centimeter," **gōngkè** "gram," **gōngchǐ** "meter," **gōngjīn** "kilogram, kilo," **gōnglǐ** "kilometer," **gōngshēng** "liter."

....

Reading

New Characters and Words

301.	转	zhuǎn/zhuàn	turn, go around, revolve
	左转	zuǒ zhuǎn	turn left
	往右转	wàng yòu zhuǎn	turn toward the right
	转进来	zhuǎnjìnlai	turn in
	转来转去	zhuànlái zhuànqù	turn back and forth
302.	跟	gēn	with, and; heel
	我跟你	wǒ gēn nǐ	you and I
	我跟你走	wǒ gēn nǐ zǒu	I'll go with you
	跟…说	gēn...shuō	say to, tell (someone); repeat after someone
	我跟你说	wǒ gēn nǐ shuō	I say to you; let me tell you
	你跟我说	nǐ gēn wǒ shuō	repeat after me
303.	讲	jiǎng	speak, say, talk about, explain
	讲话	jiǎnghuà	speak
	跟…讲	gēn...jiǎng	say to, tell (someone something)
	我跟你讲	wǒ gēn nǐ jiǎng	I say to you; let me tell you
	讲中国话	jiǎng Zhōngguo huà	speak Chinese
304.	具	jù	implement, tool
	家具	jiājù	furniture
	家具店	jiājù diàn	furniture store
305.	手	shǒu	hand
	左手	zuǒshǒu	left hand
	右手	yòushǒu	right hand
	左手边	zuǒshǒubiān	left-hand side
	右手边	yòushǒubiān	right-hand side
306.	房	fáng	house; room; (surname)
	房子	fángzi	house
	房间	fángjiān	room

A. SENTENCES

一、这个事儿我已经跟你讲过很多次了，你怎么不听？

二、在那个中文中心里面一定得讲中国话，不可以讲外国话。

三、林先生在房间里走来走去，好像有很多问题还没解决的样子。

四、那个地方离这儿不远，你先往左转，再往右转，很快就到了。

五、我们这儿十月的天气最好，你来得正是时候，别错过！

六、我今天得去家具店买几件家具，你要不要跟我一起去？

七、我不小心，错过了三点钟的那班公共汽车，只好等三点半的了。

八、弟弟，别那样动你的手，实在太难看了，我跟你讲过很多次了！

九、你的房间是几号？在左手边，在右手边？我找来找去，怎么找也
找不着！

十、王大海说他有一个问题，就是："没有家具的房子怎么能住呢？"

B. CONVERSATIONS

一、

何大安：小谢，我是小何。我跟你讲，我转来转去怎么找也找不到你
说的那条路。

谢百里：你现在在哪里？

何大安：我在你说的那个小学门口打电话给你。

谢百里：好，你听我讲。你往"中美公司"那边走，就会看到一家家具
店。店不太大，不要错过。从那条路转进来左手边就是我们
住的房子。

何大安：好，知道了。一会儿见！

二、

房先生：钱小姐，你家里的家具都很好看。是在哪儿买的？

钱小姐：我们是在和平家具店买的。

房先生：和平家具店在哪儿？离这儿远吗？

钱小姐：不太远，很近。要是从这里走的话，一直往前走，到了公共
汽车站往左转，然后一直往前走就到了。

房先生：那好。有时间我一定去看看。谢谢你了，再见！

钱小姐：不谢。明天见！

C. NARRATIVES

我要跟你们讲一讲我小时候的房子。这已经是很久以前的事了，但是
我到现在还记得很清楚。那时候我跟我家里人住在北京城外头一个叫
房山的地方。我们住的房子不大，只有两个小房间，不过我那时候还
很小，所以对我来说那个房子好像很大！房子里家具也不多，但是我
们也不需要那么多东西。房子的左手边有一个中学，右手边有一家小
店。我们后来在对面买了一个大一点的房子，可是我觉得那个房子住
起来没有以前的房子那么好。我真喜欢我小时候的房子！

Notes

A3. 好像有很多问题还没解决的样子 "It appeared that he had a lot of problems that he hadn't yet solved."

A8. 难看 **nánkàn** "be ugly, unattractive"

A9. 找不着 **zhǎobuzháo** "can't find"

B2. 不谢 **búxiè** "don't thank me" or "you're welcome"

C1. 很久以前的事 "a matter from long ago"

Kāikǒu qǐng jiǎng Pǔtōnghuà
"Open your mouths and please speak Standard Chinese"
(sign on a building in Yinchuan)

PART TWO

Conversation 🎧 LISTEN

Situation: An American businessman in Taipei stops at a gasoline station for a fill-up.

1. **GAS STATION ATTENDANT:** 欢迎光临！请问，你加什么油？
   Huānyíng guānglín! Qǐng wèn, nǐ jiā shémme yóu?
   Welcome! Excuse me, what kind of gas do you want?

2. **AMERICAN BUSINESSMAN:** 九五。二十公升。嗨，我看还是加满好了。
   Jiǔ wǔ. Èrshigōngshēng. M, wǒ kàn hái shi jiāmǎn hǎole.
   95. Twenty liters. Uh, I think you might as well just fill it up.

3. **GAS STATION ATTENDANT:** 好的。请看，现在从零开始。 *(after filling car with gas)*
   好了，一共四百七十五元。
   **Hǎode. Qǐng kàn, xiànzài cóng líng kāishǐ. Hǎole, yígòng sìbǎi
   qīshiwǔyuán.**
   All right. Look, it's now starting from zero. O.K., that makes 475 NT in all.

4. **AMERICAN BUSINESSMAN:** 这是五百块。
   Zhè shi wǔbǎikuài.
   This is 500 NT.

5. **GAS STATION ATTENDANT:** 请问，你的统一编号是……
   Qǐng wèn, nǐde tǒngyī biānhào shi…
   Excuse me, your unified serial number is…

6. **AMERICAN BUSINESSMAN:** 不必了。
   Búbìle.
   It's not necessary.

7. GAS STATION ATTENDANT: 不必了？ *(returns with change)*

好，找你二十五元。谢谢！

Búbìle? Hǎo, zhǎo nǐ èrshiwǔyuán. Xièxie!

It's not necessary? O.K., here's 25 NT in change. Thank you!

8. AMERICAN BUSINESSMAN: 好像油价又要涨了？

Hǎoxiàng yóujià yòu yào zhǎngle?

It looks likes the price of gas is going up again?

9. GAS STATION ATTENDANT: 欸，对啊。从明天起油价又要调整了，所以今天
加油的车特别多。你看，大排长龙哦！

**Èi, duì a. Cóng míngtiān qǐ yóujià yòu yào tiáozhěngle, suóyi jīntiān
jiāyóude chē tèbié duō. Nǐ kàn, dà-pái-cháng-lóng ó!**

Yeah, that's right. Starting tomorrow, the price of gas is going to be
adjusted again, so today there're especially many cars filling up. Just
look at how they've formed a long line!

New Vocabulary

欢迎光临	**huānyíng guānglín**	"we welcome your honorable presence"
油	**yóu**	oil
加油	**jiāyóu**	add gasoline, buy gas
公升	**gōngshēng**	liter
看	**kàn**	think, consider
满	**mǎn**	be full
加满	**jiāmǎn**	fill up
元	**yuán**	dollar (monetary unit)
统一	**tǒngyī**	unite, unify
编号	**biānhào**	serial number
统一编号	**tǒngyī biānhào**	unified serial number
油价	**yóujià**	price of gasoline
涨	**zhǎng**	rise, go up
欸	**èi**	"yeah"
从…起	**cóng...qǐ**	starting from…
调整	**tiáozhěng**	adjust
特别	**tèbié**	especially
大排长龙	**dà-pái-cháng-lóng**	form a long line

Supplementary Vocabulary

骑	qí	ride, straddle (bicycle, motorcycle, horse)
摩托车	mótuōchē	motorcycle
停车	tíngchē	park a car, park
停车场	tíngchēchǎng	parking lot
加油站	jiāyóuzhàn	gasoline station
汽油	qìyóu	gasoline
价钱	jiàqián	price
特	tè	especially

Notes on the Conversation

Yòu yào...le "will...again"

In line 8 of the conversation take the sentence **Yóujià yòu yào zhǎngle** "The price of gas is going to rise again" or line 9 **Yóujià yòu yào tiáozhěngle** "The price of gas is going to be adjusted again." **Yòu** "again," which normally means "again" for past situations, is used in spite of this being a future situation because the sense is that "the price of gas has gone up time and time again in the past and now here we go again." The **le** at the end of this pattern indicates anticipated change in a future situation. Examples: **Tāmen yòu yào lái le** "They're coming again," **Tīngshuō míngtiān yòu yào xiàyǔ le** "I heard tomorrow it's going to rain again."

Cóng...qǐ "beginning from"

Cóng means "from" and **qǐ** literally means "rise" or "arise." The pattern **cóng...qǐ** means "beginning from, starting from." A time word, place word, or question word fills the slot between the **cóng** and the **qǐ**. Examples: **cóng míngtiān qǐ** "starting tomorrow," **cóng xiàge yuè qǐ** "starting next month." In this pattern, the **qǐ** can occur by itself, as in the previous examples, or it can be suffixed to a one-syllable verb, as in **Wǒ zhēn bù zhīdào gāi cóng nǎr shuōqǐ** "I really don't know where I should start (talking) from" or **Yào jiějué wèntí, yīnggāi cóng nǎr zuòqǐ?** "If you want to solve problems, from where should you begin (doing things)?"

Reading

New Characters and Words

307.	加	jiā	add
	加州	Jiāzhōu	California
308.	油	yóu	oil; gasoline
	加油	jiāyóu	add gasoline, refuel; "Hang in there!"

加油站	**jiāyóuzhàn**	gas station
汽油	**qìyóu**	gasoline
309. 满	**mǎn**	be full; fill
加满	**jiāmǎn**	add to the point where something is full
满人	**Mǎnrén**	Manchu (Chinese minority people)
310. 特	**tè**	especially
特别	**tèbié**	especially
311. 价	**jià**	price
价钱	**jiàqián**	price
油价	**yóujià**	price of gasoline
半价	**bànjià**	half price
讲价钱	**jiǎng jiàqián**	discuss a price, bargain
讲价	**jiǎngjià**	discuss a price, bargain
312. 停	**tíng**	stop
停车	**tíngchē**	stop a car; park
停车场	**tíngchēchǎng**	parking lot

A. SENTENCES

一、汽车加满了油比较好。

二、你前天刚加了油，怎么今天又要加油了？

三、我的汽车快没有油了，我需要找一个加油站加油。

四、上班的人得买全票，不过学生和老人可以买半价票。

A gas station on Xinsheng South Road in Taipei

五、 我们的公司只有一个小停车场，所以停车就成了一个很大的问题。

六、 从下个星期一起，油价要贵很多，我看我得开始走路或是坐公车了。

七、 美国很多地方不能讲价，只有买房子或者买汽车的时候可以讲价。

八、 满人原来住在中国的东北，可是现在北京市和河北省也有不少满人住在那里。

九、 听说最近加州和美国西岸其他的州，汽油的价钱特贵。

十、 到现在你们大概都已经知道了，王大海特别喜欢到动物园去看动物。

B. CONVERSATIONS

一、

姐姐： 妹妹，你喜欢你的老师吗？

妹妹： 我不喜欢她。

姐姐： 你为什么不喜欢她呢？

妹妹： 因为她讲话很不清楚。第一次她说三加三是六，后来她又说二加四也是六……

二、

小李： 小王，你去过加州吗？

小王： 我就是加州人。我是在加州出生的，也是在那儿长大的。

小李： 加州怎么样？听说西岸的天气不错。

小王： 对，那儿的气候特别好，不冷也不热，但是加州买东西比较贵。

小李： 听说最近加州的油价特贵，是真的吗？

小王： 是的。以前还好，可是从今年起，汽油和其他东西的价钱都越来越贵了，所以现在不少人需要加油的时候就到别的州去加，不在加州加油。

C. NARRATIVES

一、 我们家住在美国西岸的加州。这是一个汽车特别多的州，所以很多路口都有加油站。前天我的车子快没有油了，所以我就停在一个加油站准备要加油，但是那里的油价实在太贵了，所以我决定再去别家看看。还好，对面就有一个加油站，但是那里的油价比第一家还要贵。然后我转来转去，去了十几家加油站，价钱都很贵，最后我的车子没有油了！最近油价越来越贵，我看以后车子就停在家里，坐公车或者走路去上班比较好。

二、 东山大学很小，有汽车的人也不太多，但是这个大学有一个特别大的停车场。离那儿不远还有一个大学叫西山大学。西山大学很大，开车的人也特别多，但是西山大学的停车场特别小，天天都会停满，还有很多人怎么找也找不到停车的位子。听说西山大学的林校长今天要去见东山大学的高校长。不知道两位大学校长能不能解决停车的问题？

Notes

A4. 全票 means "full-price ticket" while 半价票 means "half-price ticket."

A5. 成 here means "become."

A6. 油价要贵很多 "The price of oil is going to become much more expensive."

A10. 到现在 here means "by now."

C1a. 州 **zhōu** "district," "prefecture," "state." In the word 加州 "California," the syllable 加 **jiā** represents the "Ca-" sound in "California" and 州 means "state," so 加州 literally means "the state of California."

C1b. 还好 literally, means "still good." When followed by a statement, as here, it means "luckily" or "fortunately" and implies the situation could have been worse (i.e., there might not have been another gas station nearby).

C1c. 对面就有一个加油站 "Right on the other side there was a gas station" or "There was a gas station right across from where I was." The 就 here implies "as close as that; that close," so in this context 就 could be translated as "right."

C1d. 十几家加油站 literally, means "ten plus a few gas stations," which in good English we could render as "over a dozen gas stations." The actual number is at least 11 and at most 19. 几 is used here to mean "few," "several," or "some."

C2a. 停满 literally, "park to the point where it (the parking lot) is full."

C2b. 停车的位子 means "a place for parking" or "a parking spot."

C2c. 不知道 here means 我不知道. In contexts like this, the pronoun 我 is frequently omitted. It would be acceptable to translate this 不知道 as "I don't know," but an even better translation would be "I wonder if…"

Shopping

PART ONE

Conversation 🎧 LISTEN

Situation: Sam White, an American graduate student doing research in Beijing, is returning to his dorm on a hot summer day when he notices an ice pop seller.

1. ICE POP SELLER: 冰棍儿，冰棍儿！五毛钱一根儿。
   Bīnggùnr, bīnggùnr! Wǔmáo qián yìgēnr.
   Ice pops, ice pops! Fifty cents apiece.

2. WHITE: 买两根儿。
   Mǎi liǎnggēnr.
   I'll take two.

3. ICE POP SELLER: 奶油的还是小豆的？
   Nǎiyóude háishi xiǎodòude?
   Cream or red bean?

4. WHITE: 一样一根儿吧。
   Yíyàng yìgēnr ba.
   Why don't we make it one of each.

5. **ICE POP SELLER**: 一共一块。
      Yígòng yíkuài.
      In all that will be one yuan.

6. **WHITE**: 给您五块。
      Gěi nín wǔkuài.
      This is five yuan.

7. **ICE POP SELLER**: 找您四块。您拿好!
      Zhǎo nín sìkuài. Nín náhǎo!
      Here's four yuan in change. Hold them carefully!

New Vocabulary

冰	**bīng**	ice
冰棍	**bīnggùn(r)**	ice pop
根	**gēn(r)**	(for long, thin things)
奶油	**nǎiyóu**	cream
还是	**háishi**	or
小豆	**xiǎodòu**	red bean
样	**yàng**	kind, variety
拿	**ná**	hold, take
拿好	**náhǎo**	hold well, hold firmly

Supplementary Vocabulary

读	**dú**	read aloud; study
读书	**dúshū**	study
念书	**niànshū**	study
专业	**zhuānyè**	major, specialization
主修	**zhǔxiū**	major in; major
系	**xì**	department

Notes on the Conversation

Amount of money per item

In line 1, consider the expression **wǔmáo qián yìgēnr** "fifty cents a piece" (ice pops). The pattern for indicating how much one of a certain category of items costs is: Money Amount + **yī** + Measure. More examples: **bákuài qián yíge** "eight dollars each" (watermelons), **shíkuài qián yìbǎ** "ten dollars each" (umbrellas), **yìqiānkuài yìtái** "a thousand dollars each" (computers). An alternate pattern **yī** + Measure + Money Amount exists, so it would also be possible to say **yìgēnr wǔmáo qián** with the same meaning.

Choice-type questions with <u>A háishi B</u> "A or B"

One common way to ask about alternatives in choice-type questions is with the pattern **A háishi B** "A or B?" **Háishi** means "or." Examples: **Zhèige háishi nèige?** "This one or that one?," **Jīntiān háishi míngtiān?** "Today or tomorrow?," **Nǐ yào dàde háishi xiǎode?** "Do you want the big one or the small one?" Note that **háishi** alone is sufficient to create choice-type questions; question particle **ma** is *not* added to choice-type questions containing **háishi**.

Two words for "or": <u>háishi</u> vs. <u>huòshi</u>

It's important to compare and contrast **háishi** "or" with several other words that also translate as "or," namely, **huòshi** and its variants **huòzhě** and **huò**. The key difference is that **háishi** is used to express "or" in choice-type questions where the speaker is giving the listener alternatives and asking the listener to choose one of those alternatives. On the other hand, **huòshi**, **huòzhě**, and **huò** are used to express "or" in statements (or occasionally in questions that ask about something else, not which of several alternatives). The following pair of sentences should help clarify the difference: **Tā yào qù Běijīng háishi Táiběi?** "Does she want to go to Beijing or Taipei?" vs. **Tā yào qù Běijīng huòshi Táiběi** "She wants to go to Beijing or Taipei."

Reading

New Characters and Words

313.	根	gēn	(measure for long, thin things)
	一根毛	yìgēn máo	a (strand of) hair (on the body)
	根本	gēnběn	basically, fundamentally
	根本 + NEGATIVE	gēnběn	not at all, completely not
314.	拿	ná	take, hold
	拿好	náhǎo	hold on to well, hold firmly
	加拿大	Jiā'nádà	Canada
	加拿大人	Jiā'nádà rén	Canadian person
315.	专	zhuān	special; expert
316.	业	yè	business, industry, study (can't be used alone)
	专业	zhuānyè	major (in college)
	作业	zuòyè	homework
317.	办	bàn	do, handle, take care of
	办事	bànshì	take care of matters
	怎么办?	Zěnme bàn?	"What should be done?"
318.	法	fǎ/fá	way, method
	法子	fázi	way, method

办法	**bànfǎ**	way of managing or handling something
想法	**xiǎngfǎ**	way of thinking, idea, opinion
做法	**zuòfǎ**	way of doing something
法国	**Fǎguo**	France
法国人	**Fǎguo rén**	French person
法文	**Fǎwén**	written French

A. SENTENCES

一、 你说得不对，我根本没有说过这样儿的话！

二、 在中国，大一的学生就已经决定了要学什么专业。

三、 我的表哥姓高，是一位天文专家，你可能听说过他。

四、 你不可以拿我的东西，以后请你不要拿我这里的东西！

五、 这个大学有生物和比较文学专业，但是没有天文。

六、 对不起，我还得去办点儿事，先走了，明天见！

七、 你没有钱买车票我也没有办法，因为我也没带钱。

八、 我上个星期到加拿大去了，但是天气不好，根本没办法出门。

九、 中国有很多"美国专家，"美国也有很多"中国专家，"但是有的问题专家也没法子解决。

十、 王大海好高兴，他今天早上在他家外头的地上找到了一百块钱。

B. CONVERSATIONS

一、

男生： 要学法文的话，去法国好还是去加拿大好？

女生： 我们的老师是法国人，她说法国的法文听起来比较好听。

男生： 听说小何下个月要去法国。

女生： 小何最近太忙了，我看他根本还没决定去还是不去。

二、

小文： 小李，我有个大问题，真不知道怎么办。

小李： 你有什么问题？

小文： 这个月我们不是要决定专业了吗？家里要我学生物专业，可是我要学的是比较文学专业。

小李： 那，你能不能学两个专业？也学生物，也学比较文学。这样你家里人高兴，你也能学你喜欢的专业。

小文： 对，这是一个好办法。

C. NARRATIVES

一、 刚刚走的那个人是我一个大学同学。他是一个比较文学专家。他
刚刚来我家拿一点儿东西。因为他还有一点儿事得办，所以先走
了。他可能明天还要再来我家找我。

二、 我在高中的时候很喜欢生物，后来也喜欢天文。可是到了大学，
我越来越喜欢文学，特别是法国文学。现在我的专业是法文，明
年我要到法国或是加拿大去多学一点法文。我真的很喜欢法文，
不过以后要找什么样儿的工作，我现在根本不知道。

Notes

A2.   The adverb 就 here implies "as early as then" or "that early."

A7.   你没有钱买车票我也没有办法 "If you don't have money to buy a bus ticket, there's nothing I can do about it" or "There's nothing I can do about your not having money to buy a bus ticket."

A9.   有的问题专家也没法子解决 "Some problems even specialists have no way to solve." The 也 here implies "even."

A10.   地上, composed of the noun 地 and the localizer 上, means "on the ground."

B2.   也学生物, 也学比较文学 "Study both biology and comparative literature." 也…也 is a pattern meaning "both…and."

PART TWO

Conversation 🎧

Situation: Jonathon Little, an American who is working as an intern in a law office in Beijing, goes to a department store to purchase some ballpoint pens.

1. **LITTLE:** 我想试试这种圆珠笔，行吗？
   Wǒ xiǎng shìshi zhèizhǒng yuánzhūbǐ, xíng ma?
   Could I try out this kind of ball-point pen?

2. **CLERK:** 行。你要红的、蓝的还是黑的？
   Xíng. Nín yào hóngde, lánde, háishi hēide?
   Sure. Do you want a red one, a blue one, or a black one?

3. **LITTLE:** 蓝的吧。多少钱一支？
   Lánde ba. Duōshǎo qián yìzhī?
   A blue one, I guess. How much are they each?

4. **CLERK:** 两块钱一支。
   Liǎngkuài qián yìzhī.
   They're two yuan each.

5. **LITTLE:** 有便宜点的吗？
   Yǒu piányi diǎnde ma?
   Do you have cheaper ones?

6. **CLERK:** 有。这样儿的一块五一支。
   Yǒu. Zhèiyangrde yíkuài wǔ yìzhī.
   We do. This kind is one dollar fifty apiece.

7. LITTLE: *(tries out the cheaper pen)*

你给我两支。我还想买一本儿汉英字典、一张北京市地图和一份报纸。

Nǐ gěi wǒ liǎngzhī. Wǒ hái xiǎng mǎi yìběn Hàn-Yīng zìdiǎn, yìzhāng Běijīng shì dìtú hé yífèn bàozhǐ.

Give me two of them. I also want to buy a Chinese-English dictionary, a map of Beijing and a newspaper.

8. CLERK: 对不起，我们这儿不卖这些东西。字典和地图，您可以到隔壁的书店去买。买报纸，您得去邮局或报亭。

Duìbuqǐ, wǒmen zhèr bú mài zhèixiē dōngxi. Zìdiǎn hé dìtú, nín kéyi dào gébìde shūdiàn qù mǎi. Mǎi bàozhǐ, nín děi qù yóujú huò bàotíng.

Sorry, we don't sell these things here. The dictionary and the map you can go to the bookstore next door to buy. To buy a newspaper you'll have to go to a post office or a newspaper kiosk.

9. LITTLE: *(after paying for pens and receiving change from clerk)*

谢谢。

Xièxie.

Thank you.

10. CLERK: 不客气，希望你下次再来。你还要点儿什么吗？

Bú kèqi, xīwàng nǐ xiàcì zài lái. Nǐ hái yào diǎnr shémme ma?

You're welcome, hope you come again next time. Would you like anything else?

11. LITTLE: 不要了，谢谢。

Bú yàole, xièxie.

No, thank you.

12. CLERK: 不要了，啊。

(notices that Little has forgotten to take the pens)

别忘了这个！

Bú yàole, à. Bié wàngle zhèige!

So you don't want anything else. Don't forget this!

New Vocabulary

试	shì	try
种	zhǒng	kind
笔	bǐ	writing instrument
圆珠笔	yuánzhūbǐ	ball-point pen
支	zhī	(for pens, pencils)
本	běn(r)	(for books, dictionaries)
汉英	Hàn-Yīng	Chinese-English
字典	zìdiǎn	dictionary
市	shì	city, municipality

地图	dìtú	map
份	fèn(r)	(for newspapers, magazines)
报纸	bàozhǐ	newspaper
些	xiē	some
这些	zhèixiē	these
隔壁	gébì	next door
书	shū	book
书店	shūdiàn	bookstore
报亭	bàotíng	newspaper kiosk

Supplementary Vocabulary 🎧

铅笔	qiānbǐ	pencil
纸	zhǐ	paper
本子	běnzi	notebook
杂志	zázhì	magazine

Notes on the Conversation

Measures

Every Chinese noun must be preceded by a measure if it's counted or specified. There are two basic patterns: Number + Measure + Noun, as in **liǎngge rén** "two people"; and Specifier + Measure + Noun, as in **zhèizhāng zhuōzi** "this table." There are many specific measures, each limited to certain nouns or categories of nouns. Some measures have fairly clear meanings, e.g., **zhāng**, which is used for flat things, or **tiáo**, which is used for long, narrow things. However, many measure words are arbitrary and are best learned together with the noun they modify. The general measure **ge** can be used with many nouns; as a general strategy, use **ge** when you're not sure what the appropriate measure for a noun is. Though use of the specific measure is preferred, **ge** will be understood and will be less jarring than an incorrect measure or no measure. Examples with the new measures in this lesson: **zhèizhī qiānbǐ** "this pencil," **nèiběn shū** "that book," **něizhāng dìtú** "which map?," **wǔfèn bàozhǐ** "five newspapers," **měizhāng zhǐ** "each piece of paper." There are a few common Chinese measures that typically occur alone without a following noun and which translate into English nouns. Examples: **tiān** "day," **nián** "year," **suì** "year of age." For "one day" be careful to say **yìtiān**, for "two years" say **liǎngnián**, and for "ten years of age" say **shísuì**.

....

Xiē as Measure in zhèixiē, nèixiē, and něixiē

In line 8 in the conversation, note **zhèixiē dōngxi** "these things." The measure **xiē** indicates plural and has the basic meaning "some." There are three common combinations of Specifier + **xiē** which you should learn: **zhèixiē** "these," **nèixiē** "those," and **něixiē** "which?" These can all be used to modify a following noun (**Zhèixiē dōngxi shi wǒde** "These things are mine"), or they can be used alone as pronouns with the noun omitted (**Zhèixiē shi wǒde** "These are mine"). **Zhèixiē** has an alternate form

zhèxiē, **nèixiē** has an alternate form **nàxiē**, and **něixiē** has an alternate form **nǎxiē**. Also, **xiē** is never used if a specific number is mentioned, so to say "these three books," you must say **zhèisānběn shū** without any **xiē**.

....

More on Question Words used as Indefinites

In line 10, look at the question **Nǐ hái yào diǎnr shémme ma?** "Would you like something else?" At first glance, this may look to you as though it meant "What else do you want?" But surely you remember the rule that if there is a Question Word in a sentence that is meant as a question, then there is no **ma** at the end of the sentence. But here there *is* a **ma**, so what is going on? It just so happens that if a Question Word like **shémme** "what" or **shéi** "who" occurs in a sentence that is already a question because of a **ma** at the end or because of an affirmative-negative verb construction like **yào bu yào**, then the Question Word no longer asks a question but rather carries an indefinite sense. In this case, instead of meaning "what?," **shémme** means "something" or "anything"; and instead of meaning "who?," **shéi** means "someone" or "anyone."

....

Reading

New Characters and Words

319.	想	**xiǎng**	think; want to, would like to
	想想看	**xiángxiang kàn**	try and think
	想要	**xiǎngyào**	want to, would like to
320.	种	**zhǒng**	kind
	这种	**zhèizhǒng**	this kind
	哪种	**něizhǒng**	which kind?
	一种	**yìzhǒng**	a kind of
321.	书	**shū**	book
	一本书	**yìběn shū**	one book
	书店	**shūdiàn**	bookstore
	书房	**shūfáng**	study
	看书	**kànshū**	read a book
322.	些	**xiē**	some
	有些人	**yǒu xiē rén**	(there are) some people (who…)
	这些	**zhèixiē**	these
	那些	**nèixiē**	those
	哪些	**něixiē**	which ones?
	一些	**yìxiē**	some
323.	报	**bào**	newspaper
	报上	**bàoshang**	in the newspaper
	看报	**kànbào**	read a newspaper

324. 纸   **zhǐ**   paper
     一张纸   **yìzhāng zhǐ**   a piece of paper
     报纸   **bàozhǐ**   newspaper

A. SENTENCES

一、你想买什么样的钟？这种还是那种？

二、我天天早上第一件事就是看报，你呢？

三、这些东西是谁的？请你快一点从地上拿走。

四、那张纸上是不是有我的名字？

五、我想加个油，你说哪种汽油比较好？

六、我记得那家书店的左手边好像有一个家具店。

七、我在报上看到，你们有一些家具想卖，是不是？

八、《百家姓》是一本书的名字，这本书里头都是中国人的姓。

九、这种本子好像有两百张纸，那种好像只有一百五十张。

十、王大海去书店买了书和报纸，所以现在没有钱买饭了。

B. CONVERSATIONS

一、

李明　：今天的报纸你拿到了吗？

林文子：没有。你呢？

李明　：我也没拿到。是不是今天没有报纸呢？

林文子：不可能的！天天都有报纸，今天怎么会没有呢？

二、

边小姐：你去过和平街上的书店吗？

万先生：还没有时间去。你呢？

边小姐：我已经去过几次了。我觉得那家书店还不错。

万先生：我很想去看看。那儿都卖一些什么样儿的东西？

边小姐：书、报、本子、纸都有，价钱也不贵。

C. NARRATIVES

一、我因为小的时候没有朋友，所以特别喜欢看书跟报纸。我最喜欢去的地方就是书店。我去一回书店，就一定会买几本书，所以我的书房里书特别多！那个时候，我已经决定长大以后要在书店里工作。我觉得我一定会很喜欢这种工作的。

二、我们学校一共有两个书店，一个在东门，一个在西门。这两个书店一个比较大，里边卖的东西很多，可是离我家很远；还有一个比较小，里边卖的东西比较少，可是离我家很近。上个星期日我去这个小书店买一本书，书名是《为什么中国人会这样，外国人会那样？》，作者是王定和先生。可是小书店没有我要的这本书，所以我只好明天到大书店去找找看。

Notes

A3. 请你快一点从地上拿走 literally, "Please you more quickly take them away from the ground" or, in idiomatic English, "Please pick them up off the ground as fast as you can." The resultative verb compound 拿走 means "take away."

A5. 加个油 literally, "add a gasoline" is a more relaxed and casual way to say 加油 "add gas," "fill up," or "tank up." If you're talking about having a meal, instead of saying 吃饭 you could also say 吃个饭, with essentially the same meaning.

A7a. Note that in English one says "*in* the newspaper," but in Chinese one says 报上 literally, "*on* the newspaper."

A7b. 你们有一些家具想卖 "You have some furniture that you want to sell."

A8. 《百家姓》 **Bǎi Jiā Xìng** *The Book of One Hundred Family Names*. This is a well-known Classical Chinese text composed during the Song Dynasty that lists all the Chinese surnames that existed at the time, most of which are still in use today. The brackets 《 》 are called 书名号 and indicate book and article titles.

B1a. 拿到 is a resultative compound verb that means "get," so 你拿到了吗？ means "Did you get it?"

B1b. 不可能的！ is an exclamation meaning "Impossible!" The final 的 is optional; one could also say just 不可能！

C2. 书名 **shūmíng** "book title"

A kiosk on the campus of the Beijing Language and Culture University

LESSON 4
Buying Vegetables and Fruits

PART ONE

Conversation 🎧

Situation: Rosy Huang, a Chinese-American woman living for a year in Taipei, goes shopping for tomatoes.

1. HUANG:
老板，蕃茄怎么卖？
Lǎobǎn, fānqié zěmme mài?
Sir, how much are the tomatoes?

2. VEGETABLE SELLER:
半斤二十五块。
Bànjīn èrshiwǔkuài.
25 NT for half a catty.

3. HUANG:
怎么这么贵啊？
Zěmme zhèmme guì a?
How come they're so expensive?

4. VEGETABLE SELLER:
太太，这是今天才到的。保证新鲜。
Tàitai, zhè shi jīntiān cái dàode. Bǎozhèng xīnxiān.
Ma'am, these just arrived today. I guarantee they're fresh.

5. HUANG:
给我半斤好了。
Gěi wǒ bànjīn hǎole.
Then give me half a catty.

6. VEGETABLE SELLER: 好，半斤。要不要买点沙拉菜或是芹菜？这些都是从美国进口的，比梨山的好，又漂亮又脆。

Hǎo, bànjīn. Yào bu yào mǎi diǎn shālācài huòshi qíncài? Zhèixiē dōu shi cóng Měiguo jìnkǒude, bǐ Lí Shānde hǎo. Yòu piàoliang yòu cuì.

O.K., half a catty. Would you like to buy some lettuce or celery? These are both imported from the U.S., and they're better than those from Li Shan. They both look nice and they're crisp.

7. HUANG: 今天不要了。就买蕃茄吧。

Jīntiān bú yàole. Jiù mǎi fānqié ba.

Not today. I'll just buy the tomatoes.

8. VEGETABLE SELLER: 好。

Hǎo.

Fine.

9. HUANG: *(gives him the money)*

二十五块。

Èrshiwǔkuài.

25 NT.

9. VEGETABLE SELLER: 好，多谢。再来啊！

Hǎo, duō xiè. Zài lái a!

O.K., thanks. Come again!

New Vocabulary

蕃茄	**fānqié**	tomato
斤	**jīn**	catty (unit of weight)
怎么这么…	**zěmme zhèmme…**	how come so…
才	**cái**	not until, just
保证	**bǎozhèng**	guarantee
新鲜	**xīnxiān**	be fresh
沙拉	**shālā**	salad
菜	**cài**	vegetable
沙拉菜	**shālācài**	lettuce
芹菜	**qíncài**	Chinese celery
进口	**jìnkǒu**	import
梨	**lí(r)**	pear
梨山	**Lí Shān**	Pear Mountain, Li Shan
漂亮	**piàoliang**	be pretty, look nice
脆	**cuì**	be crisp
多谢	**duō xiè**	"many thanks"

Supplementary Vocabulary

蔬菜	**shūcài**	vegetable
青菜	**qīngcài**	green vegetable
白菜	**báicài**	cabbage
菜场	**càichǎng**	market
出口	**chūkǒu**	export

Notes on the Conversation

Zěmme zhèmme… "how come…so…."

Zěmme means "how come" and **zhèmme** means "so." The whole expression **zěmme zhèmme…** means "how come (something or somebody is or does something) so…." This pattern is most commonly followed by a stative verb but can also be followed by an auxiliary verb or regular verb. There is frequently a final particle **a** at the end of the sentence. Instead of **zhèmme** you can also use **nèmme** with the same meaning of "so" but referring to something further away. Examples: **Zhèjiān wūzi zěmme zhèmme lěng a?** "How come this room is so cold?," **Tā zěmme nèmme xǐhuan chī táng a?** "How come he likes to eat candy so much?," **Nǐ zěmme zhèmme pà tā a?** "How come you're so scared of him?"

Cái vs. jiù

Cái and **jiù** are both adverbs that sometimes translate as "then" but they have very different meanings. Depending on the context, **cái** can be translated as "then and only then," "not until then," or "only." **Jiù**, on the other hand, can be translated as "then," "then already," and "as early as." The essential difference between the two is that **cái** means later or more than expected, while **jiù** means earlier or fewer than expected. Like all regular adverbs, **cái** and **jiù** occur after the subject and before the verb. Contrast the following two sentences: **Xiǎo Wáng yīnggāi qīdiǎn dào, kěshì tā liùdiǎn bàn jiù láile** "Little Wang was supposed to arrive at 7:00, but he came at 6:30 (that early)" vs. **Xiǎo Lǐ yīnggāi qīdiǎn dào, kěshì tā qīdiǎn bàn cái lái** "Little Li was supposed to arrive at 7:00, but he didn't come until 7:30." More examples with **cái**: **Zhōu Tàitai míngtiān cái lái** "Mrs. Zhou won't come until tomorrow," **Bái Xiānsheng jīnnián cái dào Měiguo** "It wasn't until this year that Mr. Bai came to the U.S.," **Wǒ gàosu ta sāncì, tā cái dǒng** "He didn't understand until I had told him three times." After **cái** a verb doesn't have a **-le** suffixed to it. Also, the English translation of a phrase with **cái** often calls for a negative verb plus "until," but in the Chinese there is no negative.

Reading

New Characters and Words

325.	才	**cái**	not until, then and only then, just
326.	斤	**jīn**	catty (unit of weight, about 1⅓ lbs.)
	半斤	**bànjīn**	half a catty

公斤	**gōngjīn**	kilogram
327. 菜	**cài**	vegetable; dish of food
中国菜	**Zhōngguo cài**	Chinese food
生菜	**shēngcài**	lettuce
菜场	**càichǎng**	food market, marketplace
菜市场	**càishìchǎng**	food market, marketplace
328. 白	**bái**	be white; (surname)
白菜	**báicài**	cabbage
白天	**báitiān**	during the day, daytime
白人	**Báirén**	White (person), Caucasian
长白山	**Chángbái Shān**	Changbai Mountains
329. 保	**bǎo**	protect; guarantee
330. 证	**zhèng**	evidence; proof
保证	**bǎozhèng**	guarantee

A. SENTENCES

一、我同屋保证这次一定会早到，但是他最后还是很晚才到。
二、我今天白天在外面特别忙，晚上只想在家里看报，不想再出门了。
三、我们在机场等了快两个钟头，小白才到。
四、从前中国人不太喜欢吃生菜，可是最近几年他们好像越来越喜欢吃了。
五、到了加拿大我才知道这个比中国还大的地方人口比北京还少。
六、这本书写得特别好，我保证你会喜欢！
七、这种车子是从外国进口的，又好看又好开。
八、日本往外国出口很多汽车，从外国进口很多吃的东西。
九、有些美国人觉得美国汽车没有从外国进口的汽车那么好。
十、王大海到菜场给他的动物买了十公斤的白菜，但是动物不吃。

B. CONVERSATIONS

一、
张太太：白菜怎么卖？
卖菜的：白菜……半斤二十五块。
张太太：半斤二十五块？怎么这么贵？
卖菜的：太太，这种白菜是从日本进口的，今天才到的。比台湾的好，保证好吃。

A vegetable stand in Tai Po, Hong Kong

张太太：好，给我一斤好了。这是五十块。
卖菜的：好，多谢。你拿好！再来！

二、
李安：小白，你怎么这么晚才来？
白喜：我都忘了今天我是要来找你的。
李安：下次你得记得，别再忘了！
白喜：放心吧。我下次一定很早就来。
李安：好吧，你可不能忘了你今天说的话。
白喜：没有问题，我可以保证！

C. NARRATIVES

一、我跟你讲，我以前是什么菜都吃，只有白菜不吃。后来因为听朋友说从日本进口的白菜特别好吃，所以就决定买一些吃吃看。今天早上我就买了差不多三斤。很贵，但是真好吃！我先生也喜欢，他问我："这种白菜特别好吃，你在哪里买的？"朋友，你也去买一点儿从日本进口的白菜吧。我保证你一定会喜欢吃！

二、我们家住在湖北省老河口市。离我们家不远有两个菜市场。一个在路的左手边，叫四号路菜市场，一个在路的右手边，叫王家台菜市场。 四号路菜市场的菜很多都是从外国进口的，又贵又不好吃。王家台菜市场卖的差不多都是本地菜，比进口的菜好吃，也没有进口的菜那么贵。要是我们家的人去买菜的话，我保证他们会去王家台菜市场，不会去 四号路菜市场。

Notes

A5. 这个比中国还大的地方人口比北京还少 "This place that is even bigger than China has a population even smaller than Beijing." This is a topic-comment structure. A literal translation would be "This compared to China even bigger place, population compared to Beijing even fewer."

A7. 从···进口 **cóng... jìnkǒu** "import from"

A8. 往···出口 **wǎng...chūkǒu** "export to"

B2a. 我都忘了今天我是要来找你的 "I completely forgot that I was going to come looking for you today." The 都 here functions as an intensifier.

B2b. 你可不能忘了 "You really can't forget." The adverb 可 here is also an intensifier and could be translated as "really" or "indeed."

C1. 我以前是什么菜都吃 literally, "I used to be in a situation of eating any vegetable" or, in idiomatic English, "It used to be that I would eat any vegetable."

PART TWO

Conversation

Situation: Ellen Anderson, an American student who is studying Chinese in Beijing, shops for pears at a fruit stand.

1. ANDERSON:
请给我约二斤鸭梨儿，给挑新鲜一点儿的。
Qǐng gěi wǒ yāo èrjīn Yālír. Gěi tiāo xīnxiān yidianrde.
Please weigh out two catties of Ya pears for me. Pick out fresher ones.

2. FRUIT VENDOR:
要一块钱一斤的，还是要一块五一斤的？
Yào yíkuài yìjīnde háishi yào yíkuài wǔ yìjīnde?
Do you want the one yuan per catty ones or the 1.50 per catty ones?

3. ANDERSON:
我要一块五的。
Wǒ yào yíkuài wǔde.
I want the 1.50 ones.

4. FRUIT VENDOR:
一块五的比一块的大得多。还要别的吗？买点儿香蕉怎么样？
Yíkuài wǔde bǐ yíkuàide dàde duō. Hái yào biéde ma? Mǎi diǎnr xiāngjiāo zěmmeyàng?
The 1.50 ones are much bigger than the one yuan ones. Do you want anything else? How about buying some bananas?

5. ANDERSON:
香蕉多少钱一斤？
Xiāngjiāo duōshǎo qián yìjīn?
How much are bananas per catty?

6. **FRUIT VENDOR:**   两块二一斤。
   Liǎngkuài èr yìjīn.
   They're 2.20 per catty.

7. **ANDERSON:**   您给我来两斤吧。一共多少钱?
   Nín gěi wǒ lái liǎngjīn ba. Yígòng duōshǎo qián?
   Why don't you give me two catties. How much is it in all?

8. **FRUIT VENDOR:**   总共是七块四。
   Zǒnggòng shi qīkuài sì.
   In all it's 7.40.

9. **ANDERSON:**   给您十块。
   Gěi nín shíkuài.
   This is ten yuan.

10. **FRUIT VENDOR:**   找您两块六。请您点一下。
    Zhǎo nín liǎngkuài liù. Qǐng nín diǎn yíxiàr.
    Here's 2.60 in change. Please count your change.

11. **ANDERSON:**   谢谢。再见!
    Xièxie. Zàijiàn!
    Thank you. Goodbye!

12. **FRUIT VENDOR:**   再见!
    Zàijiàn!
    Goodbye!

New Vocabulary

约	yāo	weigh out
鸭梨	Yālí(r)	Ya pear
挑	tiāo	pick out, select
香蕉	xiāngjiāo	banana
来	lái	bring, give
总共	zǒnggòng	in all
点	diǎn	count, check

Supplementary Vocabulary

水果	shuǐguǒ	fruit
苹果	píngguǒ	apple
橘子	júzi	orange
桃子	táozi	peach
葡萄	pútao	grape
包	bāo	wrap

包起来	**bāoqilai**	wrap up
穷	**qióng**	be poor
有钱	**yǒuqián**	be rich
听到	**tīngdào**	hear
看见	**kànjian**	see
听见	**tīngjian**	hear

Notes on the Conversation

Bǐ followed by Stative Verb + -de duō

Look at line 4 in the conversation. You already learned that the coverb **bǐ** is used to express unequal comparison as in **Zhèige bǐ nèige dà** "This one is bigger than that one." In this lesson we learn how to form sentences like "This one is *much* bigger than that one." This is said by beginning with a basic **bǐ** sentence and then adding **-de duō** after the stative verb at the end of the sentence. The pattern is: Topic + **bǐ** + Object + Stative Verb + **-de duō**, for example, **Zhèige bǐ nèige hǎode duō** "This one is much better than that one." More examples: **Zhèizhǒng běnzi bǐ nèizhǒng běnzi piányide duō** "This kind of notebook is much cheaper than that kind of notebook," **Zhèizhǒng píngguǒ bǐ nèizhǒng píngguǒ hǎochīde duō** "This kind of apple tastes much better than that kind of apple." If the stative verb of the sentence is itself **duō**, then it's possible to have the combination **duōde duō**: **Zhèige dàxuéde xuésheng bǐ nèige dàxuéde xuésheng duōde duō** "There are many more students at this college than at that college."

Reading

New Characters and Words

331.	总	**zǒng**	collect, sum up; always
	总共	**zǒnggòng**	altogether, in all
332.	包	**bāo**	wrap; (surname)
	包起来	**bāoqilai**	wrap up
	公事包	**gōngshìbāo**	briefcase, attaché case
333.	水	**shuǐ**	water
	冷水	**lěng shuǐ**	cold water
	热水	**rè shuǐ**	hot water
	香水	**xiāngshuǐ(r)**	perfume
	口水	**kǒushuǐ**	saliva
334.	果	**guǒ**	fruit
	水果	**shuǐguǒ**	fruit

335.	语	**yǔ**	language (can't be used alone)
	国语	**Guóyǔ**	Mandarin (language)
	日语	**Rìyǔ**	Japanese (language)
	法语	**Fǎyǔ**	French (language)
	越南语	**Yuènányǔ**	Vietnamese (language)
	美语	**Měiyǔ**	American English
	外国语	**wàiguoyǔ**	foreign language
	北京外国语大学	**Běijīng Wàiguoyǔ Dàxué**	Beijing Foreign Studies University
336.	言	**yán**	speech, word (can't be used alone)
	语言	**yǔyán**	language
	语言学	**yǔyánxué**	linguistics
	方言	**fāngyán**	dialect
	北京语言大学	**Běijīng Yǔyán Dàxué**	Beijing Language & Culture University

A. SENTENCES

一、我总共只去过中国两回。你去过几回了？

二、他会讲国语、日语和越南语，不知道他会不会讲其他的语言？

三、手里拿着公事包的那位老师叫包美生，是学语言学的。

四、李校长总共会说三种外国语：日语、法语跟美语。

五、我前天好像在菜场看见李老师在买水果。

六、为什么有钱的人越来越有钱，没钱的人越来越没钱？

七、我大哥说因为很久没下雨，所以现在很多种水果跟菜都比以前贵得多。

八、北京语言大学叫"北语，"北京外国语大学叫"北外，"现在清楚了吧？

九、老毛刚刚生气了，要是我是你的话，会离他远一点儿！

十、王大海很难过，他给他的女朋友买了从法国进口的香水，可是她不喜欢。

B. CONVERSATIONS

一、

小何：今天我们家没有热水，只有冷水。

老班：有冷水就不错了。我们家停水了，根本没有水！

A fruit market in Hong Kong

二、

哥哥：我买的车比你的车好看得多。

弟弟：可是我的车比你的车快得多。

哥哥：我的车比你的车大得多！

弟弟：对，可是你的车比我的车贵得多！

哥哥：对，那是因为我的钱比你的钱多得多！

C. NARRATIVES

一、我以后要是有钱，一定天天开进口的车子去公司上班，晚上吃进口的菜和进口的水果。我以后总共要七个房子，这样我可以一天住一个。星期六的房子得比其他的房子大得多，因为那一天我可能要请朋友来我家住。有钱多好！

二、中国总共有几百种方言，但是大方言只有七、八种。北京话、上海话、广东话、台湾话和湖南话都是这些大方言的一种。大方言还分成很多小方言，要是你学过语言学你就知道这些小方言也叫"次方言"。有几位西方的语言学专家说，其实中国的大方言就是语言，不是方言，因为要是你只会北京话，没学过其他方言的话，你根本不可能知道一个说那种方言的人在讲什么。不过因为中国是一个大国，不是好几个小国，所以中国人很少这么说，他们还是觉得说这都是"方言"比较好。

Notes

A3. 手里拿着公事包的那位老师 "that teacher who is holding a briefcase in his/her hand"

B1. 停水 tíngshuǐ "stop the water; suffer a disruption of the water supply"

C1. 有钱多好！literally, "To have money how good it is!" or, in more idiomatic English, "How wonderful it is to be rich!" The character 多 is used in exclamations to mean "How…!"

C2a. 都是这些大方言的一种 "are all a variety of these major dialects"

C2b. 次方言 cìfāngyán "subdialect"

C2c. 中国是一个大国不是好几个小国 "China is one large country, not a whole bunch of little countries."

LESSON 5
At The Market

PART ONE

Conversation 🎧

Situation: Cindy Han, an American student in Beijing, goes shopping for meat at a traditional Beijing market.

1. **HAN:** 请您给我称十块钱的猪肉。
   Qǐng nín gěi wǒ chēng shíkuài qiánde zhūròu.
   Please weigh out ¥10 worth of pork for me.

2. **MEAT SELLER:** 嗯。
   M.
   Uh-huh.

3. **HAN:** 那边儿的瘦一点儿，您给我切那边儿的吧。
   Nèibianrde shòu yidianr, nín gěi wǒ qiē nèibianrde ba.
   That over there is leaner, why don't you cut that over there for me.

4. **MEAT SELLER:** 其实都差不多。*(after she has cut the pork)* 还要别的吗？
   Qíshí dōu chàbuduō. Hái yào biéde ma?
   Actually, it's all about the same. Do you want anything else?

5. HAN: 不要了，就这些吧。给您钱。哦，劳驾，哪儿卖面包？
Bú yàole, jiù zhèixiē ba. Gěi nín qián. Ò, láojià, nǎr mài miànbāo?
No, just this, I suppose. Here's the money. Oh, excuse me, where do they sell bread?

6. MEAT SELLER: 面包店、食品店都卖。
Miànbāo diàn, shípǐn diàn dōu mài.
Bakeries and grocery stores both sell it.

7. HAN: 远不远？
Yuǎn bu yuǎn?
Are they far away?

8. MEAT SELLER: 近极了，一点儿也不远。就在旁边儿的胡同儿里。
Jìnjíle, yìdiǎnr yě bù yuǎn. Jiù zài pángbiānrde hútòngrli.
They're very close, not far at all. They're right in the next alley.

9. HAN: 谢谢。
Xièxie.
Thanks.

New Vocabulary

称	chēng	weigh, weigh out
猪	zhū	pig
肉	ròu	meat
猪肉	zhūròu	pork
切	qiē	cut, slice
差不多	chàbuduō	be about the same
面包	miànbāo	bread
面包店	miànbāo diàn	bakery
食品	shípǐn	food product; groceries
食品店	shípǐn diàn	grocery store
极了	-jíle	extremely
一点也不…	yìdiǎn(r) yě bù...	not at all, not the least bit
胡同	hútòng(r)	small street, lane, alley

Supplementary Vocabulary

鸡	jī	chicken
鸡肉	jīròu	chicken meat
牛	niú	cow, ox
牛肉	niúròu	beef
羊	yáng	sheep

羊肉	**yángròu**	mutton
鸭子	**yāzi**	duck
鸭肉	**yāròu**	duck meat
肥	**féi**	be fatty (of food)
虾	**xiā**	shrimp
吃素	**chīsù**	eat vegetarian food
附近	**fùjìn**	in the vicinity, nearby

Notes on the Conversation

-jíle as verb suffix to express "extremely"

The suffix **-jíle** is often attached to stative verbs to indicate "extremely." This suffix is most commonly attached to one-syllable stative verbs like **hǎo** "be good" and **màn** "be slow," but it may also be attached to two-syllable stative verbs like **hǎochī** "be good to eat" and **hǎokàn** "be attractive." The basic pattern is: Subject + Stative Verb + **-jíle**, for example, **Miànbāo diàn jìnjíle** "The bakery is extremely close." More examples: **Hǎojíle!** "Great!," **Wǒ zuìjìn mángjíle** "Recently I've been extremely busy," **Tā gāoxìngjíle** "She was extremely happy." **-Jíle** is sometimes also used with regular verbs like **xǐhuan** as in **Wǒ xǐhuanjíle** "I like it extremely much." If you use **-jíle**, don't use **hěn** or **fēicháng**; also, **-jíle** is usually not negated with **bù**.

....

Yìdiǎnr yě bù... "not the least bit..."

The common pattern **yìdiǎn(r) yě bù** means "not even by a little, not the least bit, not at all." It may be followed by stative verbs, auxiliary verbs, and other kinds of verbs. Examples: **Yìdiǎnr yě bù yuǎn** "It's not far at all," **Wǒ yìdiǎn yě bú lèi** "I'm not at all tired," **Wǒ yìdiǎnr yě bù xǐhuan tā** "I don't like her at all." In this pattern, **dōu** can be substituted for **yě**, for example, **Wǒ juéde Zhōngwén yìdiǎn dōu bù nán** "I feel that Chinese isn't at all difficult." If the verb is **méiyou**, then **méiyou** is used instead of **bù**; a preposed object may be added between the **yìdiǎn(r)** and the **yě** or **dōu**. Example: **Wǒ yìdiǎn qián yě méiyou** "I don't have any money at all." Similarly, in the case of negative completed action, **méi(you)** is used instead of **bù**. Example: **Tā yìdiǎn yě méiyou biàn** "He hasn't changed at all."

....

Reading

New Characters and Words

337.	切	**qiē**	cut, slice
338.	肉	**ròu**	meat
339.	牛	**niú**	ox, cow; (surname)
	牛肉	**niúròu**	beef
	牛油	**niúyóu**	butter

340.	极	jí	utmost, very, extremely
	…极了	-jíle	extremely
	近极了	jìnjíle	extremely close
	好极了	hǎojíle	great, fantastic
341.	食	shí	eat (can't be used alone)
342.	品	pǐn	goods, product (can't be used alone)
	食品	shípǐn	food product, groceries
	食品店	shípǐn diàn	grocery store

A. SENTENCES

一、请放心，在上海的菜场买从美国进口的食品一点儿都不难。
二、这种进口的面包真是好吃极了，比美国的白面包好吃得多。
三、今天温州出太阳了，但是又冷又干，报上说最高温度8度，最低温度3度。
四、那个人说机场离这儿近极了，但是他不是本地人，我觉得他可能讲错了。
五、小牛是我大学时候的同屋，我今天能有机会再见到他，真是高兴极了！
六、食品店的牛肉都是进口的，贵极了，还是到市场去买本地的牛肉吧。
七、有的中国人不吃牛肉，还有的人只吃菜根本不吃肉。
八、那家食品店早上几点开门，晚上几点关门？他们卖什么样的食品？
九、弟弟，准备好了没有？你要记得，切肉的时候一定得小心！
十、因为王大海喜欢动物，所以他只吃菜，一点儿肉也不吃。

B. CONVERSATIONS

一、
王太太：李太太，您到哪儿去？
李太太：我先生的两个朋友刚从南京来。我去菜场买点儿东西。
王太太：我刚从市场回来，今天那儿的牛肉真是好极了。
李太太：是吗？我得赶快去买几斤。

二、
李太太：请问，您这儿的牛肉多少钱一斤？
卖肉的：三块八，保证肉好。
李太太：好，我要五斤……可是，对不起，我不要这块。您给我切那块，好不好？

卖肉的：这块看起来也不错，其实哪块都差不多。

李太太：请您包起来，谢谢。

卖肉的：好。一共是十九块。

李太太：这是二十块。

卖肉的：找您一块，您拿好。

C. NARRATIVE

一、小李原来在一家食品店工作。可是，他后来又找到了别的工作。他现在这个工作是在一个市场里，天天都在那儿卖肉，忙极了。他早上很早就得去上班，晚上很晚才下班回家。他跟我们说，有的时候一天得切一千多斤的牛肉！

二、我小学三年级的时候，有一次切肉，不小心切到了我小妹的手。从那之后，她有一年没跟我讲话！现在我已经长大了，切肉、切菜根本不会切到人。不过我切肉、切菜的时候，我小妹还是离我很远！

Notes

A6.　市场 **shìchǎng** "market" or "marketplace"

C2.　从那之后 literally, "from after that" or, in idiomatic English, "after that" or "since then"

A stand selling fish at an outdoor market in Hong Kong

PART TWO

Conversation 🎧

Situation: Su Ning, a young Taiwanese woman, asks her American housemate Holly Young if she would like to go to the supermarket with her.

1. SU: Holly, 我要去超市买点东西。你要不要和我一起去?
Holly, wǒ yào qù chāoshì mǎi diǎn dōngxi. Nǐ yào bu yào hàn wǒ yìqǐ qù?
Holly, I'm going to the supermarket to buy some stuff. Do you want to go together with me?

2. YOUNG: 好啊。我也正想买点咖啡、土司什么的。
Hǎo a. Wǒ yě zhèng xiǎng mǎi diǎn kāfēi, tǔsī shemmede.
Sure. I was just thinking of buying some coffee, white bread, and so forth.

3. SU: *(after they arrive at the supermarket)*

这样好了,为了节省时间,你买你的,我买我的。我们五分钟
以后在出口的柜台见,怎么样?
**Zhèiyang hǎole. Wèile jiéshěng shíjiān, nǐ mǎi nǐde, wǒ mǎi wǒde. Wǒmen wǔfēn
zhōng yǐhòu zài chūkǒude guìtái jiàn, zěmmeyàng?**
How about this? To save time, you buy your things and I'll buy mine. In five minutes we'll
meet at the counter by the exit. How about it?

4. YOUNG: 好主意!
Hǎo zhǔyì!
Good idea!

5. SU: *(after they've finished shopping)*

你觉得台湾跟美国的超市比起来怎么样?
Nǐ juéde Táiwān gēn Měiguode chāoshì bíqilai zěmmeyàng?
How do you feel supermarkets in Taiwan compare with those in America?

6. **YOUNG:** 都差不多。大概比美国的小一点，也不像在美国那么普遍。

Dōu chàbuduō. Dàgài bǐ Měiguode xiǎo yìdiǎn, yě bú xiàng zài Měiguo nèmme pǔbiàn.

About the same. Probably a bit smaller than in America, and not so widespread as in America.

7. **SU:** 可能要慢慢来吧。我想以后会一年比一年普遍的。

Kěnéng yào mànmān lái ba. Wǒ xiǎng yǐhòu huì yìnián bǐ yìnián pǔbiànde.

All in its own good time. I think in the future they'll become more widespread each year.

New Vocabulary 🎧

超市	chāoshì	supermarket
和	hàn	with (Taiwanese pronunciation)
咖啡	kāfēi	coffee
土司	tǔsī	white bread
…什么的	…shemmede	…and so on
为了	wèile	in order to, for
节省	jiéshěng	save
出口	chūkǒu(r)	exit
柜台	guìtái	counter
主意	zhǔyì	idea, plan
比起来	bíqilai	compare
A跟B比起来	A gēn B bǐqǐlái	comparing A and B
像	xiàng	resemble, be like
普遍	pǔbiàn	be widespread, common
慢慢来	mànmān lái	"take one's time"
一…比一…	yī…bǐ yī…	one…compared with the next
会…的	huì…-de	be likely to, would, will

Supplementary Vocabulary 🎧

入口	rùkǒu	entrance
节省	jiéshěng	be frugal

Notes on the Conversation

…shemmede "and so on"

The common sentence ending **…shemmede** "and so on," "and so forth" is attached to the end of a series of two or more nouns (or occasionally other words) when you wish to indicate that there exist more members of the same series but don't want to list them all. Examples: **Tā mǎile zìdiǎn, bàozhǐ, dìtú shemmede** "She bought dictionaries, newspapers, maps, and so on," **Wǒ xūyào báicài, qíncài, fānqié shemmede** "I need cabbage, celery, tomatoes, and so forth," **Wǒmen jīntiān yào chīfàn, mǎi dōngxi, kàn wǒ biǎojiě shemmede** "Today we're going to have a meal, go shopping, visit my cousin and so forth."

Wèile to express purpose

One way to express purpose is with the coverb expression **wèile** "in order to, so as to, to, for." The pattern is: **Wèile** + purpose clause + main clause. Examples: **Wèile jiéshěng qián, tāmen juédìng bù chī zǎofàn le** "So as to save money, they decided not to eat breakfast," **Wèile néng mǎidào piào, tā yídàzǎo jiù qù páiduì le** "To be able to buy a ticket, she went to stand in line very early in the morning," **Wèile xué zuì biāozhǔnde Zhōngwén, tā bāndao Běijīng qule** "To learn the most standard Chinese, he moved to Beijing."

A gēn B bǐqǐlái "comparing A and B"

In line 5, look at the question **Táiwān gēn Měiguode chāoshì bíqilai zěmmeyàng?** "How do supermarkets in Taiwan compare with those in America?" This is actually an abbreviation of a fuller form **Táiwānde chāoshì gēn Měiguode chāoshì bíqilai zěmmeyàng?** "Taiwan's supermarkets compared with America's supermarkets how are they?" The pattern **A gēn B bǐqǐlái** "comparing A and B" is used to compare two items with each other. Some sort of a comment or, as here, question then follows. Examples: **Zhèrde gēn nàrde bíqilai zěmmeyàng?** "How do the ones here compare with the ones there?," **Nǐ juéde Běijīngde tiānqi gēn Huáshèngdùnde tiānqi bíqilai zěmmeyàng?** "What do you think of Beijing's weather compared to Washington's weather?"

Huì…-de "be likely to, would, will"

The pattern **huì…-de** "be likely to, would, will" expresses a speaker's conviction that something will most likely be a certain way. The **huì** and the **-de** surround the predicate of the sentence. Example: **Táiwānde chāoshì huì yìnián bǐ yìnián pǔbiànde** "Taiwan's supermarkets will become more widespread each year." The **huì…-de** pattern is especially common in Southern Mandarin. **Huì** can also be used alone with basically the same meaning, but the addition of final **-de** lends additional assurance or assertion to the statement. More examples: **Xiǎo Liú huì láide** "Little Liu will come," **Xiǎo Zhào bú huì láide** "Little Zhao isn't likely to come," **Dōngxi yídìng huì zhǎodàode** "I'm sure the things will be found."

Yī + Measure + bǐ + yī + Measure

In line 7, look at the sentence **Wǒ xiǎng yǐhòu huì yìnián bǐ yìnián pǔbiànde** "I think in the future they're likely to become more widespread each year." The meaning of the pattern **yī** + Measure + **bǐ** + **yī** + Measure is "(measure) by (measure)" or "one (measure) at a time." More examples: **Měiguode shū yìnián bǐ yìnián guì** "Books in America are getting more expensive year by year," **Nǐde Zhōngwén yìtiān bǐ yìtiān hǎo!** "Your Chinese is getting better day by day!," **Zhèixiē dìtú, yìzhāng bǐ yìzhāng piàoliang** "These maps, one is more attractive than the next."

Reading

New Characters and Words

343.	土	tǔ	earth
	土司	tǔsī	white bread
	土地	tǔdì	soil, earth, land, territory
344.	节	jié	restrict, control; economize
	节省	jiéshěng	save; be frugal, thrifty
345.	入	rù	enter (can't be used alone)
	入口	rùkǒu	entrance
	进入	jìnrù	enter, come in
346.	主	zhǔ	master, host, lord; main
	主张	zhǔzhāng	advocate, be in favor of
347.	意	yì	meaning, intention (can't be used alone)
	主意	zhǔyì	idea, plan
348.	思	sī	think (can't be used alone)
	意思	yìsi	meaning
	有意思	yǒu yìsi	be interesting
	没意思	méi yìsi	be uninteresting
	不好意思	bù hǎo yìsi	be embarrassing, be embarrassed

A. SENTENCES

一、中文难极了，可是我觉得学起来很有意思。

二、中文跟日文比起来，你觉得哪种比较难学？

三、小姐，你走错了，这儿是出口，入口在那边。

四、牛先生看起来像一头牛，可是高先生不高，白先生也不白。

五、我弟弟、妹妹都主张卖我们家的那块土地，可是我哥哥不想卖。

六、你节省一点儿，先别买汽车。你还年轻，慢慢来，以后还有机会买。

七、我们的中文老师好极了，所以我们班上的同学，中文一天比一天好。

八、不好意思，我的中文不好，请问，"禁止携犬进入"这六个字是什么意思？

九、他们家土地不少但是没钱，所以那次他们需要钱的时候，没有别的办法，只好卖了一些土地，这样才解决了问题。

十、有一天早上，王大海跟他的同屋说："我有一个好主意，星期六早上我们都去动物园，你们觉得怎么样？"

B. CONVERSATIONS

一、

小牛：八点一刻了，我们吃早饭吧！

小白：好主意。你准备吃什么？

小牛：我早饭喜欢吃土司。

小白：你吃干土司？

小牛：不，土司加一点牛油就很好吃了。你呢？你准备吃什么？

小白：我吃一点水果就行了。

二、

太太：为了节省时间，你进市场买你的牛肉、白菜什么的，我开车去加油站加油。我们差不多半个小时以后在市场的入口见，怎么样？

先生：好主意。市场看起来好像人很多，所以你慢慢加你的油吧。如果半个小时以后我还没出来的话，你等我一会儿，好吗？

太太：好，没问题。

An elderly couple shopping for meat in a Beijing supermarket

C. NARRATIVES

一、我有两个哥哥、一个弟弟。我长得比较像大哥，弟弟长得比较像二哥。大哥比我大四岁，可是看起来我的年纪比他大，所以有的人不太清楚谁是哥哥，谁是弟弟。你看得出来吗？

二、星期天我出去买报纸，在书店看见了我的老朋友张国林。他说正想去我家里找我呢。我们两个人好久没见了，我觉得他好像一年比一年老了。从书店出来，他就和我一起回家了。我太太看到我的老朋友来了，也很高兴。她一定要张国林在我们家吃中饭。为了买到最好的牛肉和白菜，她去了离我们家比较远的市场，然后给我们准备了很好吃的中饭。

Notes

A8a. 禁止 **jìnzhǐ** "forbid, prohibit, ban"

A8b. 犬 **quǎn** "canine, dog". 犬, to be differentiated from the character 太, is a formal, written-style Chinese word for colloquial 狗 **gǒu** "dog." The street sign 禁止携犬进入 **Jìnzhǐ xié quǎn jìnrù** means literally, "Forbid bring dogs enter," or in more idiomatic English, "It is not permitted to enter if you are bringing a dog."

Purchasing Shoes and Clothing

PART ONE

Conversation 🎧

Situation: Rosy Huang, a Chinese-American woman living with her family in Taipei for a year, wants to purchase a pair of black high-heel shoes.

1. HUANG:	我需要一双黑色的高跟鞋。 **Wǒ xūyào yìshuāng hēisède gāogēnxié.** I need a pair of black high-heel shoes.
2. SHOE SALESMAN:	你穿几号的？ **Nǐ chuān jǐhàode?** What size do you wear?
3. HUANG:	我在美国穿七号的。不知道你们的号码跟美国的号码一样不一样？ **Wǒ zài Měiguo chuān qíhàode. Bù zhīdào nǐmende hàomǎ gēn Měiguode hàomǎ yíyàng bu yíyàng?** In America I wear size seven. I wonder if your sizes are the same as or different from American sizes?

4. SHOE SALESMAN: 号码不一样啦，不过我可以帮你试试看。这双大小怎么样？

Hàomǎ bù yíyàng la, búguò wǒ kéyi bāng nǐ shìshi kàn.

(takes out a pair of shoes for her to try on) **Zhèishuāng dàxiǎo zěmmeyàng?**

The sizes are different, but I can help you try some on and see. How is the size of this pair?

5. HUANG: 好像太小了。有没有大一号的？

Hǎoxiàng tài xiǎole. Yǒu méiyou dà yíhàode?

They seem too small. Do you have any that are one size larger?

6. SHOE SALESMAN: 这双大一号，你试试看。

Zhèishuāng dà yíhào, nǐ shìshi kàn.

This pair is one size bigger, try it on.

7. HUANG: 这双刚好。这双卖多少钱？

Zhèishuāng gāng hǎo. Zhèishuāng mài duōshǎo qián?

This pair is just right. How much does this pair sell for?

8. SHOE SALESMAN: 一千八。

Yìqiān bā.

1,800 NT.

9. HUANG: 嗯，漂亮是漂亮，但是一千八太贵了。少算一点，好不好？

M, piàoliang shi piàoliang, dànshi yìqiān bā tài guìle. Shǎo suàn yidian, hǎo bu hǎo?

Hm, they do look nice, but 1,800 NT is too expensive. Could you reduce the price a little?

10. SHOE SALESMAN: 刚上市的，没有办法。

Gāng shàngshìde, méiyou bànfa.

They just came on the market, nothing I can do.

11. HUANG: 那我再看看。

Nà wǒ zài kànkan.

Then I'll look around some more.

12. SHOE SALESMAN: 好的。有需要欢迎再来。

Hǎode. Yǒu xūyào huānyíng zài lái.

O.K. If you need anything, you're welcome to come again.

New Vocabulary

双	**shuāng**	pair
高跟鞋	**gāogēn(r)xié**	high-heel shoes
穿	**chuān**	put on, wear (shoes, clothes)
不知道	**bù zhīdào**	(I) wonder
号码	**hàomǎ(r)**	number

一样	yíyàng	one kind; the same
A跟B一样	A gēn B yíyàng	A is the same as B
帮	bāng	help
算	suàn	figure, calculate
上市	shàngshì	come on the market
需要	xūyào	need
大小	dàxiǎo	size

Supplementary Vocabulary

| 完全 | wánquán | completely |
| 袜子 | wàzi | sock |

Notes on the Conversation

A gēn B yíyàng to express similarity

The pattern **A gēn B yíyàng** "A is the same as B" (literally, "A and B are one kind") is a common pattern for expressing that things are the same or different. Examples: **Zhèige gēn nèige yíyàng** "This one is the same as that one," **Zuò gōngchē gēn zuò diànchē yíyàng** "Taking the bus would be the same as taking the trolley," **Zài zhèr chīfàn gēn zài nàr chīfàn dōu yíyàng** "Eating here would be the same as eating there." To indicate in what respect the two things compared are similar, a verb can be added after the **yíyàng**. Examples: **Wǒ gēn nǐ yíyàng gāo** "I'm as tall as you," **Wǒ gēn nǐ yíyàng xǐhuan chī Zhōngguo cài** "I like eating Chinese food as much as you do." To express that two things aren't the same, put **bù** before **yíyàng** and say **A gēn B bù yíyàng**. Examples: **Zhèige gēn nèige bù yíyàng** "This one isn't the same as that one," **Nèiliǎngzhǒng chē bù yíyàng guì** "Those two kinds of cars aren't equally expensive." To make questions, either add **ma** or use an affirmative-negative verb construction. Examples: **Zhèige gēn nèige yíyàng ma?** "Is this one the same as that one?," **Zhèizhǒng gēn nèizhǒng yíyàng bu yíyàng?** "Is this kind the same as that kind?"

Stative Verbs followed by quantity expressions

A stative verb may be followed by a quantity expression that limits or otherwise clarifies its meaning. Examples: **Dà yíhào** "It's one number (or size) bigger," **Zhèige guì wǔkuài** "This one is five dollars more expensive," **Nèibān huǒchē màn liǎngge zhōngtóu** "That train is two hours slower."

Concessive clauses with X shi X, ...

Look at line 9 in the conversation: **Piàoliang shi piàoliang, dànshi yìqiān bā tài guìle** "As for being pretty, they (shoes) are pretty all right, but 1,800 is too expensive." In concessive clauses with **X shi X, ...**, speakers concede certain aspects of an argument before making their main point. The **X** can be a stative verb, some other kind of verb, or even a phrase. The second clause, where the main point is made, is usually introduced by **dànshi** "but," **kěshi** "but," **búguò** "however," or **jiù shi** "it's just that." The concessive clause can be translated with "all right," "to be sure," or sometimes just by contrastive stress. More examples: **Nèige dìfang yuǎn shi yuǎn, dànshi wǒ hái shi xiǎng qù** "That place is far away to be sure, but I still want to go," **Gōngzuò máng shi máng, kěshi dàjiā dōu hěn gāoxìng** "Work is busy all right, but everyone is happy," **Wǒ qù shi qùguo, kěshi méi kànjian tā** "As far as going there is concerned, I did go but I didn't see her."

....

Reading

New Characters and Words

349.	双	**shuāng**	pair
	一双	**yìshuāng**	a pair
	双号	**shuānghào**	even number
	双人房	**shuāngrénfáng**	double room
350.	鞋	**xié**	shoe
	一双鞋	**yìshuāng xié**	a pair of shoes
	雨鞋	**yǔxié**	rain shoes
	高跟鞋	**gāogēnxié**	high-heel shoes
	鞋店	**xiédiàn**	shoe store
	鞋厂	**xiéchǎng**	shoe factory
351.	黑	**hēi**	black
	黑人	**Hēirén**	Black (person)
352.	色	**sè**	color
	黑色	**hēisè**	the color black
	白色	**báisè**	the color white
353.	穿	**chuān**	put on, wear (shoes, clothes)
354.	算	**suàn**	reckon, calculate
	算钱	**suànqián**	calculate money, figure a price

A. SENTENCES

一、你看，我的票跟你的票不一样；我的是黑色的，你的是白色的。

二、这双白色的鞋太小了，我能不能换一双大一号的？

三、那双黑鞋是从法国进口的，所以价钱才这么贵。

四、那家鞋厂一个月出口五万双雨鞋到美国去。

五、你看！你这双手看起来跟你哥哥的完全一样。

六、穿高跟鞋走路不好走，我得找一双别的鞋。

七、白菜刚上市，一斤五十块。不贵，买一点儿吧！

八、我们决定买二十斤白菜，请您算一算一共多少钱。

九、中文跟日文原来是两种完全不一样的语言。

十、你们大概已经知道，王大海这个人跟你、跟我都很不一样。

B. CONVERSATIONS

一、

万老师：何山明，听说你下星期要去张家口，是吗？

何山明：对，我要到那儿去看我的表哥。

万老师：什么时候回来？

何山明：我星期四或者星期五就回来了。

万老师：张家口是个很有意思的地方。你表哥住在张家口市还是张家口县？

何山明：他住在万全县，离张家口市很近。

万老师：你去那儿一定要多穿一点儿，听说现在冷得要死！

何山明：好，那我一定多穿一点儿。谢谢老师！

万老师：别忘了写你的作业！

何山明：请老师放心，我不会忘的。

二、

买鞋的：请问，你们有没有七号半的鞋？

卖鞋的：七号半？我找找看。对不起，七号半的刚卖完。

买鞋的：问题不大，我也能穿八号的。有八号的吧？

卖鞋的：你等一下，我看看。对不起，八号的也卖完了。九、十、十一、十二号的也都卖完了。

买鞋的：你们这是什么样儿的鞋店？你们根本没有鞋！

卖鞋的：我们最近雨鞋和高跟鞋特别多。你多买几双，我可以少算你一点。怎么样，你要几双？

C. NARRATIVE

一、我跟姐姐住在一起。明天我要开始在一家进出口公司上班了。在台北，上班的小姐差不多都穿高跟鞋，可是我只有一双高跟鞋，姐姐也只有一双高跟鞋，怎么办呢？我穿八号的鞋子，姐姐跟我一样也穿八号的鞋子。所以为了节省一点钱，我们一个人买黑色的高跟鞋，一个人买白色的高跟鞋。她可以穿我的鞋，我也可以穿她的鞋。这样问题就解决了，我们好像多了好几双鞋一样！

二、"您好！我是万国语言中心的白老师。您可以在我们中心学中文、日文、越南文和法文，白天或者晚上都可以。我们也有老师可以到您家去。我们中心的电话是65158263。万国语言中心在北京市新街口东街小学的对面，不难找，很多公车都到，所以交通根本不是问题。您有时间，可以先来看看。您先拿一张我们中心的名片吧。以后您有时间一定来看看！"

Notes

A3. 所以价钱才这么贵 *"that's* why the price is so expensive." The adverb 才 here empha-sizes the reason why the black shoes are so expensive.

A6. 不好走 literally, "not easy to walk" or "hard to walk (in)." The stative verb 好 here means "easy to."

B2. 问题不大 literally, "Problem is not big" is the equivalent of English "No problem." Another way to express this, of course, would be 没问题.

C1. 我们好像多了好几双鞋一样 "It's as though we have quite a few more pairs of shoes." 多 here functions not as a stative verb, as it normally does, but as a regular verb meaning "become many; increase."

C2. 新 **xīn** "new." 新街口 is the name of a neighborhood in Beijing.

A shoe store along Heping East Road in Taipei

PART TWO

Conversation 🎧

Situation: Rosy Huang, a Chinese-American woman living with her family in Taipei for a year, goes shopping at a children's clothing store.

1. HUANG: 小姐，你们有没有小男生穿的长裤?
Xiáojie, nǐmen yǒu méiyou xiǎo nánshēng chuānde chángkù?
Miss, do you have long pants that little boys wear?

2. CLERK: 有，请过来看看。小孩几岁了?
Yǒu, qǐng guòlai kànkan. Xiǎoháir jǐsuì le?
Yes, please come over and take a look. How old is the child?

3. HUANG: 六岁多，快七岁了。
Liùsuì duō, kuài qísuì le.
He's six, almost seven.

4. CLERK: 穿九号应该没有问题。看看这条。
Chuān jiǔhào yīnggāi méiyou wèntí. Kànkan zhèitiáo.
Size nine should be no problem. Take a look at this pair.

5. HUANG: 颜色还不错，但是不知道会不会太大或太小?
Yánsè hái bú cuò, dànshi bù zhīdào huì bu huì tài dà huò tài xiǎo?
The color is fine, but I wonder if it's going to be too big or too small?

6. CLERK: 没关系。假如不合适的话，七天以内可以拿来换。
Méi guānxi. Jiǎrú bù héshìde huà, qītiān yǐnèi kéyi nálai huàn.
That's O.K. If it doesn't fit, you can bring it here within seven days for exchange.

7. HUANG: 多少钱？

Duōshǎo qián?

How much is it?

8. CLERK: 这种裤子本来是五百四一条，这个礼拜刚好打对折，只要两百七。

Zhèizhǒng kùzi běnlái shi wǔbǎi sì yìtiáo, zhèige lǐbài gānghǎo dǎ duìzhé, zhǐ yào liǎngbǎi qī.

These pants originally were 540 NT per pair, this week they just happen to be 50% off, only 270 NT.

9. HUANG: 好，我买一条。可以刷卡吗？

Hǎo, wǒ mǎi yìtiáo. Kéyi shuākǎ ma?

All right, I'll buy a pair. Can I use a credit card?

10. CLERK: 对不起，我们不收信用卡。

Duìbuqǐ, wǒmen bù shōu xìnyòngkǎ.

I'm sorry, we don't accept credit cards.

11. HUANG: 好吧，那我给你现金。这是三百块。

Hǎo ba, nà wǒ gěi nǐ xiànjīn. Zhè shi sānbǎikuài.

O.K., then I'll give you cash. This is 300 NT.

12. CLERK: 好的，请稍候。找您三十，发票在里面。谢谢！欢迎再来。

Hǎode, qǐng shāo hòu. Zhǎo nín sānshí. Fāpiào zài lǐmiàn. Xièxie! Huānyíng zài lái.

O.K., just a minute, please. Here's 30 NT in change. The receipt is inside. Thank you! Please come again.

New Vocabulary

小男生	**xiǎo nánshēng**	young male student, little boy
长裤	**chángkù**	long pants
过来	**guòlai**	come over
假如	**jiǎrú**	if
假如…的话	**jiǎrú...-de huà**	if...
合适	**héshì**	be the right size, fit
…以内	**...yǐnèi**	within...
拿来	**nálai**	bring here
裤子	**kùzi**	pants
本来	**běnlái**	originally
刚好	**gānghǎo**	just, as it happens
打折	**dǎzhé**	give a discount
对折	**duìzhé**	50% discount
打对折	**dǎ duìzhé**	give a 50% discount
刷卡	**shuākǎ**	imprint a credit card

收	shōu	accept
信用卡	xìnyòngkǎ	credit card
现金	xiànjīn	cash
请稍候	qǐng shāo hòu	"please wait briefly"
发票	fāpiào	itemized bill; receipt

Supplementary Vocabulary

短	duǎn	be short (not long)
短裤	duǎnkù	short pants
衣服	yīfu	clothes
衬衫	chènshān	shirt
裙子	qúnzi	skirt
小女生	xiǎo nǚshēng	little girl
戴	dài	put on, wear (watch, hat, jewelry)
表	biǎo	watch (for telling time)
手表	shǒubiǎo	wristwatch
过去	guòqu	go over, pass by
拿去	náqu	take away
搬过来	bānguolai	move over
拿过去	náguoqu	take over
…之内	…zhīnèi	within…

Notes on the Conversation

Jiǎrú…-de huà "if"

The pattern **jiǎrú…-de huà** "if" works the same way and has the same meaning as the patterns **yàoshi…-de huà** and **rúguǒ…-de huà**. These patterns all indicate that if a certain condition is met, a certain result will occur. **Yàoshi** is very colloquial and is used mostly in northern China, while **jiǎrú** and **rúguǒ** can be used everywhere Chinese is spoken. The clause with **jiǎrú** (or **yàoshi** or **rúguǒ**) precedes the condition while **-de huà**, which literally means "the words that," follows it (**-de huà** is common but can be omitted). Examples: **Jiǎrú míngtiān tiānqi hǎode huà, wǒ yídìng qù** "If the weather tomorrow is good, I'll definitely go," **Jiǎrú tā bù láide huà, nǐ dǎsuan zěmme bàn?** "What do you plan to do if she doesn't come?," **Jiǎrú míngtiān bù héshìde huà, hòutiān yě kéyi** "If tomorrow isn't convenient, the day after tomorrow is O.K., too."

....

Time Expression + yǐnèi

The pattern Time Expression + **yǐnèi** means "within a certain period of time." Unlike English, in Chinese the time expression always comes first. Examples: **yìnián yǐnèi** "within one year," **sāntiān yǐnèi** "within three days," **yíge yuè yǐnèi** "within a month." **Zhīnèi**, in the Supplementary Vocabulary of this lesson, has the same meaning and is used in the same way as **yǐnèi**, for example, **shítiān zhīnèi** "within ten days."

....

Dǎzhe "give a discount"

Dǎzhé indicates that a discount is being given off the original price. A number indicating for how many tenths of the original price the item will be sold is inserted between the **dǎ** and the **zhé**. The pattern is: **dǎ** + number of tenths + **zhé**. Examples: **dǎ jiǔzhé** "sell at 9/10 of the original price" (i.e., 10% discount), **dǎ qīzhé** "sell at 7/10 of the original price" (= 30% discount), **dǎ bāwǔzhé** "sell at 85% of the original price" (= 15% discount). Don't confuse the number of tenths of the original price (the Chinese point of view) with the percentage amount of the discount (the American point of view). For example, **dǎ liùzhé** means "sell at a 40% discount" (not "sell at a 60% discount"). Instead of **dǎ wǔzhé** "sell at a 50% discount" you can also say **dǎ duìzhé** "sell at half price." **Dǎzhé** can also be used alone, as in **Néng bu néng dǎzhé?** "Could you give a discount?"

....

Chinese equivalents of English "wear"

There are two Chinese verbs that translate as "put on" or "wear": **dài**, in this lesson, and **chuān**, which was introduced earlier. The distinction is that **chuān**, which literally means "pass through," is used for wearing things that have an opening in them like shirts, pants, and shoes (since a part of the body must "pass through" an opening when you wear them). On the other hand, **dài** is used for things that don't have an opening like hats, jewelry, and glasses. Grammatically, both **dài** and **chuān** are action verbs more like English "put on" than like "wear." Therefore, to say "I'm wearing…" say **Wǒ chuānle...** or **Wǒ dàile...** with a completed action **-le**; to say "I'm not wearing…" say **Wǒ méi chuān...** or **Wǒ méi dài....**

....

Reading

New Characters and Words

355.	应	yīng	should, ought
356.	该	gāi	should, ought
	应该	yīnggāi	should, ought
357.	衣	yī	clothing (can't be used alone); (surname)
	毛衣	máoyī	sweater
	大衣	dàyī	overcoat
	雨衣	yǔyī	raincoat
358.	服	fú	clothing (can't be used alone)
	衣服	yīfu	clothes
359.	如	rú	if; be like, equal
	如果	rúguǒ	if
	如果…的话	rúguǒ...de huà	if
360.	内	nèi	inside, within

⋯以内	**...yǐnèi**	within
⋯之内	**...zhīnèi**	within
内衣	**nèiyī**	underwear

A. SENTENCES

一、如果下雨的话，应该穿雨衣跟雨鞋。
二、下一站就是动物园儿了，您该准备下车了！
三、那个女的好像在叫我，你看我应该不应该过去？
四、我下星期六刚好有时间，到你家去应该没有问题。
五、地上本来没有路，走的人多了，也就有了路了。
六、这双鞋，您如果不喜欢的话，只要是五天之内都可以拿来换。
七、小何，这些牛肉和白菜你拿过去给对面的王老太太，好不好？
八、今天是老高的生日，朋友准备送他大衣、毛衣、内衣什么的。
九、我知道我应该节省一点，所以我决定从明年起不买贵的衣服了。
十、王大海因为没有钱买手表，所以到哪儿去都带着一个小钟。

B. CONVERSATIONS

一、

美国人：房应国老先生死了，你觉得我应不应该到房家去看看房太太？
中国人：我觉得你应该去。
美国人：听说在中国，人死了要穿白色的衣服，是真的吗？
中国人：对，有时候是这样子，可是也不一定。你是外国人，你穿黑
　　　　衣服、黑鞋就可以了。

二、

年家平：李老师，不好意思，今天的作业我忘了。
李老师：你忘了？那你什么时候能给我呢？
年家平：我两天之内一定给老师，真对不起。
李老师：两天之内？不行！你最晚明天早上八点给我，要不然太晚了。

C. NARRATIVE

一、广州在中国的南方。以前有不少朋友跟我讲过，那个地方热得要
　　死，所以去年一月我去那儿看我表哥的时候，我想天气一定很热
　　吧。但是我错了，刚好我去的那个星期广州的天气冷极了，还天
　　天下大雨。我应该带的很多衣服，像大衣、毛衣、雨衣、雨鞋什么
　　的，都没有带。所以我在那儿的那几天就觉得很冷。我保证下次如
　　果还去广州的话，一定会多带一点儿衣服，特别是一月去的话。

二、 很久没看到白老师的儿子了。三年前他跟白老师一起来学校的时候还很小。今天看到他，好像不是以前的那个小男孩儿了。三年时间他就长这么大了！我想他应该上学了，可是白老师说他明年才可以上学。他长得那么高，看起来好像有六、七岁的样子，其实他还不到五岁。

Notes

A3.　好像在叫我 "it seems she's calling me"

B1.　人死了要穿白色的衣服 "When a person dies, you should wear white clothing."

C2.　三年时间他就长这么大了！ "In three years' time he has grown to be so big!" or "In the space of three years he's gotten so big!" Be sure to pronounce 长 here as **zhǎng** "grow."

Street scene in Hong Kong

Ordering a Meal in a Restaurant

PART ONE

Conversation 🎧

Situation: Dave Warres, an American student in Beijing, and his Chinese roommate, Li Xiaodong, have decided to go out for lunch. They're trying to decide where to eat.

1. **LI:** 你看咱们在哪个饭馆儿吃?
   Nǐ kàn zámmen zài něige fànguǎnr chī?
   Which restaurant do you think we should eat at?

2. **WARRES:** 随便，哪个都行。
   Suíbiàn, něige dōu xíng.
   As you like, any one is fine.

3. **LI:** 那家人少，咱们就在那儿吧。 *(they enter and sit down)*
   你先看看菜单儿，看看你想吃什么。
   Nèijiā rén shǎo, zámmen jiù zài nàr ba. Nǐ xiān kànkan càidānr, kànkan nǐ xiǎng chī shémme.
   That one doesn't have many people, why don't we eat there. You look at the menu first; see what you'd like to eat.

4. WARRES: 什么都可以。你点吧。
           Shémme dōu kéyi. Nǐ diǎn ba.
           Anything's fine. Why don't you order.

5. WAITRESS: 两位要点儿什么？
           Liǎngwèi yào diǎnr shémme?
           What would the two of you like?

6. LI: 一个鱼香肉丝、一个蚂蚁上树、一个麻婆豆腐。差不多了。
         再来两碗鸡蛋汤。
         Yíge Yúxiāng Ròusī, yíge Mǎyǐ Shàngshù, yíge Mápó Dòufu. Chàbuduōle. Zài lái liǎngwǎn jīdàn tāng.
         One Fish Fragrant Meat Shreds, one Ants Climbing a Tree, and one Pockmarked Old Woman's Tofu. That's about it. And bring two bowls of egg soup.

New Vocabulary

咱们	**zámmen**	we (you and I)
饭馆	**fànguǎn(r)**	restaurant
随便	**suíbiàn**	"as you wish"
菜	**cài**	dish of food
菜单	**càidān(r)**	menu
点	**diǎn**	order, choose
肉丝	**ròusī(r)**	meat shred
鱼香肉丝	**Yúxiāng Ròusī**	Fish Fragrant Meat Shreds
蚂蚁	**mǎyǐ**	ant
树	**shù**	tree
蚂蚁上树	**Mǎyǐ Shàngshù**	Ants Climbing a Tree
豆腐	**dòufu**	tofu
麻婆豆腐	**Mápó Dòufu**	Pockmarked Old Woman's Tofu
碗	**wǎn**	bowl
蛋	**dàn**	egg
鸡蛋	**jīdàn**	chicken egg
汤	**tāng**	soup
鸡蛋汤	**jīdàn tāng**	egg soup

Supplementary Vocabulary

刀子	**dāozi**	knife
叉子	**chāzi**	fork

勺子	sháozi	spoon
饭碗	fànwǎn	rice bowl
用	yòng	use; with
洗	xǐ	wash
洗手间	xǐshǒujiān	bathroom
筷子	kuàizi	chopsticks
点菜	diǎncài	order dishes of food
够	gòu	be enough

Notes on the Conversation

Zámmen as inclusive "we"

In line 1 of this conversation we encounter the last of the personal pronouns, **zámmen**. This pronoun, which in rapid speech is often contracted to **zám** or even **zém**, is used primarily in Beijing and environs to indicate "inclusive we/our/us," referring to both the speaker and the person(s) spoken to. For those Chinese speakers who use **zámmen**, **wǒmen** has a separate meaning of "exclusive we/our/us" that does not include the person(s) spoken to. As an example, study this sentence: **Nǐmen shi Měiguo rén, wǒmen shi Zhōngguo rén, kěshi zámmen dōu shi tóngxué!** "You are Americans and we (not including you) are Chinese, but we (including you) are all classmates!" Since the majority of Chinese speakers use **wǒmen** for both inclusive and exclusive "we," it would be fine for you to use only **wǒmen**, but you should be able to understand **zámmen** if you hear it.

More on Question Words used as Indefinites

In line 2, consider the phrase **Něige dōu xíng** "Any one (restaurant) will do." As you've seen before, Chinese Question Words can sometimes function as indefinites. There is a pattern Question Word + **dōu** + Verb in which the Question Word takes on an indefinite meaning of "any" or "every." The Question Word may serve as the topic of the sentence or it may serve as the preposed object. More examples: **Shéi dōu rènshi tā** "Everyone knows her," **Jǐsuì dōu kéyi** "Any age is fine," **Duōjiǔ dōu méi guānxi** "It doesn't matter how long," **Nǎr dōu shi rén!** "There were people everywhere!," **Tā shéi dōu xǐhuan** "She likes everyone," **Wǒ shémme dōu chī** "I eat everything," **Wǒ nǎr dōu zhǎoguo** "I've looked everywhere."

Reading

New Characters and Words

361. 随	suí	follow; (surname)
362. 便	biàn	convenient
随便	suíbiàn	"as you wish"; be casual, informal
便鞋	biànxié	slipper

大便	**dàbiàn**	defecate (literally, "big convenience"); feces
小便	**xiǎobiàn**	urinate (literally, "small convenience"); urine
363. 用	**yòng**	use; with; need to
用完	**yòngwán**	finish using
不用	**bú yòng**	don't need to
不用谢	**bú yòng xiè**	"you don't need to thank me"
不用找了	**bú yòng zhǎole**	"you don't need to give change"
公用	**gōngyòng**	public
公用电话	**gōngyòng diànhuà**	public telephone
364. 够	**gòu**	be enough
365. 爸	**bà**	dad, daddy
爸爸	**bàba**	dad, daddy
366. 妈	**mā**	mom, mommy
妈妈	**māma**	mom, mommy

A. SENTENCES

一、今天我们请你吃饭，你就随便点吧。

二、那个东西怎么用？我不会。听说用起来不太好用。

三、你妈妈也在这家工厂工作，是吗？

四、我跟老林说他不用谢我，可是他不听，一定要谢。

五、你随便在哪儿等我都可以，要是能离车站近一点儿是最好。

六、他三岁的时候爸爸、妈妈都死了，所以是在我们家长大的。

七、美国的菜市场不但卖吃的东西，也卖用的东西。

八、如果两双便鞋不够你们穿，你要跟我讲，我们家里还有几双。

九、我们一家五口点三个菜够吗？我们再多点几个菜吧！

十、真有意思，王大海用右手写字，但是用左手吃饭。

B. CONVERSATIONS

一、

中国人：你看我们在哪儿吃？

美国人：随便，哪儿都行。

中国人：那家人少，我们就在那儿吃吧。你想吃什么？

美国人：什么都可以。你点吧。

中国人：好。那我就点菜好了。

二、

外国学生：公用电话您用完了吗？

本地人　　：我还没用完。

外国学生（过了一会儿）：您现在用完了吧？

本地人　　：用完了。您可以用了。

外国学生：谢谢。

本地人　　：不用谢。

C. NARRATIVES

一、　我爸爸、妈妈都是台湾人。我跟我哥哥是在台湾出生，在美国长大的，所以我们两个应该算是美国人吧。我跟哥哥都会讲国语，可是我们在一起的时候还是讲美国话的时间比较多。我爸爸的美国话不太好，所以我用国语跟爸爸讲话。我妈妈美国话讲得很好，有时候我用美国话跟妈妈讲话，但是她一定用国语跟我讲话。

二、　在中国吃饭根本不成问题，哪儿都有吃饭的地方。如果你到大饭店，可以随便点菜，想吃什么就吃什么，像北京菜、广东菜、四川菜、上海菜差不多都有，保证好吃。你也可以到小吃店买一点小吃，又好吃又不贵，如果吃不完的话，还可以包起来带回家去吃。要不然你也可以到菜市场或食品店去买点儿水果拿回家去吃。在中国出去吃饭也不用带很多钱，带几十块现金就够了。

Notes

A2.　不太好用 "not very easy to use"

A5.　要是能离车站近一点儿也好 literally, "If it could be closer to the bus station it would also be good" or "It would be great if it could be fairly close to the bus station."

A10.　用右手写字 literally, "Use right hand to write characters" or, in idiomatic English, "Write with his right hand." In Chinese the coverb 用 is often used where in English we would use the preposition "with."

C1.　我们两个应该算是美国人吧 "I suppose the two of us ought to be considered Americans."

C2a.　不成问题 **bù chéng wèntí** "not become a problem," "not be a problem"

C2b.　小吃店 **xiǎochī diàn** "snack shop"

C2c.　小吃 **xiǎochī** "snack"

PART TWO

Conversation

Situation: Li and Warres finish ordering their meal (continued from the previous lesson).

1. LI:
麻婆豆腐少放点儿辣椒，我怕这位美国朋友受不了。
Mápó Dòufu shǎo fàng diǎnr làjiāo, wǒ pà zhèiwèi Měiguo péngyou shòubuliǎo.
For the Pockmarked Old Woman's Tofu don't put in too many hot peppers, I'm afraid my American friend wouldn't be able to stand it.

2. WARRES:
多放点儿也没关系，我能吃辣的。
Duō fàng diǎnr yě méi guānxi, wǒ néng chī làde.
It's O.K. if you put in a lot, I can eat hot spicy foods.

3. WAITRESS:
好嘞。主食要什么？米饭还是馒头？
Hǎo lei. Zhǔshí yào shémme? Mǐfàn háishi mántou?
All right. What do you want for your main food? Rice or steamed buns?

4. LI:
四两米饭、两个馒头。
Sìliǎng mǐfàn, liǎngge mántou.
Four ounces of rice and two steamed buns.

5. WAITRESS:
喝点儿什么？
Hē diǎnr shémme?
What would you like to drink?

6. LI:
有啤酒吗，您这儿？
Yǒu píjiǔ ma, nín zhèr?
Do you have beer here?

7. WAITRESS: 有。

Yǒu.

Yes.

8. LI: 那就先来一瓶吧。就这些了吧。我们有急事，麻烦您快点儿上菜。

Nà jiù xiān lái yìpíng ba. Jiù zhèixiē le ba. Wǒmen yǒu jíshì, máfan nín kuài dianr shàngcài.

Then why don't you first bring us one bottle. That's all, I guess. We're in a great hurry, so please bring the food as fast as you can.

9. WAITRESS: 行。

Xíng.

O.K.

New Vocabulary

放	**fàng**	put, place
辣椒	**làjiāo**	hot pepper
怕	**pà**	fear, be afraid of
受	**shòu**	endure, suffer
受不了	**shòubuliǎo**	not to be able to endure
辣	**là**	be peppery hot
嘞	**lei**	(sentence final particle)
好嘞	**hǎo lei**	"all right," "O.K."
主食	**zhǔshí**	staple food, main food
米	**mǐ**	rice (uncooked)
米饭	**mǐfàn**	rice (cooked)
馒头	**mántou**	steamed bun
两	**liǎng**	ounce (50 grams)
喝	**hē**	drink
酒	**jiǔ**	liquor
啤酒	**píjiǔ**	beer
瓶	**píng**	bottle
急事	**jíshì**	urgent matter
上菜	**shàngcài**	bring food to a table

Supplementary Vocabulary

酸	**suān**	be sour
甜	**tián**	be sweet

苦	**kǔ**	be bitter
咸	**xián**	be salty
瓶子	**píngzi**	bottle

Notes on the Conversation

Duō and shǎo before verbs to indicate "more" and "less"

In line 1, consider the phrase **shǎo fàng diǎnr làjiāo** "put in fewer hot peppers" and, in line 2, **duō fàng diǎnr yě méi guānxi** "if you put in more it's also O.K." The stative verbs **duō** and **shǎo** can be used as adverbs directly before verbs to indicate "more" and "less." In this pattern, **yìdiǎn(r)** or some other quantity expression is often added after the verb. If both **yìdiǎn(r)** and an object are present, then the object is placed after the **yìdiǎn(r)**. The basic patterns are: **Duō** + Verb + **yìdiǎn(r)** + Object and **Shǎo** + Verb + **yìdiǎn(r)** + Object. Examples: **duō kàn yìdiǎnr shū** "study more," **shǎo chī diǎnr** "eat a little less," **duō chuān diǎnr yīfu** "wear more clothes," **duō zhù jǐtiān** "stay a few more days," **duō zuòshì, shǎo shuōhuà** "do more and talk less."

....

The resultative ending -liǎo "be able to"

Also in line 1, look at the resultative compound verb **shòubuliǎo** "be unable to endure." The resultative ending **-liǎo** means "be able to" or "have the physical ability to." It can be used only in conjunction with the potential infixes **-de-** "be able to" and **-bu-** "not be able to." More examples: **Nǐ kāideliǎo chē ma?** "Are you able to drive?" (for example, when asked of people who may have had too much alcohol), **Jīntiān wǒ zǒubuliǎo nèmme yuǎnde lù** "Today I can't walk that far," **Wǒ Zhōngwén bù hǎo, xiěbuliǎo nèmme chángde bàogào** "My Chinese isn't good, I can't write that long a report."

....

Reading

New Characters and Words

367.	受	**shòu**	stand, endure, bear; receive
	受不了	**shòubuliǎo**	can't stand, can't endure
368.	米	**mǐ**	uncooked rice; (surname)
	米饭	**mǐfàn**	cooked rice
	米	**mǐ**	meter
369.	系	**xì**	relate to; department
	关系	**guānxi**	relationship, relevance
	中美关系	**Zhōngměi guānxi**	U.S.-China relations
	没关系	**méi guānxi**	"it doesn't matter"
	法文系	**Fǎwén xì**	Department of French
	转系	**zhuǎnxì**	transfer to another department

370.	急	jí	be nervous, excited; in a hurry
	急事	jíshì	urgent matter
	着急	zháojí	worry, get excited
371.	喝	hē	drink
	喝水	hēshuǐ	drink water
372.	酒	jiǔ	liquor, wine, spirits
	喝酒	hējiǔ	drink an alcoholic beverage
	米酒	mǐjiǔ	rice wine
	白酒	báijiǔ	clear liquor or spirits; white wine

A. SENTENCES

一、喝一点儿酒没关系，但是不能多喝。

二、你现在吃不完没有关系，等一会儿再吃吧。

三、她们是不是有什么急事？怎么这么早就要走了？

四、小牛，你看起来比我高。我一米七八。你有多高？

五、喝酒以后不可以开车！你长这么大，怎么还不知道呢？

六、米饭是中国南方人的主食，没有米饭他们会吃得很不高兴。

七、我真受不了生物专业，所以决定明年从生物系转到比较文学系。

八、不好意思，可是我还是想问你：金小姐跟李先生是什么关系？

九、在美国年满二十一岁才可以喝酒，在中国年满十八岁就可以喝了。

十、王大海不喜欢喝酒，白酒、米酒什么的，他都不喝。

B. CONVERSATIONS

一、

小文：小李，你先吃了饭再走吧。

小李：不行，我有一些急事得现在去办。

小文：那没关系，你先去办你的事吧。

小李：好。再见，明天见！

小文：再见，慢走。

二、

金老师：小车，你喜欢你们学校的饭吗？

车大山：我一点儿都不喜欢。我吃了快一年了，已经受不了了。

金老师：真的吗？为什么这么不喜欢呢？

车大山：我也不太清楚。可能吃来吃去都是差不多一样的，所以就不喜欢了。

金老师：那，你最想吃什么？

车大山：我就想吃我妈妈做的菜。我们家里的米饭也特别香。

C. NARRATIVE

一、 我大哥很喜欢吃米饭。他早饭、中饭、晚饭都吃米饭，每次都吃好几两呢，要是有一天没吃米饭他就受不了。有时候，他不吃菜也不吃肉，只吃米饭！我二哥跟大哥很不一样，他不是特别喜欢吃米饭，可是很喜欢喝酒。没有米饭、没有菜跟肉都没关系，但是一定要有酒，要不然他就不高兴。有时候我想：这么不一样的两个人，怎么会都是我的哥哥呢？

二、 美国进口的东西太多，出口的东西太少，这已经成了一个很大的问题。今年美国的国会有人主张美国应该多出口一些东西到外国去，我觉得这个想法很对。不过今天我在报上看到，国会也有人主张少从外国进口东西，或者一、两年之后可能根本不进口外国的东西，特别是从中国来的东西，这个想法我觉得是不对的，不是解决问题的好办法。

Notes

A5.　你长这么大 literally, "You've grown so big" or, in idiomatic English, "You're all so grown up." Be sure you pronounce 长 as **zhǎng** "grow."

A6.　他们会吃得很不高兴 literally, "They'll eat in such a way that they're very unhappy" or, in idiomatic English, "They won't enjoy their meal at all."

B1.　你先吃了饭再走吧 "Why don't you eat first before leaving?"

C1a.　好几两 "quite a few ounces"

C1b.　这么不一样的两个人 "two people who are so different"

C2.　国会 **Guóhuì** "Congress" (the national legislative body of the U.S. government)

Mápó Dòufu or "Pockmarked Old Woman's Tofu"

Mǎyǐ Shàngshù or "Ants Climbing a Tree"

Jīdàn Tāng or "Egg Soup"

Arranging a Banquet

PART ONE

Conversation 🎧

Situation: Professor Michael Vitale, who directs a study abroad program in Beijing, arranges a welcoming banquet for his new students at a local restaurant.

1. **VITALE:**
劳驾，我想定桌酒席。

Láojià, wǒ xiǎng dìng zhuō jiǔxí.

Excuse me, I'd like to make a reservation for a banquet.

2. **RESTAURANT MANAGER:**
什么时候？多少人？

Shémme shíhou? Duōshǎo rén?

When? For how many people?

3. **VITALE:**
十二号，星期六，晚上六点。我估计差不多有二十个人参加。

Shí'èrhào, xīngqīliù, wǎnshang liùdiǎn. Wǒ gūjì chàbuduō yǒu èr-shíge rén cānjiā.

The twelfth, Saturday, at 6:00 P.M. I reckon there will be about twenty people attending.

4. **RESTAURANT MANAGER:**
我看分成两桌好，您觉得怎么样？

Wǒ kàn fēnchéng liǎngzhuō hǎo, nín juéde zěmmeyàng?

I think dividing into two tables would be best, what do you think?

5. **VITALE:**   行啊。
                        Xíng a.
                        Fine.

6. **RESTAURANT MANAGER:** 您打算定什么标准的？有每人十元的、二十元的。
                        高级一点儿的话，也有每人四十元的、五十元的。
                        Nín dǎsuan dìng shémme biāozhǔnde? Yǒu měi rén shíyuánde, èrshí-
                        yuánde. Gāojí yìdiǎnrde huà, yě yǒu měi rén sìshíyuánde, wǔshíyuánde.
                        What price level do you plan to book? There are 10 and 20 yuan per
                        person ones. A little higher class, there are also 40 and 50 yuan per
                        person ones.

7. **VITALE:**   哦，每人四十元的吧。
                        Ò, měi rén sìshíyuánde ba.
                        Oh, I guess one at 40 yuan for each person.

New Vocabulary

定	dìng	reserve, book
桌	zhuō	(for banquets)
酒席	jiǔxí	banquet
估计	gūjì	reckon, estimate
参加	cānjiā	take part in
分	fēn	divide, separate
分成	fēnchéng	divide into
打算	dǎsuan	plan
标准	biāozhǔn	level, standard
高级	gāojí	be high-class

Supplementary Vocabulary

主席	zhǔxí	chairman
西餐	Xīcān	Western-style food
中餐	Zhōngcān	Chinese-style food
做饭	zuòfàn	cook

Notes on the Conversation

Dìng "reserve"

Note the expression **dìng zhuō jiǔxí** "reserve a banquet." Here are some other things that you can reserve with the verb **dìng: dìng zhuōzi** "reserve a table," **dìng fángjiān** "reserve a room," **dìng piào** "reserve a ticket," and **dìng yíge shíjiān** "reserve a time."

··

Fēnchéng "divide into"

The postverb **-chéng** means "into." Like all postverbs, it's attached to a regular verb. Here are more examples of postverb constructions with the postverb **-chéng: huànchéng** "exchange for," **gǎichéng** "change into," **kànchéng** "see as," **qiēchéng** "slice into," **shuōchéng** "say as," **xiěchéng** "write into," and **zuòchéng** "make into."

··

Reading

New Characters and Words

373.	桌	zhuō	table; (for banquets)
	分成三桌	fēnchéng sānzhuō	divide into three tables
	桌子	zhuōzi	table
	一张桌子	yìzhāng zhuōzi	a table
374.	席	xí	feast, banquet; (surname)
	酒席	jiǔxí	banquet, feast
	一桌酒席	yìzhuō jiǔxí	a banquet
	主席	zhǔxí	chairperson
	毛主席	Máo Zhǔxí	Chairman Mao
375.	参	cān	participate (can't be used alone)
	参加	cānjiā	take part in, participate, join
376.	每	měi	every, each
	每天	měitiān	every day
	每位	měiwèi	each person (polite)
	每人	měirén	each person
377.	元	yuán	yuan, dollar; (surname; name of a dynasty)
	五十元	wǔshíyuán	50 yuan
	多少元	duōshǎo yuán	how many dollars?
	美元	Měiyuán	U.S. dollar
378.	做	zuò	do; make
	做饭	zuòfàn	cook, make food

做衣服	**zuò yīfu**	make clothes
做买卖	**zuò mǎimài**	do business
做事	**zuòshì**	do things, work
做菜	**zuòcài**	cook, make food
做准备	**zuò zhǔnbèi**	make preparations

A. SENTENCES

一、 他爸爸过百岁生日，他办了十桌酒席，请了一百多个人，我们都去参加了。

二、 你跟你爸爸是两个人，他做什么，你不一定就得做什么。

三、 你如果以后想做那种买卖的话，应该早一点做准备。

四、 那个房间好是好，但是家具还不够，需要加一张桌子。

五、 这家饭店看起来很高级，可是我们穿的衣服太随便了，带的钱可能也不够，我看我们还是去别家好了。

六、 她以前在一家外国公司做事，现在在家里做一点儿小买卖。

七、 定一桌酒席八百元，你定两桌我算你一千五，你觉得怎么样？

八、 我觉得男人也应该会做饭、做衣服什么的，你说呢？

九、 毛主席是1893年在湖南省出生的，1976年在北京市死的。

十、 王大海记得他定过一桌酒席，只是他忘了是哪天，在哪里。

B. CONVERSATIONS

一、

张小姐： 你明天要不要去参加那个酒席？

席先生： 我明天太忙了，可能不去了。你打算去吗？

张小姐： 我打算去。听说那个饭店特别高级！

席先生： 我也听说了，不过我实在没办法，只好下次再去了。

二、

包明生： 桌子上的水果是你带来的吗？

车一文： 对，是我带来的，不过你可以吃。

包明生： 小李也可以吃一个吧？

车一文： 没有问题！你们随便拿吧。

包明生： 谢谢！

车一文： 不用谢！

三、
老师：哪个月有二十八天？
学生：每个月都有二十八天！

C. NARRATIVE

一、汽车公司的张主席下个星期日要请我们工厂里的工人去饭店参加一个酒席。听说那家饭店很高级，不过也很贵，一桌好像要一千多元。我表姐几个月以前去过那家饭店，她说菜做得好吃极了，饭店里面也特别好看。我觉得张主席请的每一个人都一定会去的，不可能有人不参加。

二、我们家住在加州Monterey Park，那个地方中国人特别多。明天我爸爸以前的小学校长要来我们家住几天，所以我爸爸、妈妈打算定几桌酒席。酒席定在了一家特别高级的饭店，应该会有一百多个人参加，大概要分成十桌左右。听说每桌菜差不多两百美元，还得再加上酒什么的，所以总共可能要两千多美元，很贵的。我跟我妹妹也想去参加，但是爸爸、妈妈没请我们！

Notes

A2.　他做什么，你不一定就得做什么 "You don't necessarily have to do what he does."

A7.　定一桌酒席 "Make a reservation for one table for a banquet." Some Chinese write **dìng** with the character 定 while others prefer the character 订.

C2.　酒席定在了一家特别高级的饭店 "The banquet was reserved at an especially high-class restaurant." The postverb 在 has here been attached to the verb 定 and a completed action 了 has been suffixed to the 在.

PART TWO

Conversation

Situation: Professor Vitale and the restaurant manager discuss the menu for the banquet (continued from the previous lesson).

1. RESTAURANT MANAGER: 菜是您自己点呢，还是由我们配呢？

   Cài shi nín zìjǐ diǎn ne, háishi yóu wǒmen pèi ne?

   Will you order the dishes yourself, or should they be arranged by us?

2. VITALE: 我对你们东北风味儿的菜不太熟悉，还是您给我们配吧。

   Wǒ duì nǐmen Dōngběi fēngwèirde cài bú tài shúxi, hái shi nín gěi wǒmen pèi ba.

   I'm not very familiar with your Manchurian cuisine; it might be better if you arranged it for us.

3. RESTAURANT MANAGER: 好吧。四个冷盘、八道菜、一个汤，还有一道甜食，行吗？

   Hǎo ba. Sìge lěngpán, bādào cài, yíge tāng, hái yǒu yídào tiánshí. Xíng ma?

   All right. Four cold dishes, eight hot dishes, a soup, and a dessert. Will that do?

4. VITALE: 可以，可以。

   Kéyi, kéyi.

   Fine.

5. RESTAURANT MANAGER: 请留下您的姓名、地址、电话，以便我们同您联系。

Qǐng liúxià nínde xìngmíng, dìzhǐ, diànhuà, yǐbiàn wǒmen tóng nín liánxì.

Please leave your name, address, and phone number, so that we can contact you.

6. VITALE: 好，这是我的名片。麻烦您！

Hǎo, zhè shi wǒde míngpiàn. Máfan nín!

All right, this is my name card. Much obliged!

New Vocabulary 🎧

自己	zìjǐ	oneself
由	yóu	by
配	pèi	coordinate, arrange
对	duì	to, toward
东北	Dōngběi	the Northeast, Manchuria
风味	fēngwèi(r)	special local flavor
熟悉	shúxi	be familiar
对···熟悉	duì...shúxi	be familiar with...
冷盘	lěngpán(r)	cold dish
道	dào	(for courses of food)
甜食	tiánshí	dessert
留下	liúxià	leave behind
以便	yǐbiàn	so that, in order to
同	tóng	with
联系	liánxì	contact
同···联系	tóng...liánxì	contact (someone)

Supplementary Vocabulary 🎧

盘子	pánzi	dish, plate
炒饭	chǎofàn	fried rice
炒面	chǎomiàn	fried noodles

Notes on the Conversation

The coverb yóu "by, from"

Examine the coverb **yóu** in the question **Cài shi nín zìjǐ diǎn ne, háishi yóu wǒmen pèi ne?** "Will you order the dishes yourself or should they be arranged by us?" **Yóu** means "by" or "from" and indicates the person who performs the action of the verb or who is responsible. More examples of **yóu**: **Zhèijiàn shì yóu nǐ lái guǎn** "This matter (can) be handled by you," **Zhèijiàn shìr yóu wǒ lái zuò ba** "Let me do this."

....

Duì...shúxi "be familiar with"

Look at the sentence **Wǒ duì nǐmen Dōngběi fēngwèirde cài bú tài shúxi** "I'm not very familiar with your Manchurian cuisine." The pattern **duì...shúxi** means "be familiar with." Notice that it's **duì...shúxi** and not *****gēn...shúxi**, as you might expect from the vantage point of English. Also, the stative verb **shúxi** "be familiar" has an alternate pronunciation **shóuxi**, which is quite common and is in fact used by the speaker in the audio recording.

....

Yǐbiàn... "so as to facilitate..."

In line 5, look at the sentence **Qǐng liúxià nínde xìngmíng, dìzhǐ, diànhuà, yǐbiàn wǒmen tóng nín liánxì** "Please leave your name, address, and phone number, so that we can contact you." **Yǐbiàn** "so as to facilitate," "so that," "in order that" is a somewhat formal way to indicate purpose. **Yǐbiàn** is similar in meaning to **wèile** but is more formal; unlike **wèile**, it can never occur at the beginning of a sentence. Another difference is that **yǐbiàn** can be followed by nouns or pronouns as well as verbs, but **wèile**, in the sense of "in order to," must be followed by a verb. Another example with **yǐbiàn**: **Yǐnyòngde cáiliào yīng zhùmíng chūchù, yǐbiàn cházhèng** "For materials cited one should indicate the source, so as to facilitate verification."

....

Tóng...liánxì "contact (someone)"

The pattern **tóng...liánxì** means "contact (someone)." Instead of **tóng**, **gēn** and **hé** can also be used. In English the verb "contact" is transitive and takes a direct object ("contact him"). The Chinese verb **liánxì**, on the other hand, is intransitive and can't take an object; it must always be used with a coverb like **tóng**. Examples of the pattern **tóng...liánxì**: **Qǐng nín zǎo yìdiǎn tóng tā liánxì** "Please contact her as soon as possible," **Qǐng liúxià nínde diànhuà yǐbiàn wǒmen tóng nín liánxì** "Please leave your phone number so that we can contact you."

....

Reading

New Characters and Words

379. 自	zì	self; from (can't be used alone)
380. 己	jǐ	self (can't be used alone)
自己	zìjǐ	oneself
我自己	wǒ zìjǐ	I myself
381. 风	fēng	wind
382. 味	wèi	taste; smell; flavor
风味	fēngwèi(r)	local taste; special flavor
383. 由	yóu	from; by
由她决定	yóu tā juédìng	decided by her

自由	zìyóu	freedom; be free
384. 留	liú	keep; leave behind
留下	liúxià	leave behind
留学	liúxué	study abroad
留学生	liúxuéshēng	student who studies abroad

A. SENTENCES

一、今天外面的风不知道为什么这么大，还下着雨呢。
二、她的爸爸、妈妈都比较喜欢四川和北京风味的菜。
三、你是打算自己一个人去香港吗？要不要同我一起去？
四、这个问题不能由我们自己决定，一定得由校长决定才行。
五、这几道菜还真有风味！也都是她们自己做的。
六、请您留下您的姓名和电话以便我们通知您。
七、我下星期不太忙，应该有很多时间，这件事由我来做吧！
八、何小山原来打算同他的女朋友一起去加拿大留学，可是因为她钱不够，所以他只好自己一个人去了。
九、你们现在是大学生，很自由，以后参加工作了，就不像现在这么自由了！
十、王大海这个人对动物特别好，对人不一定那么好。

B. CONVERSATIONS

一、
小何：你比较喜欢吃什么风味的菜？
小李：我还是比较喜欢吃上海风味的菜。广东风味的菜也不错。
小何：你是不是上海人？
小李：其实，我是湖北人，不是上海人，但是我就是喜欢吃上海菜。

二、
温老师：外头这么大的风，您也不穿一件毛衣吗？
文老师：毛衣我今天忘了带了，没关系。
温老师：您先用我这件大衣吧。
文老师：那你不就没有衣服穿了吗？
温老师：我这儿还有一件毛衣。
文老师：好吧，那我就先穿一下您的大衣了。真是多谢您了！
温老师：哪儿的话。

C. NARRATIVES

"王先生、张小姐，你们好！我姓林，我们上个月在台中见过面，你们还记得我吧？今天晚上实在很高兴见到二位，我知道你们是大忙人，你们能找时间来参加今天晚上的酒席，我们特别高兴！能不能请你们先在酒席入口那里留下你们的姓名和电话，以便我们知道今天总共来了多少人。对，放一张名片在桌子上就可以了。好，我看一下，因为我们今天请了一百多人，所以要分成十四桌，你们二位坐在第三桌。我现在带你们进去，好吗？你们跟着我来吧。我们今天点的菜有几道是川菜，有几道是广东菜，还有几道是东北风味儿的菜，都是很特别的菜，保证你们喜欢吃。还有从法国进口的酒。等一下请你们多吃一点儿，多喝一点儿！"

Notes

A4.　一定得由校长决定才行 "It definitely must be decided by the school president; only that will do." The phrase 才行 at the end of a sentence means "only that will do," with "that" referring back to what was mentioned in the previous clause.

A7.　这件事由我来做吧 literally, "This matter by me come do it" or, in more idiomatic English, "Let me take care of this matter." The verb 来 here does not literally mean "come," but indicates in a general way the speaker's intention to do something.

A9a.　参加工作 literally, "participate in work" or, in idiomatic English, just "work"

A9b.　你们⋯⋯以后⋯⋯不像现在这么自由 "In the future, you won't be as free as you are now." Be sure to remember the pattern A 不像 B 这么 C "A is not as C as B."

B2.　哪儿的话 literally, "Words from where?" This is a polite response to "Thanks," and is a functional equivalent of "You're welcome."

C1.　二位 "The two of you." This is especially polite usage. It would not be wrong to say 两位.

C2.　大忙人 "very busy person"

C3.　以便我们知道今天总共来了多少人 "So that we know how many people came today in total." Note that in the clause 来了多少人, the subject 人 and the verb 来了 are inverted. This sometimes occurs in the case of unspecified subjects.

C4.　你们跟着我来吧 "Why don't you all just come and follow me."

C5.　等一下请你们多吃一点儿 "In a while (when the eating begins) please eat a lot." Note that 等一下 here does not mean "wait" but rather "in a while."

LESSON 9
Peking Duck

PART ONE

Conversation 🎧

Situation: Professor Jiang Zixiang has invited Professor Peter McCoy and his wife, as well as several other guests, to a welcoming banquet at a duck restaurant in Beijing.

1. PROFESSOR JIANG: 我先来简单地说几句。今天啊，我们大家在这儿聚餐是欢迎莫教授和夫人来我们学校工作。祝莫教授在这里工作顺利，生活愉快！现在我们来敬他们二位一杯！

Wǒ xiān lái jiǎndānde shuō jǐjù. Jīntiān a, wǒmen dàjiā zài zhèr jùcān shi huānyíng Mò Jiàoshòu hé fūren lái wǒmen xuéxiào gōngzuò. Zhù Mò Jiàoshòu zài zhèli gōngzuò shùnlì, shēnghuó yúkuài! Xiànzài wǒmen lái jìng tāmen èrwèi yìbēi!

I'll first simply say a few words. Today all of us have gathered here for a meal to welcome Professor and Mrs. McCoy to our school to work. We wish Professor McCoy that his work here go smoothly and that his life be happy! Now let's show our respect and toast the two of them with a glass of wine!

2. PROFESSOR McCOY: 谢谢大家，谢谢，谢谢！我们很高兴有机会到中国
来，同时也非常感谢大家几个星期来给我们的帮助和
照顾。恐怕以后麻烦大家的地方还很多。

Xièxie dàjiā, xièxie, xièxie. Wǒmen hěn gāoxìng yǒu jīhui dào Zhōngguo lái. Tóngshí yě fēicháng gǎnxiè dàjiā jǐge xīngqī lái gěi wǒmende bāngzhù hé zhàogu. Kǒngpà yǐhòu máfan dàjiāde dìfang hái hěn duō.

Thank you, everyone. We're very pleased to have the chance to come to China. At the same time, we also very much appreciate the help and care you've given us the past few weeks. I'm afraid in the future we'll still need to call on you frequently.

New Vocabulary

来	lái	(indicates one is about to do something)
简单	jiǎndān	be simple
地	-de	(adverbial marker)
句	jù	sentence, phrase
大家	dàjiā	everybody, everyone
聚餐	jùcān	get together for a meal
莫	Mò	Mo (surname)
夫人	fūren	madam, lady
祝	zhù	wish
顺利	shùnlì	be smooth
生活	shēnghuó	life
愉快	yúkuài	be happy
敬	jìng	respectfully toast, drink to
杯	bēi	glass, cup (for beverages)
同时	tóngshí	at the same time
非常	fēicháng	extremely
感谢	gǎnxiè	thank
帮助	bāngzhù	help
照顾	zhàogu	care

Supplementary Vocabulary

句子	jùzi	sentence
照顾	zhàogu	take care of
小孩子	xiǎo háizi	small child
快乐	kuàilè	be happy

Notes on the Conversation

-de as adverbial modifier to express manner

If there is an adverbial expression of two or more syllables that precedes a verb, a **-de** is usually added after the adverbial expression and before the verb. This is especially common in the case of two-syllable stative verbs. When **-de** is added to the stative verb, it makes the stative verb into an adverb that expresses manner. For example, **jiǎndān** means "be simple," but **jiǎndānde** means "simply," as in **jiǎndānde shuō jǐjù** "to simply say a few sentences." More examples: **rènzhēnde liànxí** "diligently practice," **hěn kuàide guò mǎlù** "quickly cross the street."

Time Expression + (yǐ)lái "(in) the last..."

In line 2, notice the expression **jǐge xīngqī lái** "in the past few weeks." The pattern Time Expression + **(yǐ)lái** means "(in) the last..." or "(during) the past...." Examples: **zhèijǐge yuè yǐlái** "the last few months," **zhèijǐtiān yǐlái** "these past few days," **duō nián lái** "for many years."

Reading

New Characters and Words

385.	非	**fēi**	not; Africa
	南非	**Nánfēi**	South Africa
386.	常	**cháng**	often; common (surname)
	常常	**chángcháng**	often
	平常	**píngcháng**	usually, ordinarily
	非常	**fēicháng**	extremely
387.	简	**jiǎn**	simple (can't be used alone); (surname)
388.	单	**dān**	single; odd-numbered; list (can't be used alone)
	简单	**jiǎndān**	be simple
	菜单	**càidān**	menu
	单位	**dānwèi**	work unit; organization
	名单	**míngdān**	name list, list of names
	单子	**dānzi**	list
	单号	**dānhào**	odd number
	单人房	**dānrénfáng**	single room
389.	句	**jù**	phrase; sentence
	一句话	**yíjù huà**	a phrase; a sentence
	句子	**jùzi**	sentence
390.	活	**huó**	to live; alive
	生活	**shēnghuó**	life; live

A. SENTENCES

一、老师，请问，这个句子是什么意思？

二、这几年以来，中国人的生活越来越好了。

三、那位同学一句中文都不会，可是他的日语讲得非常好。

四、大家好！谢谢你们来参加今天晚上的酒席，我先来简单地说几句……

五、先生，我们可以看看菜单吗？你们今天有没有什么比较特别的菜？

六、大家好！我姓简。我非常高兴今年能有机会到中国来跟你们一起工作！

七、因为美国的大学非常好，还有工作的机会比较多，所以美国的外国留学生特别多。

八、最简单的中国字是"一"；最难写的中国字可能是"齉"nàng，真的非常难写！

九、我觉得法语很难，比西语难得多，你为什么说法语很简单呢？

十、王大海同时有两个女朋友，他的两个女朋友知道了这件事，都非常生气。

B. CONVERSATIONS

一、

姐姐：妹妹，在北京开车要特别小心。

妹妹：姐姐，我知道，你放心！我会非常小心的。

二、

老何：我还有几句话想跟大家说……

小李：老何，你刚才已经说了很多，我们吃饭吧！

三、

小林：小王，你平常几点上班，几点下班？

小王：我应该八点上班，但是我常常会晚一点儿到。

小林：是吗？那你几点才到呢？

小王：我有的时候晚十分钟，有的时候晚半个钟头。

小林：你的上司不会不高兴吗？

小王：我的上司？他一句话也没说！

C. NARRATIVES

一、我常常同时做很多不一样的事。我喜欢吃饭的时候看报，或是做
饭的时候讲电话，或是走路的时候想我第二天应该做的事。我妈
妈常常说我这个人都是"一半在这儿，一半在那儿"。

二、我们家喜欢过简单的生活。我们不需要住大房子，小房子就够我
们住了。因为房子小，所以我们不需要买很多很贵的家具。因
为我们平常都走路，所以我们也不需要买很大的汽车，小车就行
了。我们也很少去那些很高级的饭店或者买很多从外国进口的衣
服什么的。我们不做这些事，还是可以过得非常高兴。我们家的
人都觉得过简单的生活真的比较好！

Notes

A8.   The word 齉 **nàng**, which means "have a nasal twang," contains a total of 36 strokes and is
thus the character with the largest number of strokes that can be found in modern Chinese
dictionaries.

A9.   西语 **Xīyǔ** "Spanish." This is an abbreviation of 西班牙语 **Xībānyáyǔ**.

B3.   上司 **shàngsi** "boss, superior"

Inside a restaurant in Beijing

PART TWO

Conversation 🎧 LISTEN

Situation: The host and guests continue eating and drinking (continued from the previous conversation).

1. **PROFESSOR McCOY:** 我提议为了主人和在座各位的健康干一杯！
   Wǒ tíyì wèile zhǔrén hé zàizuò gèwèide jiànkāng gān yìbēi!
   I propose a toast to the health of the host and everyone here.

2. **PROFESSOR JIANG:** 莫教授，您尝尝这个菜！
   Mò Jiàoshòu, nín chángchang zhèige cài.
   Professor McCoy, try this dish.

3. **PROFESSOR McCOY:** 谢谢，我自己来。嗨，味道真不错。
   Xièxie, wǒ zìjǐ lái. M, wèidao zhēn bú cuò.
   Thank you, I'll help myself. Mmm, it tastes really good.

4. **CHINESE GUEST:** 莫教授、莫夫人，我来敬您二位一杯。中国菜你们还
   吃得惯吗？
   **Mò Jiàoshòu, Mò Fūren, wǒ lái jìng nín èrwèi yìbēi. Zhōngguo cài nǐmen
   hái chīdeguàn ma?**
   Professor McCoy, Mrs. McCoy, let me drink a toast to the two of you. So how
   do you like eating Chinese food?

5. **MRS. McCOY:** 我们很喜欢吃。来，我们也敬您一杯！
   Wǒmen hěn xǐhuan chī. Lái, wǒmen yě jìng nín yìbēi!
   We like to eat it very much. Come, let's also drink a toast to you!

6. **PROFESSOR JIANG:** 这是鸭胗肝儿。您吃得来吗？
   Zhè shi yā zhēn'gānr. Nín chīdelái ma?
   This is duck gizzard and liver. Do you like it?

7. PROFESSOR McCOY: 不错。越吃越好吃！
Bú cuò. Yuè chī yuè hǎochī!
It's good. The more I eat, the better it tastes!

8. PROFESSOR JIANG: 欸，烤鸭来了！莫教授，您以前吃过烤鸭没有？
Èi, kǎoyā láile! Mò Jiàoshòu, nín yǐqián chīguo kǎoyā méiyou?
Hey, the duck is here! Professor McCoy, have you ever eaten roast duck before?

9. PROFESSOR McCOY: 早就听说过，但一直没吃过。
Zǎo jiù tīngshuōguo, dàn yìzhí méi chīguo.
I heard of it long ago, but have never eaten it before.

New Vocabulary 🎧

提议	tíyì	propose
主人	zhǔrén	host
在座	zàizuò	be present (at a banquet or meeting)
各	gè-	each, every
健康	jiànkāng	health
干杯	gānbēi	drink a toast
尝	cháng	taste
来	lái	(verb substitute)
味道	wèidao	taste
吃惯	chīguàn	be used to eating something
鸭胗肝	yā zhēn'gān(r)	duck gizzard and liver
吃得来	chīdelái	can or like to eat something
越···越···	yuè...yuè...	the more...the more...
烤	kǎo	bake, roast
烤鸭	kǎoyā	roast duck
早就	zǎo jiù	long ago
但	dàn	but
一直	yìzhí	always, all along

Supplementary Vocabulary 🎧

醉	zuì	become drunk
喝醉	hēzuì	get drunk
干杯	gānbēi	"Cheers!," "Bottoms up"

Notes on the Conversation

Yuè…yuè… "the more…the more…."

You're already familiar with the pattern **yuè lái yuè…** "more and more…," as in **yuè lái yuè rè** "hotter and hotter." Now, in this lesson, you learn the related pattern **yuè…yuè…** "the more…the more…." as in **Yuè chī yuè hǎochī** "The more I eat, the better it tastes." The slots after the two **yuè** are filled by some kind of verb. More examples: **Yǔ yuè xià yuè dà** "The more it rained, the heavier the rain became," **Tā yuè lǎo yuè qíguài!** "The older he gets, the stranger he gets!," **Zhèige háizi yuè dà yuè cōngming** "The older this child gets, the smarter she is." In the preceding examples, the subject of the two **yuè** is the same. However, it's also possible to have sentences where the subject of each **yuè** is different. For example: **Wǒ juéde Zhōngwén yuè xué yuè yǒu yìsi** "I feel that the more you study Chinese, the more interesting it gets." In addition to **yuè…yuè…**, you can also use the negative patterns **yuè…yuè bù…** or **yuè bù…yuè bù**. For example: **Nèiběn shū wǒ yuè kàn yuè bù xǐhuan** "That book, the more I read it, the less I liked it."

....

Affirmative-negative questions with -guo and méiyou

Note the **méiyou** at the end of the question **Nín yǐqián chīguo kǎoyā méiyou?** "Have you ever eaten roast duck before?" This question form, with **méiyou** at the end of the sentence, is the preferred affirmative-negative question form for verbs with **-guo** in Northern China. Some more examples: **Nǐ qùguo Nánjīng méiyou?** "Have you ever been to Nanjing?," **Tā xuéguo Zhōngwén méiyou?** "Has she ever studied Chinese?"

....

Reading

New Characters and Words

391.	各	gè	each, every
	各位	gèwèi	each person (polite)
	各国	gèguó	each country; the various countries
392.	客	kè	visitor, guest
	客人	kèrén	guest
	主客	zhǔkè	main guest
	不客气	bú kèqi	"you're welcome"
	客家人	Kèjiā rén	Hakka (person)
	客家话	Kèjiā huà	Hakka (language)
393.	习	xí	practice (can't be used alone); (surname)
	习近平	Xí Jìnpíng	Xi Jinping (President of the PRC, 2013–)
	习主席	Xí Zhǔxí	Chairman Xi
	学习	xuéxí	learn, study; study, studies
394.	惯	guàn	be used to, accustomed to

吃惯	**chīguàn**	be used to eating something
吃得惯	**chīdeguàn**	can get used to eating something
吃不惯	**chībuguàn**	can't get used to eating something
习惯	**xíguàn**	be accustomed to; custom, habit
395. 认	**rèn**	recognize; know; admit
396. 识	**shí**	know; recognize (can't be used alone)
认识	**rènshi**	become acquainted with; recognize; know

A. SENTENCES

一、各国的语言和生活习惯都不一样。

二、我认识的中国字，有的会写，有的还不会。

三、客家人讲客家话，他们的生活习惯跟别的中国人也不完全一样。

四、你们在哪儿学习中文？学了多长时间了？中文是不是越学越有意思？

五、有的人习惯用左手拿东西，有的人习惯用右手拿东西，我觉得都一样。

六、习近平主席是在北京出生的，也是在北京长大的，所以他说一口北京话。

七、各位同学，你们如果已经学到这个地方了，就已经认识三百九十六个中国字了！

八、在法国，喝酒已经成了一种生活习惯，如果家里有客人也常请客人喝酒。

九、要是你认识差不多一千五百个中国常用字，你就可以开始看一点中文的书和报纸了。

十、你们都认识王大海吧？他正在写一本书，越写越长。

B. CONVERSATIONS

一、

主人：谢太太早！

客人：李太太早！

主人：请进，请进。

客人：谢谢。

主人：请坐，请坐。请喝一点儿水，请吃一点儿水果。

客人：谢谢。（过了半小时之后）李太太，时间不早了，我等一下还有一点儿别的事，该走了。今天谢谢您了！

主人：您不多坐一会儿吗？

客人：我真得走了。谢谢您了！

主人： 不客气，慢走！

客人： 再见，再见！

二、

小方： 小文，一直没机会问你，你老家在哪儿？

小文： 我老家在河北省同口，是个小地方，你大概没听说过。我是前年开始在中山大学学习的。

小方： 你来广州这么久了，现在已经习惯广州的气候了吧？

小文： 刚来的时候，不太习惯。这儿七、八月热得我受不了。不过，住的时间越久也就越习惯了。

小方： 对了，你认不认识我的同学小简？他叫简长文。

小文： 我认识他。他家离我住的地方特别近，我们早上常常一起坐公车到中大来。

C. NARRATIVES

一、 我一直记得我小学三年级的白老师。白老师对人特别好。她可能早就忘了我了，但我还常常想起她，一直想找个机会回去看看她。今天早上，我妈妈打电话给我，说白老师上个星期死了。听到她这样说，我心里非常难过。太晚了！所以说，我们想要做什么，不要等，快快去做，要不然可能会错过机会的。

二、 小明常听到妈妈跟爸爸说："别老喝醉，别老喝醉。" 有一次，小明问他爸爸"喝醉"是什么意思？他爸爸说："你看见坐在那边的那两个人没有？你如果喝醉了的话，就会看到四个人。" 小明看了一下，说："可是爸爸，只有一个人坐在那里……"

Notes

C1a. 对人特别好 "is/was especially good to people"

C1b. 想起她 "think of her"

C1c. 我们想要做什么 "if we want to do something." 想要 is here one word, not two. It is a two-syllable auxiliary verb that means "want," the same as either 想 or 要 alone.

C1d. 快快去做 "go and do it quickly." Monosyllabic stative verbs like 快 "be quick" are often reduplicated to function as adverbs, e.g., 快快 "quickly."

C2a. 妈妈跟爸爸说 "(his) mother says/said to (his) father"

C2b. 老 "always" or "constantly"

C2c. 喝醉 **hēzuì** "drink to the point of drunkenness, get drunk"

More Peking Duck and Making Dumplings

PART ONE

Conversation

Situation: Professor Jiang explains to Professor McCoy how to eat Peking Duck (continued from the previous conversation).

1. **PROFESSOR JIANG:** 您得先拿张薄饼，把甜面酱涂在饼上，再放上葱，然后把鸭肉放在中间。把饼卷起来就可以吃了。

   Nín děi xiān ná zhāng báobǐng, bǎ tiánmiànjiàng túzai bǐngshang, zài fàng-shang cōng, ránhòu bǎ yāròu fàngzai zhōngjiān. Bǎ bǐng juánqilai jiù kéyi chīle.

   You have to first take a pancake and spread the sweet flour sauce onto the pancake, then put on scallions, and after that put the duck meat in the middle. Roll up the pancake and you can eat it.

2. **PROFESSOR McCOY:** 好，我试试看。嗯，好吃极了！

   Hǎo, wǒ shìshi kàn. M, hǎochījíle!

   All right, let me try. Mmm, it's delicious!

3. **ANOTHER CHINESE** *(as she puts more food on Mrs. McCoy's plate):*
   GUEST

   莫夫人，您吃得太少了。再来一点儿这个菜吧！

   Mò Fūren, nín chīde tài shǎole. Zài lái yidianr zhèige cài ba!

   Mrs. McCoy, you're not eating enough. Have a little more of this dish!

4. MRS. McCOY: 我已经吃了很多了。别仅给我夹菜，您自己也吃啊！

Wǒ yǐjīng chīle hěn duōle. Bié jǐn gěi wǒ jiācài, nín zìjǐ yě chī a!

I've already had a lot. Don't only serve me food; you yourself eat, too!

5. PROFESSOR JIANG: 莫教授，您怎么不吃了？多吃点儿吧！

Mò Jiàoshòu, nín zěmme bù chīle? Duō chī diǎnr ba!

Professor McCoy, how come you're not eating anymore? Have some more!

6. PROFESSOR McCOY: 我吃得太多了，实在吃不下了。今天的菜太丰富了！非常感谢主人以及在座的各位！

Wǒ chīde tài duōle, shízài chībuxiàle. Jīntiānde cài tài fēngfùle! Fēicháng gǎnxiè zhǔrén yǐjí zàizuòde gèwèi!

I've eaten too much, I really can't eat any more. There was so much food today! Very special thanks to our hosts and to everyone here!

New Vocabulary

薄	báo	be thin (in dimensions)
饼	bǐng	pancake, biscuit
薄饼	báobǐng	pancake
先…再…	xiān…zài…	first…then…
把	bǎ	(moves object before verb)
面	miàn	flour; pasta, noodles
酱	jiàng	thick sauce
甜面酱	tiánmiànjiàng	sweet flour sauce
涂	tú	smear, daub
葱	cōng	scallion
中间	zhōngjiān	in the middle
卷	juǎn	roll up
卷起来	juánqilai	roll up
仅	jǐn	only
夹	jiā	pick up (with chopsticks)
夹菜	jiācài	pick up food (with chopsticks)
吃不下	chībuxià	can't eat
丰富	fēngfù	be abundant
以及	yǐjí	and

Supplementary Vocabulary

厚	hòu	be thick

Notes on the Conversation

Bǎ construction to move object before verb

In the first line of the conversation, look at these three phrases: **bǎ tiánmiànjiàng túzai bǐngshang** "take the sweet flour sauce and smear it onto the pancake," **bǎ yāròu fàngzai zhōngjiān** "take the duck meat and put it in the middle," **bǎ bǐng juǎnqilai** "take the pancake and roll it up." The so-called **bǎ** construction is extremely common. It moves the object of the verb to a position before the verb and indicates that the object is being disposed of in a certain way. Consider these two sentences: **Tā guānshang mén le** "She closed the door," **Tā bǎ mén guānshangle** "She closed the door" (literally "She took the door and closed it"). In the second sentence, **bǎ** has transformed the regular Subject + Verb + Object order to Subject + **bǎ** + Object + Verb. Although both of these sentences are equally good and mean about the same thing, the version with **bǎ** is especially common and is typical of spoken Chinese. If we had to distinguish between the meaning, we could say that in the sentence with **bǎ** there is a special focus on what is being done to the door. There are several restrictions on the use of **bǎ**: the verb must be capable of having an object; the object after **bǎ** is always definite; the verb at the end of the sentence usually has a verb ending attached; the potential forms with **-de-** or **-bu-** cannot be used; and **bǎ** can't be used with verbs ending in **-jiàn** "perceive" and some verbs indicating emotions. If these rules seem complicated, just memorize a couple of sentences with **bǎ** and use them as often as you can. As always, observe how Chinese native speakers and writers use **bǎ**. Gradually, you'll gain a "feel" for **bǎ**. You're encouraged to use **bǎ** whenever you can but, when in doubt, you can always use a preposed object (as in **Shū tā fàngzai nàr le** "She put the books there"). More examples with **bǎ**: **Qǐng bǎ chēzi tíngzai tíngchēchǎng** "Please park the car in the garage," **Qǐng nǐ bǎ zhuōzi fàngzai zhèr, bǎ yǐzi fàngzai nàr** "Please put the tables here and put the chairs over there," **Nǐ zěmme yòu bǎ wǒde shēngrì gěi wàngle ne?** "How come you forgot my birthday again?"

Xiān…zài… "first…, then…"

Look at this sentence: **Nín děi xiān ná yìzhāng báobǐng, zài fàngshang cōng** "You have to first take a pancake, then put on scallions." When used alone, **xiān** means "first" and **zài** means "again." These two adverbs are commonly used together in the paired adverb pattern **xiān…zài… "first…, then…,"** which shows the sequence of two actions taking place one after another. Any kind of verb or verb phrase may fill the slots after **xiān** and **zài**. The clause with **xiān** and the clause with **zài** may have the same subject or they may have two different subjects. More examples: **Xiān xué shuō Zhōngguo huà, zài xué xiě Zhōngguo zì** "First learn how to speak Chinese, then learn how to write Chinese characters," **Wǒmen xiān xiūxi yìhuǐr zài qù, hǎo bu hǎo?** "Let's first rest a while and then go, O.K.?," **Měiguo rén xiān hē tāng zài chīfàn, Zhōngguo rén xiān chīfàn zài hē tāng** "Americans drink their soup first and then eat; Chinese people eat first and then drink their soup."

Reading

New Characters and Words

397.	把	bǎ	(measure for things with handles like umbrellas and knives); take, hold; (moves object before verb)
398.	夫	fū	man; husband
	夫人	fūren	madam, lady; another's wife (polite usage)

张夫人	**Zhāng Fūren**	Madam Zhang
表姐夫	**biǎojiěfū**	husband of older female cousin of different surname
399. 感	**gǎn**	respond; feel
感谢	**gǎnxiè**	thank
400. 及	**jí**	and; reach
以及	**yǐjí**	and
来得及	**láidejí**	have enough time
来不及	**láibují**	not have enough time
401. 更	**gèng**	even more, more
402. 笑	**xiào**	laugh, laugh at
可笑	**kěxiào**	be laughable, funny
笑话	**xiàohua**	joke; laugh at, ridicule
说笑话	**shuō xiàohua**	tell a joke
讲笑话	**jiǎng xiàohua**	tell a joke

A. SENTENCES

一、你能不能把桌子上的报纸拿给我看看？谢谢。

二、中国北方人习惯吃面，南方人更喜欢吃米饭。

三、非常感谢各位今天晚上找时间来参加这次的酒席！

四、我们现在生活过得这么好，得感谢我的表姐及表姐夫。

五、你为什么觉得美国西岸的生活比东岸的生活更有意思呢？

六、有的美国人习惯把鞋子放在桌子上，在中国这是不可以的！

七、我住的房子在一所黑色的房子跟一所白色的房子的中间，
不难找。

八、何夫人，对不起，您的车子不能停在这儿，请您把车子停在停车
场，好吗？

九、火车六点十分开，现在已经五点四十了，你还要找个地方吃晚
饭，我想大概来不及。

十、因为王大海的同学常常笑话他，所以他心里很难过。

B. CONVERSATIONS

一、

男：请问，和平食品店怎么走？

女：你走着去或者坐公车去都可以。

男：哪个更方便呢？

女：两个都行。走路去可能更快一点儿。

男： 那，我应该怎么走呢？

女： 这条街你先一直往前走，走差不多五分钟。到了第一个路口往左
转。再走差不多两、三分钟，然后在路的右手边你会看到一个加油
站跟一家大饭店。和平食品店很小，就在加油站和饭店的中间。

男： 行，那我知道了。谢谢你了！

女： 不用谢。

二、

包先生： 高先生，听说您的夫人是外语专家，会讲好多种语言！她总
共会讲几种语言呢？

高先生： 她好像一共会说七、八种吧，还会说一些中国的方言，像客
家话、广东话、台湾话什么的。

包先生： 七、八种语言？还会几种方言？真不简单！您的夫人上大学
学的是不是语言学专业？

高先生： 其实不是，她是法文专业，后来也在加拿大留了一、两年学。

包先生： 会那么多语言一定很方便。如果她需要到外国去办什么事的
话，跟老外讲话根本就不成问题。

高先生： 是的，是很方便。我们这几年以来到各国各地，认识了不知
道多少外国朋友，我太太还常常用外语跟他们讲笑话呢！

C. NARRATIVES

我小时候很喜欢笑。有时候我家里人或是我同学随便说什么或是做什
么，我都会一直笑。有时候我自己给自己讲笑话，然后就一直笑。有
一次我跟爸妈和姐姐到火车站坐火车，可是火车已经走了，我那时不
知道为什么，觉得非常好笑，就笑个不停，我的家人很不高兴。还有
一次爸妈请了很多客人，都是他们最好的朋友，爸爸说"这是我们的
小女儿美美，"我听了就开始笑，一直笑个不停。那天晚上回家以后，
爸爸很生气，打了我几下，我一直到现在还记得。他说以后不可以再
这样笑了，要不然大家会不喜欢我，以后我也会没有朋友，长大了也
会找不到工作。从那天起，我就不笑了。

Notes

A10.   心里 "in his heart"

B1.   走着去 "go by walking," "go on foot," or "walk"

B2a.   好多种语言 "many kinds of languages." The 好 here has the same meaning as 很.

B2b.   For the phrase 留了一、两年学 "studied abroad for one or two years," remember that
留学 is a verb-object compound, so other words can be inserted between the 留 and the 学.

B2c.   各国各地 "various countries and various places"

B2d.   认识了不知道多少外国朋友 "(We) became acquainted with I don't know how many foreign friends."

C1.   那时 "at that time"

C2.   笑个不停 "laugh without stopping"

C3.   下 indicates the number of times, instances, or occurrences of some action. 打了我几下 means "hit me several times."

C4.   一直到现在 "straight through in time until now, up until now"

Two ladies having High Tea at the Peninsula Hotel in Hong Kong

PART TWO

Conversation 🎧

Situation: Jenny Tai, a Chinese-American woman who is studying in Beijing, learns how to make dumplings at a Chinese friend's home.

1. CHINESE FRIEND: 珍妮，你愿意这个周末去我那儿吃饺子吗？
Zhēnní, nǐ yuànyi zhèige zhōumò qù wǒ nàr chī jiǎozi ma?
Jenny, would you like to go to my place this weekend to eat dumplings?

2. JENNY: 当然愿意啦！ *(at the friend's home)*
这就是你说的饺子吗？好漂亮！这是什么呀？
Dāngrán yuànyi la! ... Zhè jiù shi nǐ shuōde jiǎozi ma? Hǎo piàoliang! Zhè shi shémme ya?
Of course I'd like to! ... These are the dumplings you mentioned? They look great! What's this?

3. CHINESE FRIEND: 这是饺子馅儿。
Zhè shi jiǎozi xiànr.
This is the dumpling filling.

4. JENNY: 都有什么？
Dōu yǒu shémme?
What all is in it?

5. CHINESE FRIEND: 主要是肉和白菜。除了这些之外，还有些调料：葱、姜、酱油、盐和香油。
Zhǔyào shi ròu hé báicài. Chúle zhèixiē zhīwài, hái yǒu xiē tiáoliào: cōng, jiāng, jiàngyóu, yán hé xiāngyóu.
It's mainly meat and cabbage. Besides these, there are also some condiments: scallions, ginger, soy sauce, salt and sesame oil.

6. JENNY: 真香啊！闻得我都饿了。能不能先煮几个让我尝尝？

Zhēn xiāng a! Wénde wǒ dōu èle. Néng bu néng xiān zhǔ jǐge ràng wǒ chángchang?

Smells real good! Smells so good, I'm hungry. Could you boil a few first and let me taste them?

7. CHINESE FRIEND: 当然可以啦，现在我就去煮。

(returns from kitchen with a plate of dumplings)

请吃吧，别客气。

Dāngrán kéyi la, xiànzài wǒ jiù qù zhǔ. … Qǐng chī ba, bié kèqi.

Of course I can, I'll go boil them right now. … Please eat some, don't be polite.

8. JENNY: 哇，好吃极了！

Wà, hǎochījíle!

Wow, they're incredibly delicious!

9. CHINESE FRIEND: 好吃就多吃一点儿！

Hǎochī jiù duō chī yidianr!

If they're good, have some more!

New Vocabulary 🎧

愿意	**yuànyi**	be willing to, like to
周末	**zhōumò**	weekend
饺子	**jiǎozi**	dumpling
馅	**xiàn(r)**	filling
主要	**zhǔyào**	mainly
除了…之外…	**chúle…zhīwài**	besides…; except for…
调料	**tiáoliào**	condiment, seasoning
姜	**jiāng**	ginger
酱油	**jiàngyóu**	soy sauce
盐	**yán**	salt
香油	**xiāngyóu**	sesame oil
闻	**wén**	smell something
饿	**è**	be hungry
煮	**zhǔ**	boil
客气	**kèqi**	be polite
别客气	**bié kèqi**	"don't be polite"
哇	**wà**	"wow"

Supplementary Vocabulary

| 渴 | kě | be thirsty |
| 除了···以外 | chúle...yǐwài | besides...; except for... |

Notes on the Conversation

Chúle...zhīwài and chúle...yǐwài "besides; except"

The patterns **chúle...zhīwài** and **chúle...yǐwài** literally mean "removing...apart"; a common English translation is "besides" or "in addition to." What comes between the two parts of the pattern can be a noun, pronoun, or verb phrase. The main clause that follows often contains the adverbs **hái**, **yě**, or **yòu**. Some more examples of **chúle...zhīwài** and **chúle...yǐwài**: **Chúle Xībānyáyǔ zhīwài, tā hái huì Fǎyǔ hé Déyǔ** "Besides Spanish, she also knows French and German," **Chúle tā yǐwài, wǒ hái yǒu biéde péngyou** "Besides her, I also have other friends," **Tā chúle bù xǐhuan chī ròu yǐwài, yě bù xǐhuan chī yú** "Besides not liking to eat meat, he also doesn't like to eat fish." If a sense of exclusion is indicated through the use of a negative verb or words like "all," then **chúle...zhīwài** and **chúle...yǐwài** are often best translated into English as "except." Examples: **Chúle nǐ yǐwài, wǒ méiyou biéde péngyou** "I don't have any other friends except you," **Chúle tā zhīwài, wǒmen dōu qùguo Chángchéng le** "Except for her, we've all been to the Great Wall."

....

-de to indicate extent

Another function of the particle **-de** when it appears after a verb is to indicate the extent of the action of the verb. The example in the conversation is **Wénde wǒ dōu èle** "(I) have smelled them to the extent that I've even become hungry." The pattern is: Subject + Verb + **-de** followed by a phrase expressing extent or result. More examples: **Wǒ mángde méi shíjiān shuìjiào** "I'm so busy I don't have time to sleep," **Tā qìde shuōbuchū huà lái** "She was so angry that she couldn't speak," **Tā gāoxìngde dōu tiàoqilaile** "He was so happy that he jumped up."

....

Reading

New Characters and Words

403.	愿	yuàn	wish, want (can't be used alone)
	愿意	yuànyi	like to; be willing to
404.	当	dāng	should (can't be used alone)
	当然	dāngrán	of course
	应当	yīngdāng	should, ought
405.	除	chú	remove
	除了···以外	chúle...yǐwài	besides; except for
	除了···之外	chúle...zhīwài	besides; except for

406.	让	**ràng**	let; make; cause
	让你久等了	**ràng nǐ jiǔ děngle**	"made you wait a long time"
407.	调	**tiáo**	adjust; blend
408.	料	**liào**	material
	料子	**liàozi**	fabric
	调料	**tiáoliào**	seasoning

A. SENTENCES

一、老白是湖北人，当然会说湖北话。

二、小李说笑话说得每个人都笑个不停。

三、小姐，请问，你知不知道这件衣服是用什么料子做的？

四、除了小林和小方之外，好像其他同学不太愿意再去动物园。

五、那个老外很客气，常常用中文说"您好"、"请"和"谢谢"。

六、谁都不愿意天天只工作、做饭、做家事，那样的生活太没意思。

七、我的主意是这个菜不要加这种调料了，不知道你觉得怎么样？

八、小高不但人长得好看，也很会讲话，还会调酒；女孩子当然特别喜欢他。

九、同学们，你们应当对王老太太客气一点儿，以后别让她生这么大的气。

十、王大海对他的女朋友说："除了你以外，我还有谁呢？"

B. CONVERSATIONS

一、

男生：你明天有事吗？

女生：没什么特别的事。

男生：你愿意和我一起吃中饭吗？

女生：当然愿意。几点？在哪里？

男生：十二点半在首都饭店门口见，怎么样？

女生：没问题。先谢谢你！

男生：你谢我什么？我又没说要请你！

女生：什么？我听错了吗？你……你……你不请我？

男生：放心，我当然要请你！

A plate of **shuǐjiǎo** or "boiled dumplings"

二、

李老师：高老师，真对不起，让您久等了！

高老师：没关系，没关系。我也没等多久。

李老师：实在不好意思，今天交通不太好，路上的车子太多，我应当早一点儿出来才对。

高老师：我不是已经跟你说过没关系吗？

李老师：那我得多谢你等我等了这么久了。

高老师：您别这么客气，我们又是老同事，又是老朋友。好吧，那我们进去吧，好像刚开始……

C. NARRATIVE

一、"各位先生，各位小姐，大家好！我叫何万里，我想你们大概都认识我吧？你们每一位我差不多都认识，可能有两、三位还不太认识。非常高兴大家都能来参加今晚的这个酒席。饭店的人刚刚跟我讲，很快就要上菜了。等一会儿菜上了桌子，请大家别客气，一定要多吃一点儿，多喝一点儿，好不好？现在我请大家一起先来喝点儿酒！"

二、最近几年，张太太为了她的先生，差不多什么事都愿意做。她天天除了上班以外，回家还给他先生做饭、做家事什么的，忙得不得了。可是最近几个月她的先生对她越来越冷了，后来有人说张先生在外面还交了女朋友，常常跟他的女朋友在一起。张太太知道了这件事，气得好几天都不能上班，什么事都做不了，心里非常难过。现在张太太对张先生也不那么客气了。除了不跟他说话、不给他做饭、不给他做家事之外，她根本不让他的先生回家！如果你是张太太的话，你会怎么办？

A Northern-style Chinese restaurant on Chengfu Road in Beijing

Notes

A2. 说笑话说得每个人都笑个不停 "tells jokes with the result that everybody keeps on laughing"

A3. A是用B做的 **A shi yòng B zuòde** "A is made of B" or "A is made from B"

A6. 谁都不愿意 "nobody would like to"

A8. 小高不但人长得好看，也很会讲话 "Little Gao is not only handsome, but is also very articulate."

A9. 以后别让她生这么大的气 "In the future don't make her so angry."

C1a. 今晚 **jīnwǎn** "this evening." This is a slightly more formal abbreviation of 今天晚上.

C1b. 上桌子 **shàng zhuōzi** "be put on the table"

C2a. 为了她的先生 "for her husband"

C2b. 差不多什么事都愿意做 "she was willing to do almost anything"

C2c. 做家事 **zuò jiāshì** "do housework"

C2d. 忙得不得了 **mángde bùdéliǎo** "busy to an extreme extent, extremely busy." Note that the second 得 is here pronounced **dé**, not **de** or **děi**; and that 了 is pronounced **liǎo**, not **le**.

C2e. 交 **jiāo** "become friends with" or "befriend"

C2f. 气 **qì** "be angry." The sentence 张太太⋯⋯气得好几天都不能上班 means "Mrs. Zhang got so angry that she couldn't go to work for quite a few days."

C2g. 不了 **-bùliǎo** "can't" (indicates inability to finish something successfully). The phrase 什么事都做不了 means "(She) wasn't able to do anything." Note that 了 is here pronounced **liǎo**, not **le**.

Eating with a Colleague in a Restaurant

PART ONE

Conversation 🎧

Situation: Zeng Xianfen, a Taiwanese employee at a cram school in Taipei, asks Donna Neal, an American teacher there, if she'd like to have lunch together.

1. **ZENG:** 嗨，Donna! ⋯⋯ 吃过饭没有？
Hài, Donna! Chīguo fàn méiyou?
Hi, Donna! Have you eaten yet?

2. **NEAL:** 还没。刚才补了一堂课。你呢？
Hái méi. Gāngcái bǔle yìtáng kè. Nǐ ne?
Not yet. I just made up a class. And you?

3. **ZENG:** 我也还没吃。怎么样？要不要一块儿去吃？
Wǒ yě hái méi chī. Zěmmeyàng? Yào bu yào yíkuàir qù chī?
I haven't eaten yet either. How about it? Do you want to go eat together?

4. **NEAL:** 好啊！
Hǎo a!
Sure!

5. **RESTAURANT**
   HOSTESS: *(a little later, at a restaurant)*

   欢迎光临。几位？

   Huānyíng guānglín. Jǐwèi?

   Welcome! How many?

6. **ZENG:**   两个。 *(after they've started eating)*

   鱼怎么样？好不好吃？

   Liǎngge...Yú zěmmeyàng? Hǎo bu hǎochī?

   Two... How's the fish? Is it good?

7. **NEAL:**   蛮嫩的，就是刺多了一点。

   Mán nènde, jiù shi cì duōle yidian.

   Very tender, it's just there are a few too many fish bones.

8. **ZENG:**   买单。

   Mǎidān.

   The check.

9. **NEAL:**   *(to the waitress, when they're finished)*

   多少钱？我来付吧。

   Duōshǎo qián? Wǒ lái fù ba.

   How much is it? I'll pay.

10. **ZENG:**   不，今天我请客。

    Bù, jīntiān wǒ qǐngkè.

    No, today I'm treating.

11. **NEAL:**   还是我来吧！

    Hái shi wǒ lái ba!

    Come on, let me pay.

12. **ZENG:**   唉，别客气。一顿便饭而已。

    Ài, bié kèqi. Yídùn biànfàn éryǐ.

    Oh, don't be polite. It's only a simple meal.

13. **NEAL:**   不好意思，让你破费了。改天我做东吧。

    Bù hǎo yìsi, ràng nǐ pòfèile. Gǎitiān wǒ zuòdōng ba.

    How embarrassing to let you go to such expense. Next time I'll be the host.

New Vocabulary

嗨	**hài**	"hi"
过	**-guo**	(expresses completed action)
刚才	**gāngcái**	just now, just
补课	**bǔkè**	make up a class
堂	**táng**	(for classes)
一块	**yíkuài(r)**	together
蛮⋯的	**mán...de**	quite

嫩	nèn	be tender
刺	cì	fish bone
买单	mǎidān	pay the check, figure up the bill
付	fù	pay
请客	qǐngkè	treat (someone to something)
唉	ài	(indicates strong sentiment)
顿	dùn	(for meals)
便饭	biànfàn	simple meal
破费	pòfèi	go to great expense
改	gǎi	change
改天	gǎitiān	on some other day
做东	zuòdōng	serve as host

Supplementary Vocabulary

补习班	bǔxíbān	cram school
服务员	fúwùyuán	attendant, waiter, waitress
老	lǎo	be tough (of food)
付钱	fùqián	pay money

Notes on the Conversation

-guo to express completed action

As we saw in earlier lessons, the verb suffix **-guo** can express experience, as in **Nǐ qùguo Běijīng ma?** "Have you ever been to Beijing?" A different use of **-guo** that we see in this lesson is to express a completed action, much like verb suffix **-le**. The pattern is: Verb + **-guo**, as in **chīguo** "has eaten" or "have eaten." One common and useful example of **-guo** to express completed action is in the question **Nǐ chīguo fàn le ma?** "Have you eaten?" The answer to that question would be either **Wǒ chīguo fàn le** "I've eaten" or **Wǒ hái méi chīguo fàn** "I haven't eaten yet." The context will usually make clear which of the two types of **-guo** is involved. When a non-Chinese person is asked **Nǐ chīguo Zhōngguo fàn ma?**, this would ordinarily be interpreted as "Have you ever eaten Chinese food?" On the other hand, **Nǐ chīguo fàn le ma?** would be understood as "Have you eaten (yet)?," since it wouldn't make sense to ask someone if they had ever eaten.

....

Mán...-de "quite"

While the adverb **mán** "quite," which is similar in meaning to **tǐng**, can occur alone, it's often used in the pattern **mán...-de**, which surrounds stative verbs or other types of verb phrases and means "quite, rather, very." The pattern is: **mán** + Verb + **-de**. Examples: **mán hǎochīde** "quite tasty," **mán lèide** "quite tired," **mán bú cuòde** "quite good," **mán yǒu yìside** "quite interesting." Instead of **mán...-de**, some speakers pronounce the syllable **mán** with Tone Three and say **mǎn...-de**.

....

Stative Verb + <u>le</u> + <u>(yi)dianr</u> to express excess

Look at the line in the conversation **jiù shi cì duōle yidian** "it's just that the fish bones are a little too many." A stative verb like **duō** followed by **le** plus **yidian(r)** can indicate "a little too much" or "a little too many." The basic pattern is: Stative Verb + **le** + **(yi)dianr**. More examples: **Zhèige cài hǎochī shi hǎochī, jiù shi làle yidianr** "This dish is good all right, it's just a little too spicy hot," **Nèijiā diànde dōngxi hǎo shi hǎo, jiù shi guìle yidian** "The things in that store are good enough, they're just a bit too expensive."

Reading

New Characters and Words

409.	而	ér	also, and, yet, but, moreover
	…而已	…éryǐ	only, and that is all
410.	且	qiě	moreover, and, also
	而且	érqiě	moreover, and, also
	不但…而且	búdàn…érqiě	not only…but also
411.	鱼	yú	fish
	一条鱼	yìtiáo yú	a fish
	鱼肉	yúròu	the flesh of a fish
	金鱼	jīnyú	goldfish
412.	改	gǎi	change; correct
	改错	gǎicuò	correct mistakes
	改天	gǎitiān	on some other day
	改行	gǎiháng	change one's line of work
413.	务	wù	do; matter (can't be used alone); (surname)
	服务	fúwù	serve
414.	员	yuán	member (can't be used alone)
	服务员	fúwùyuán	attendant, waiter, waitress
	专员	zhuānyuán	specialist
	学员	xuéyuán	student

A. SENTENCES

一、我刚才给校长打了一个电话，可是她不在。

二、服务员，买单！也请你把这些菜包起来，谢谢！

三、没关系，你如果今天太忙的话，我可以改天再来找你。

四、那家书店的服务非常好，我很喜欢去那儿买书，买报纸什么的。

五、服务员，请你把菜单拿来，好吗？我们已经等了很久了！

六、我的表姐以前在工厂里工作，后来改行了，现在做一点儿小买卖。

七、你不应该让白老师请你，她只是一位小学老师而已，又不是什么很有钱的人。

八、水里本来有两条金鱼，可是大的把小的给吃了，所以现在只有一条了。

九、我觉得一个老师应该常常改学生的错，不过学生不应该改别的学生的错。

十、王大海不但不喜欢吃肉，而且也不喜欢吃鱼。

B. CONVERSATIONS

一、

张东山：你去过和平饭店吗？

关雨中：我自己没去过，可是我表姐夫每次到北京来都住那家饭店。

张东山：他觉得那里的服务怎么样？

关雨中：他说服务不错，还说他们的早点特别好吃！

张东山：你表姐夫觉得那家的价钱怎么样？

关雨中：他说和平饭店不但服务好，而且价钱不贵。

张东山：那太好了！我下个月要定一桌酒席。那我大概就在和平饭店定吧。

二、

王先生：何小姐，你这里好像写错了一个字。

何小姐：让我看看。

王先生：是这个句子，第二个字。

何小姐：我看看。对不起，我真的写错了！我已经不习惯用手写中国字了！我来改一下吧。

王先生：好，谢谢你。

何小姐：不客气，这是我的错。以后我会小心一点。

C. NARRATIVES

一、有一次，一个美国人想请他的中国朋友王先生、王太太到家里来吃饭。他知道中国人讲话很客气，也听说中国话有时候前头加一个"小"字，那句话就更客气了。像"小姓"比"我姓"客气，"小儿"比"我儿子"客气，"小女"比"我女儿"客气。所以那个美国人把他在中文班上学的"请你们到家里来吃便饭"说成了"请你们到家里来吃小便饭"！当然，他的中国朋友听了，不太高兴。王先生还好，只是觉得有一点儿可笑，可是王太太真的生气了。

二、中国人的生活习惯跟美国不太一样。美国人请客，客人来了，先请他坐，然后主人大概会问客人："Would you like something to drink?"就是"你想不想喝点儿什么？"。而在中国，如果你那样问一位中国客人，他就是想喝东西，大概也会说"不用了！"所以，如果请了中国客人到家里来，根本不用问他想不想喝什么，你就拿给他一些喝的就行了。

Notes

A8.   大的把小的给吃了 literally, "The big one took the little one and ate it," or in idiomatic English, "The big one ate the little one." 把 moves the object of the verb to a position before the verb and indicates that the object is being handled in a certain way. Placing a 给 before the main verb, as here, is optional but common; the 给 strengthens the sense that something is being taken and handled in a certain way.

B2.   Because Chinese people now often write characters by computer or mobile device, they are beginning to forget how to write the less common characters by hand.

C1a.   像 here means "like." The writer is giving examples of Chinese expressions where adding the character 小 at the beginning renders the expression politer or more modest. The expression 小姓 is rarely used nowadays.

C1b.   把A说成B literally, "take A and say it so that it becomes B."

C2a.   他就是想喝东西，大概也会说"不用了！" literally, "Even if he wants to drink something, he'll probably say, 'It's not necessary!'" The pattern 就是……也 means "even if" or "even."

Cram schools on Nanyang Street in downtown Taipei

C2b.   你就拿给他一些喝的就行了 "Just bring him some things to drink and that will do." 喝的 here means 喝的东西 "things to drink" or "beverages."

PART TWO

Conversation 🎧

Situation: Larry Wells, an American who used to teach English in Taiwan, returns to Taipei for a short visit. Mr. and Mrs. Yang invite him and some other mutual friends to a dinner at their home to welcome him back.

1. MR. YANG:
今天我们替老魏接风。欢迎你回到台湾来！在座的也都是老朋友。来，我们敬老魏！
Jīntiān wǒmen tì Lǎo Wèi jiēfēng. Huānyíng nǐ huídào Táiwān lái! Zàizuòde yě dōu shi lǎo péngyou. Lái, wǒmen jìng Lǎo Wèi!
Today we're having a welcome dinner for Larry. Welcome back to Taiwan! Those present are all old friends. Come, let's toast Larry!

2. WELLS:
谢谢，谢谢，实在不敢当。
Xièxie, xièxie, shízài bù gǎn dāng.
Thank you, I really don't dare accept this honor.

3. MR. SHI:
老魏，来，我敬你！干杯怎么样？
Lǎo Wèi, lái, wǒ jìng nǐ! Gānbēi zěmmeyàng?
Larry, come, here's to you! Bottoms up, O.K.?

4. MR. WELLS:
量浅，量浅。你干，我随意吧。
Liàng qiǎn, liàng qiǎn. Nǐ gān, wǒ suíyì ba.
I'm not much of a drinker. You drink bottoms up, I'll just have a little.

5. MR. SHI:
欸，你是海量。来，干杯，干杯！
Éi, nǐ shi hǎiliàng. Lái, gānbēi, gānbēi!
Hey, your capacity is limitless. Come on, bottoms up!

6. MR. WELLS:　恭敬不如从命。那我先干为敬了！
　　　　　　Gōngjìng bù rú cóng mìng. Nà wǒ xiān-gān-wéi-jìngle!
　　　　　　It's better to obey than to show respect. So I'll drink bottoms up first to show
　　　　　　my respect!

New Vocabulary

替	tì	for
魏	Wèi	Wei (surname)
接风	jiēfēng	give a welcome dinner
回来	huílai	come back
回到	huídào	come back to
敢	gǎn	dare to
不敢当	bù gǎn dāng	"don't dare accept"
浅	qiǎn	be shallow
量浅	liàng qiǎn	"capacity is shallow"
随意	suíyì	"as you like"
海	hǎi	ocean, sea
海量	hǎiliàng	"ocean capacity"
不如	bù rú	not be as good as
恭敬不如从命	gōngjìng bù rú cóng mìng	"to show respect is not as good as following orders"
先干为敬	xiān-gān-wéi-jìng	drink bottoms up before someone else to show respect

Supplementary Vocabulary

河	hé	river
湖	hú	lake
深	shēn	be deep
石	Shí	Shi (surname)
石头	shítou	stone
雨量	yǔliàng	rainfall
回去	huíqu	go back

Notes on the Conversation

A bù rú B "A isn't as good as B"

Gōngjìng bù rú cóng mìng "to show respect is not as good as following orders" is a set expression, but you should learn the common and useful grammatical pattern **A bù rú B** "A isn't as good as B" that is contained in it. The literal meaning of **bù rú** is "not be as good as," "not be equal to," or "be inferior to." It is a bit formal in style. More examples: **Nǐ bù rú tā** "You're not as good as she is," **Zhèr bù rú nàr** "It's not as good here as it is there," **Wǒ zuòcài bù rú wǒ bàba** "I can't cook as well as my father," **Tā Zhōngwén shuōde bù rú tā tàitai hǎo** "He doesn't speak Chinese as well as his wife." At the beginning of a sentence or phrase, **bù rú** sometimes is used to make a polite suggestion and can imply "it would be better to...." Example: **Xiàyǔ le, bù rú míngtiān zài qù** "It's raining; it would be better to go tomorrow."

Reading

New Characters and Words

415.	替	tì	replace, substitute; for
416.	接	jiē	receive, meet, welcome
	接风	jiēfēng	give a welcome dinner
	替···接风	tì...jiēfēng	give a welcome dinner for
	接电话	jiē diànhuà	receive or take a phone call
417.	敢	gǎn	dare
	不敢当	bù gǎn dāng	"don't dare accept"
418.	量	liàng	capacity, amount
	海量	hǎiliàng	"ocean capacity," great capacity for drinking liquor
	雨量	yǔliàng	rainfall
	酒量	jiǔliàng	capacity for drinking alcohol
419.	深	shēn	be deep; dark (of colors)
	深色	shēnsè	dark in color, dark-colored
	深水	shēn shuǐ	deep water
420.	石	shí	rock, stone (can't be used alone); (surname)
	石头	shítou	stone

A. SENTENCES

一、"简开石先生，简开石先生，请快到前面来接电话！"

二、那位法国老太太的先生死了以后，她天天都穿深色的衣服。

三、小石，你先别着急，那件事我替你办就是了，你可以放心。

四、 时间不早了，而且家里还有好多事得做，不如早点儿回去吧！

五、 林夫人刚回国，我们星期六晚上替她跟她先生接风，你能参加吗？

六、 我们学校前边的那条河很深，不过好像水里头没有什么鱼，只有很多石头！

七、 我每到一个新地方，都喜欢随意走走看看，多认识几个本地人，交几个新朋友。

八、 一个学习外语的学生如果不敢开口说话，那么他一定学不好。

九、 中国东边和南方各省雨量都很多，比较起来北方雨量就少得多，所以中国北方各省都特别干。

十、 王大海不喝酒，可是他爸爸很会喝，王老先生的酒量根本就是海量。

B. CONVERSATIONS

一、

白先生　　：今天我们替 Larry 接风。Larry，我们都好高兴你这次回到台湾来了！大家也都是老朋友。来，我们敬 Larry！

美国主客：谢谢，谢谢，实在不敢当。

石先生　　：Larry，来，我敬你！干杯怎么样？

美国主客：量浅，量浅。你干，我随意吧。

石先生　　：你是海量！来，干杯，干杯！

美国主客：恭敬不如从命。那我先干为敬了！

二、

文老师：石老师，后天您有什么事吗？

石老师：我想一想，后天是星期五，应该没什么事吧。

文老师：我们要替张老师接风，您能来参加吗？

石老师：没问题。几点钟？在什么地方？

文老师：首都饭店。时间还没决定，不过大概是六点或是六点一刻。我明天再给您打电话通知您时间，行吗？

石老师：行。

C. NARRATIVE

一、 我的女朋友金金已经二十二岁了，可是她还不会开车。她不会开车是因为她根本不敢学！金金今年七月要开始在一家离她家很远的公司工作，每天上下班都需要开车，因为从她家到那家公司根本没有公共汽车，当然也不可能每天都打的。金金也知道，她得在两、三个月之内学会开车。我刚才跟她说，不如早一点开始学，别再等了。现在已经四月了，她还没开始学，我真替她着急！

二、老简去了加拿大好几个月，刚回北京，所以我星期六晚上替他接风。我打算请他跟我们公司的一些同事到阳明饭店吃饭。阳明饭店刚开不久，听说满高级的，他们的山东菜做得特别好。当然，我们一定会喝不少酒，我已经通知了饭店多为我们准备一些酒。老简本来就是海量，所以我想没有人敢跟他比酒量。我叫大家那天晚饭后千万别开车，打的比较好，因为我们都知道，"酒后不开车，开车不喝酒！"

Notes

A7. The 每 in this sentence means "every time that" or "whenever."

A8. 开口 **kāikǒu** "open one's mouth"

A10. 王老先生的酒量根本就是海量 "Old Mr. Wang's capacity for drinking alcohol is basically unlimited." 根本 here means "basically," "fundamentally," or "completely."

B1a. 敬 **jìng** "toast" or "drink to"

B1b. 干杯 **gānbēi** "drink a toast" or "bottoms up." Literally, this means "dry cup."

B1c. 量浅 **liàngqiǎn** literally, "capacity (for drinking alcohol) is shallow"

B1d. 恭敬不如从命 **gōngjìng bù rú cóng mìng** "showing respect is not as good as following orders"

B1e. 先干为敬 **xiān-gān-wéi-jìng** literally, "drink bottoms up before someone else to show respect." Note that 为 is here pronounced **wéi**, not **wèi** as in 为什么 **wèishenme** "why."

C1a. 在两、三个月之内 "within two or three months." The use of 在 at the beginning of a time expression followed by 之内 or 以内 is optional but not uncommon.

C1b. 学会 is a compound verb that literally means "study something to the point where you can do it." A shorter translation would be just "learn."

C1c. 别再等了 "Don't wait any longer."

C2a. 老简本来就是海量 "It goes without saying that Old Jian has a great capacity for drinking alcohol." You previously learned 本来 with the meaning "originally." In this sentence, 本来 is used with the meaning "of course" or "it goes without saying that."

C2b. 没有人敢跟他比酒量 literally, "Nobody dares to compete with him in the capacity for drinking alcohol."

C2c. 叫, which you have learned in the sense of "call" or "be named," here means "tell" or "ask" someone to do something.

C2d. 千万 **qiānwàn** "by all means" or "be sure to." 千万别开车 means "By all means don't drive" or "Whatever you do, don't drive."

LESSON 12
A Dinner Party at Home

PART ONE

Conversation 🎧 LISTEN

Situation: The eating and drinking continues (continued from the previous conversation).

1. **MR. ZHANG:** 来，老魏，我也敬你。干杯！
   Lái, Lǎo Wèi, wǒ yě jìng nǐ. Gānbēi!
   Come, Larry, let me toast you, too. Bottoms up!

2. **WELLS:** 半杯吧。 *(after a while, to Mrs. Yang)*
   大嫂，你今天预备了这么多菜啊！
   Bànbēi ba... Dàsǎo, nǐ jīntiān yùbeile zhèmme duō cài a!
   I'm going to go with half a glass. Older sister, you prepared so many dishes today!

3. **MRS. YANG:** 没什么菜，实在简单得很。不要客气！来，这是糖醋里脊，
   我记得你最爱吃的。
   **Méi shémme cài, shízài jiǎndānde hěn. Búyào kèqi! Lái, zhè shi Tángcù Lǐjī, wǒ
   jìde nǐ zuì ài chīde.**
   The food is nothing special, really very simple. Don't be polite! Here, this is Sweet
   and Sour Pork, I remember this was your favorite.

4. **WELLS:** 嗯，味儿闻着真香啊！真是两三年没吃到了。
   M, wèir wénzhe zhēn xiāng a! Zhēn shi liǎngsānnián méi chīdàole.
   Mmm, the aroma smells really great! I really haven't had it for a couple of years now.

5. MRS. YANG: 我也记得你爱吃辣的。我特地为你做了麻辣杂拌儿。你够不着吧? 我给你夹一点儿。

Wǒ yě jìde nǐ ài chī làde. Wǒ tèdì wèi nǐ zuòle Málà Zábànr. Nǐ gòubuzháo ba? Wǒ gěi nǐ jiā yidianr.

I remember too that you love to eat hot spicy food. I specially made Sesame Hot Spicy Medley for you. I guess you can't reach it? Let me serve you some.

6. WELLS: 够得着, 够得着, 我自己来!

Gòudezháo, gòudezháo, wǒ zìjǐ lái.

I can reach it, I'll help myself.

7. MR. ZHANG: *(looks at his watch)*

对不起, 我们有一点儿事, 得先走一步。我跟内人敬各位! 各位慢用, 失陪了。

Duìbuqǐ, wǒmen yǒu yidianr shì, děi xiān zǒu yíbù. Wǒ gēn nèirén jìng gèwèi! Gèwèi màn yòng, shīpéile.

Excuse us, we have something we have to do, we must leave early. My wife and I would like to toast everyone! Enjoy your meal, sorry we have to leave.

New Vocabulary

大嫂	dàsǎo	wife of oldest brother
预备	yùbei	prepare
不要客气	búyào kèqi	"don't be polite"
糖醋里脊	Tángcù Lǐjī	Sweet and Sour Pork
味儿	wèir	smell, aroma
吃到	chīdào	succeed in eating
特地	tèdì	especially
为	wèi	for
麻辣杂拌儿	Málà Zábànr	Sesame Hot Spicy Medley
够	gòu	reach (by stretching)
够不着	gòubuzháo	be unable to reach
够得着	gòudezháo	be able to reach
步	bù	step, pace
先走一步	xiān zǒu yíbù	"take one step first"
内人	nèirén	one's wife (polite)
慢用	màn yòng	"take your time eating"
失陪	shīpéi	"sorry to have to leave"

Supplementary Vocabulary

小吃	**xiǎochī**	snack
便当	**biàndāng**	box lunch

Notes on the Conversation

Stative Verb + -de + hěn "very…"

The meaning of the pattern Stative Verb + **-de** + **hěn** is "very (Stative Verb)." **Jiǎndānde hěn** literally means "simple to the extent of being very," that is, "very simple." You could also just say **hěn jiǎndān** "very simple," but the use of the Stative Verb + **-de** + **hěn** pattern adds emphasis and variety. This pattern is closely related to the pattern with **-de** that indicates extent that you learned in Lesson 10, Part 2. Examples: **Zhèrde dōngxi guìde hěn** "The things here are very expensive," **Wǒ zuìjìn mángde hěn** "I've been very busy lately," **Tāde Zhōngwén hǎode hěn** "Her Chinese is very good."

(Shi)…-de to emphasize a situation

Examine the last **-de** in **Wǒ jìde nǐ zuì ài chīde** "I remember that you loved to eat it." This **-de** emphasizes that a certain feature is part of a situation and gives a statement an air of solidity and permanence. A **shi** can optionally be placed after the subject, so you could also say **Wǒ jìde nǐ shi zuì ài chīde**. More examples: **Nǐ nèiyàng shuō shi bú duìde** "It's not right of you to speak that way," **Wáng Jiàoshòu duì yǔyánxué hěn yǒu yánjiūde** "Professor Wang is very knowledgeable about linguistics," **Wǒ yuèmǔ chīle wǔshiniánde Zhōngguo cài, xīcān tā shi chībuláide** "My mother-in-law has eaten Chinese food for 50 years, she's just not going to get used to eating Western food."

-zhe as continuous aspect suffix

In the conversation, look at the sentence **Wèir wénzhe zhēn xiāng** "The aroma smells really great!" (literally "The aroma, in my smelling it, is really fragrant"). The suffix **-zhe** can indicate continuous aspect, that an action is prolonged and continues for a period of time. When **-zhe** is suffixed onto an action verb, it often corresponds to English "-ing." More examples of **-zhe** as continuous aspect suffix: **Nǐ shóuli názhe shémme ne?** "What are you holding in your hand?," **Zhèijiàn yīfu chuānzhe tǐng shūfude** "This dress is very comfortable," **Zhànzhe bǐ zuòzhe hǎo** "Standing is better than sitting," **Mén hái kāizhe ne** "The door is still open," **Wàitou zhèng xiàzhe yǔ ne** "It's raining outside right now."

Approximate numbers

Consider the approximate number expression **liǎngsānnián** "two or three years." Approximations involving single digits can be indicated in Chinese by juxtaposing two consecutive numbers followed by a measure, without any overt expression for "or" or "and." The numbers involved can be simple numbers, money amounts, times, or numbers of people. Examples: **yìliǎngge** "one or two," **liǎngsānfēn zhōng** "two or three minutes," **sānsìtiān** "three or four days," **wǔliùge rén** "five or six people," **qībādiǎn zhōng** "7:00 or 8:00."

Reading

New Characters and Words

421. 预	yù	prepare; in advance (can't be said alone)
预备	yùbei	prepare
预备中学	yùbei zhōngxué	preparatory high school, prep school
预报	yùbào	forecast
天气预报	tiānqi yùbào	weather forecast
422. 爱	ài	love, like
爱人	àiren	spouse, husband, wife
可爱	kě'ài	be lovable, cute
最爱	zuì'ài	favorite
423. 步	bù	step, pace
走一步	zǒu yíbù	walk one step, take a step
先走一步	xiān zǒu yíbù	"take one step first," leave before others
饭后百步走，活到九十九	Fàn hòu bǎi bù zǒu, huódào jiǔshijiǔ	"After eating if you walk a hundred paces, you'll live to be 99 years old."
424. 数	shù	number, figure; several
多数	duōshù	majority
大多数	dà duōshù	great majority
数学	shùxué	mathematics
算数	suànshù	count
岁数	suìshu	age (of a person)
425. 紧	jǐn	be tight, tense
紧张	jǐnzhāng	be nervous, intense
要紧	yàojǐn	be important
不要紧	bú yàojǐn	be unimportant; "never mind"
426. 啊	a	(particle that softens the sentence)

A. SENTENCES

一、你如果现在不方便跟我讲话，不要紧，我可以改天再来。

二、不好意思，我有一点儿急事，得先走一步，各位请慢用！

三、听说你的数学特别好，我能问你一个跟数学有关系的问题吗？

四、王老先生，您好啊？好久不见了！能不能问您个问题，您今年多大岁数了？

五、 你别紧张！一步一步地来吧。你要是太紧张的话，什么事儿都办
　　 不好。

六、 天气预报说今天会下毛毛雨，不过天气预报只是预报而已，不一
　　 定准！

七、 这是我爱人特地为您预备的小吃和菜，您爱吃什么就吃什么吧，
　　 不要客气了！

八、 我姐姐、姐夫有一个儿子，今年四岁，非常可爱，因为他是牛年
　　 生的，所以大家都叫他"牛牛"。

九、 在中国请客的时候，主人常常给客人拿菜；可是大多数美国人不
　　 喜欢你给他拿菜，他们习惯自己拿。

十、 王大海，你快来接电话，校长说他有一件非常要紧的事找你！

B. CONVERSATIONS

一、

谢国平： 表姐，你们家住在哪儿啊？

李爱文： 我们住在通县，在北京城的东边儿。

谢国平： 你们家都有什么人啊？

李爱文： 我们一家三口。我和你表姐夫，还有一个女儿。

谢国平： 表姐，您在哪儿工作啊？

李爱文： 我在一家进出口公司做事。

谢国平： 表姐夫呢？

李爱文： 你表姐夫原来在一家工厂工作。因为太忙，所以他最近改行
　　　　 了，现在做点儿小买卖。

Xiǎocài or
"appetizer" choices
in a Taipei restaurant

二、
外国学生： 老师，请问，"饭后百步走，活到九十九"这句话是什么意思？
中文老师： 这句话的意思就是吃饭以后应该多走一走，才会活到比较
大的岁数。也就是说，要是你吃了饭以后都不动，就会老
得很快，可能活不到很大的年纪。

C. NARRATIVE

我的同屋小东今年大三，不过他才十七岁。他十一岁就开始上一个预备中学，十四岁就进大学了。小东的数学特别好，他妈妈说他两岁还不太会说话，可是已经会算数了！不过除了数学以外，其他很多事小东都不会。他不敢开车，坐别人开的车他也很紧张。他也不会做饭，更不会做家务什么的。穿衣服他也不知道什么衣服跟什么衣服一起穿好看。他走路想数学，吃饭也想数学，每天只想数学，因为数学就是他的最爱。我想小东的头和别人的头一定不太一样。不过，小东是个好人，对同学很好，他愿意替我们做我们的数学作业！

Notes

A3.　A跟B有关系 **A gēn B yǒu guānxi** "A is related to B"

B2a.　老 "become old, age"

B2b.　活不到很大的年纪 "won't be able to live to an old age"

C1a.　进大学 **jìn dàxué** "enter a university"

C1b.　家务 **jiāwù** "household duties" or "housework"

C1c.　头 **tóu** "head"

PART TWO

Conversation 🎧

Situation: After some more drinking, the dinner concludes (continued from the previous conversation).

1. MR. YANG: *(after returning from escorting Mr. and Mrs. Zhang to the elevator)*

老魏，来，再喝酒！我敬你！

Lǎo Wèi, lái, zài hē jiǔ! Wǒ jìng nǐ!

Larry, come on, have some more liquor! To you!

2. MR. WELLS: 我已经喝得太多了，实在是不能再喝了。我以果汁代酒好吧。

(after a while, to Mrs. Yang)

大嫂做的菜真是"色、香、味儿俱全"。馆子也比不上！

Wǒ yǐjīng hēde tài duōle, shízài shi bù néng zài hēle. Wǒ yǐ guǒzhī dài jiǔ hǎo ba... Dàsǎo zuòde cài zhēn shi "sè xiāng wèir jùquán." Guǎnzi yě bǐbushàng!

I've already had too much to drink, I really can't drink any more. I'll substitute juice for liquor...Older sister, the food you cook really is perfect in color, aroma, and taste. Not even a restaurant could compare!

3. MRS. YANG: 哪里，哪里，一点儿家常菜而已。不过呢，菜虽然不怎么样，你还是要吃饱哦！

Náli, náli, yìdiǎnr jiācháng cài éryǐ. Búguò ne, cài suīrán bù zěmmeyàng, nǐ hái shi yào chībǎo ó!

Thank you. It's just a little home-style cooking. But though the food is nothing special, you do have to get enough to eat, you know!

4. MR. WELLS: 我都已经吃撑了，实在是太好吃了。这么丰盛的一顿饭，大嫂今天辛苦了。我敬大哥、大嫂！又麻烦各位大老远地来。我敬各位！就算是门前清吧。

Wǒ dōu yǐjīng chīchēngle. Shízài shi tài hǎochīle. Zhèmme fēngshèngde yídùn fàn, Dàsāo jīntiān xīnkǔle. Wǒ jìng Dàgē, Dàsǎo! Yòu máfan gèwèi dà lǎo yuǎnde lái. Wǒ jìng gèwèi! Jiù suàn shi ménqiánqīng ba.

I've already eaten so much, I'm going to burst. It was really delicious. Such a sumptuous meal; Older Sister worked very hard today. Let me toast the two of you! And I made you all go to the trouble of coming here from far away. Here's to all of you! Let's just consider this a last "bottoms up."

5. MR. YANG: 各位请到客厅坐。喝点茶，吃点水果！

Gèwèi qǐng dào kètīng zuò. Hē diǎn chá, chī diǎn shuǐguǒ!

Everyone please go to the living room and have a seat. Drink some tea and eat some fruit!

New Vocabulary 🎧 LISTEN

以	**yǐ**	take
果汁	**guǒzhī**	juice
代	**dài**	take the place of
以A代B	**yǐ A dài B**	take A to substitute for B
色香味儿俱全	**"sè xiāng wèir jùquán"**	"color, aroma, and taste are all complete"
馆子	**guǎnzi**	restaurant
比不上	**bǐbushàng**	not be able to compare
家常菜	**jiācháng cài**	home-style cooking
虽然	**suīrán**	although
饱	**bǎo**	be full, satiated
吃饱	**chībǎo**	eat one's fill
吃撑	**chīchēng**	eat until one bursts
丰盛	**fēngshèng**	be sumptuous
辛苦	**xīnkǔ**	endure hardship
老	**lǎo**	very
算	**suàn**	consider as
门前清	**ménqiánqīng**	finish drinking up alcoholic beverages before leaving
客厅	**kètīng**	living room
茶	**chá**	tea

Supplementary Vocabulary 🎧

水	**shuǐ**	water
汽水	**qìshuǐ(r)**	soda
可乐	**kělè**	cola
餐厅	**cāntīng**	dining room (in a house); dining hall, restaurant
代课	**dàikè**	teach in place of someone else, substitute teach

Notes on the Conversation

Yǐ A dài B "substitute A for B"

Consider in the conversation the line **Wǒ yǐ guǒzhī dài jiǔ** "I'll substitute juice for wine." The pattern **yǐ A dài B** "take A to substitute for B" is a useful pattern for you to learn. It would be considered bad manners if someone at a banquet raised his or her glass to toast you and you refused entirely, since this would cause the other party to lose face. Therefore, if you really can't drink alcohol, then you can use this pattern and propose substituting some non-alcoholic beverage such as **guǒzhī** "juice," **qìshuǐ** "soda," or **chá** "tea" for the alcohol. More examples: **Wǒmen yǐ chá dài jiǔ ba** "Let's drink tea in place of wine," **Wǒ yǐ qìshuǐ dài jiǔ** "I'm substituting soda for liquor."

Topic + yě + Negative Verb

In the conversation notice the line **Guǎnzi yě bǐbushàng** "Not even a restaurant could compare." A topic followed by **yě** (or **dōu**) plus a negative verb often carries the connotation "not even." A fuller version of this would add a **lián: lián guǎnzi yě bǐbushàng**, with the same meaning. Examples: **Wǒ shínián yě xuébuhuì** "Even in 10 years I couldn't learn it," **Nǐ yìqiānkuài yě mǎibudào** "You couldn't buy it even for a thousand dollars," **Nǐ sònggěi wǒ, wǒ yě bú yào** "Even if you gave it to me as a present, I wouldn't want it."

Suīrán...kěshi "although"

To say "although" or "though," use the pattern **suīrán...kěshi**. The movable adverb **suīrán** occurs in the first or dependent clause, with **kěshi** "but" in the second or independent clause. In place of **kěshi**, you can also use **dànshi** "but" or **hái shi** "still." Examples: **Nǐ suīrán bú è, kěshi yě děi chī yidian dōngxi** "Though you're not hungry, you still have to eat something," **Tā suīrán hěn cōngming, dànshi bú tài yònggōng** "Even though he's smart, he's not very hard-working," **Suīrán tiānqi bù hǎo, wǒ hái shi yào qù** "I'm still going to go, though the weather isn't good."

Reading

New Characters and Words

427.	代	**dài**	substitute for; generation
	以A代B	**yǐ A dài B**	take A to substitute for B; substitute A for B
	代替	**dàitì**	replace, substitute
428.	课	**kè**	lesson; class
	上课	**shàngkè**	have class
	下课	**xiàkè**	end class
	中文课	**Zhōngwén kè**	Chinese class
	第一课	**dìyīkè**	lesson one
	代课	**dàikè**	teach in place of someone
	代课老师	**dàikè lǎoshī**	substitute teacher
429.	馆	**guǎn**	establishment; hotel; restaurant (can't be said alone)
	饭馆	**fànguǎn(r)**	restaurant
	馆子	**guǎnzi**	restaurant
	川菜馆子	**Chuāncài guǎnzi**	Sichuan-style restaurant
430.	虽	**suī**	though, although
	虽然	**suīrán**	although, though
	虽然…可是	**suīrán…kěshi**	although, though
	虽然…但是	**suīrán…dànshi**	although, though
431.	茶	**chá**	tea
	喝茶	**hēchá**	drink tea
	以茶代酒	**yǐ chá dài jiǔ**	"substitute tea for liquor"
	茶馆	**cháguǎn(r)**	teahouse
432.	乐	**lè**	cheerful, happy, joyful
	快乐	**kuàilè**	be happy
	生日快乐	**shēngrì kuàilè**	"birthday happiness," happy birthday
	可乐	**kělè**	cola
	可口可乐	**Kěkǒu Kělè**	Coca-Cola®
	百事可乐	**Bǎishì Kělè**	Pepsi-Cola®

A. SENTENCES

一、张老师明天有一点事不能来上课，所以何老师要替她代课。

二、小李虽然长得好看，也很有钱，可是他一点儿都不快乐。

三、可口可乐和百事可乐的味道不完全一样，哪个是哪个，你喝得出来吗？

四、喝水要紧，每个人都需要喝水；喝酒、喝茶、喝汽水都不能代替喝水！

五、你上完了这一课，就应当已经认识四百三十二个中国字了。这些字，你都认识吗？

六、有句话说："有太阳的地方就有中国人，有中国人的地方就有中国饭馆儿。"

七、在中国，喝茶已经成了一种生活习惯，人们不但自己喝茶，而且常请客人喝。

八、我的中文课应该是九点上课，九点五十下课，可是老师常常十点左右才下课。

九、妈妈，生日快乐！你是我们最爱的妈妈，在我们的心里没有谁能代替你！

十、王大海最近常常问自己，什么才是人生中最要紧的事？他虽然长这么大，但是对这个问题还是不太清楚。

B. CONVERSATIONS

一、

纪先生：老班，你从南京大老远地来看我，你自己又那么忙，真不好意思。

班先生：哪儿的话。你算是我最好的朋友，我再忙也应当来看你啊！

二、

服务员：您想喝什么？

温校长：有汽水吗，您这儿？

服务员：有。我们有百事可乐，也有七喜，您喝哪个？

温校长：有没有可口可乐？

服务员：对不起，没有可口可乐，只有百事可乐跟七喜。百事可乐行吗？

温校长：好吧，那我就喝百事可乐。

C. NARRATIVE

一、我从小就非常喜欢喝茶，喝着，喝着，一直喝到现在。上小学的时候我喜欢喝水果茶，到了国中开始喜欢喝香片，到了高中改为喝黑茶。上了大学就爱上了茶馆，常常和几个好朋友一起在那儿坐坐、说说话、喝喝茶。我现在早上起来，第一件事就是一定要喝一杯热茶。我现在什么茶都喝，不过台湾的东方美人茶是我的最爱。我实在太喜欢喝茶了，我觉得没有什么能代替茶。酒、汽水、可乐都不如茶好喝。朋友，你现在忙不忙？我请你和我一起上茶馆去，我们两个人喝喝茶、说说话，你觉得怎么样？

二、中国人请客的时候有"劝酒"的习惯。他们觉得主人，特别是男主人，应该劝客人多喝酒，这样做他们才是好主人，这样做请客才会比较有意思。所以你如果有机会参加中国人的酒席，你会常听到像"您多喝一点儿！，""您怎么喝得那么少？，""我敬您，""干杯！，""您干，我随意，""您海量，""我先干为敬，""门前清"这样的话。不过，大多数的外国人很不喜欢"劝酒"的习惯。老外觉得我要喝酒是我的事，我自己决定，用不着你来叫我怎么做。如果中国人劝你喝酒而你不想喝，该怎么办呢？你当然可以改喝一点儿别的，像茶、汽水、开水什么的。在这个时候，你可以这样说："您随意吧，我以茶代酒。" 这个意思就是说你要用茶来代替酒，这样说也很客气，而且你就可以不用喝酒。当然你也可以说"我以汽水代酒"或"我以开水代酒"。如果你不想喝酒的话，你还可以笑着说"对不起，但是我从小就受不了酒的味道"；或者你可以说你的大夫不让你喝酒；或者你的先生、太太、男朋友、女朋友不要你喝酒；或者你还太小，年纪还没满21岁，所以根本不可以喝酒。最要紧的是，不要不敢或是不好意思说你不想喝酒，特别是如果你还得开车。要不然你开车出事了，对谁都不好，是不是？

Notes

A3.　喝得出来 "be able to tell (something) by drinking (something)"

A6.　The pattern 有 A 就有 B means "wherever there is A, there is B."

A7a.　成了 "has become"

A7b.　人们 **rénmen** "people"

A9.　在我们的心里 "in our hearts"

A10a.　人生 **rénshēng** "human life." 什么才是人生中最要紧的事？ means "What is the most important thing in life?" The 才 in this question is optional but strengthens it, so that literally the meaning is more like "What really is the most important thing in life?"

A10b.　长这么大 "has grown to be so big" or "has grown to be so old" (长 is here pronounced **zhǎng**)

B1.　我再忙也应当来看你 "No matter how busy I might be, I should still come visit you." The pattern 再 + Verb + 也 or 都 means "no matter."

C1a.　从小 **cóng xiǎo** "from the time I was little, from childhood"

C1b. 喝着，喝着，一直喝到现在 "Keep on drinking and drinking all the way up until now." The use of a verb plus 着 reduplicated in this way indicates a high degree of frequency. Another example is 说着，说着 "keep on talking and talking."

C1c. 国中 **guózhōng** "junior middle school"

C1d. 香片 **xiāngpiàn** "scented tea"

C1e. 改为喝 means "change to drinking" (some other beverage that is different from what one was drinking before)

C1f. 杯 **bēi** "cup" or "glass"

C1g. 东方美人茶 **Dōngfāng Měirén Chá** "Oriental Beauty Tea" (name of a variety of black tea from Taiwan)

C1h. 不如茶好喝 "is not as good to drink as tea"

C2a. 劝 **quàn** means "urge," "encourage," or "advise." The verb-object compound 劝酒 **quànjiǔ** means "urge someone to drink alcohol."

C2b. 用不着 **yòngbuzháo** means "don't need, have no need for, there is no need to." 用不着你来叫我怎么做 "There's no need for you to tell me what to do."

C2c. 改喝 "change to drinking" (some other beverage)

C2d. 笑着说 means "say while smiling, say with a smile."

C2e. 大夫 **dàifu** means "(medical) doctor." 大 is here pronounced **dài**, not **dà**.

C2f. 出事 **chūshì** "have something go wrong, have an accident"

C2g. 对谁都不好 "be good for nobody"

On the Telephone

PART ONE

Conversation 🎧

Situation: Jim Donovan calls his friend Wang Dapeng to ask if Wang would like to accompany him to a musical event at the Beijing International Club.

1. **WANG:** *(answering the telephone, which is ringing)*
   喂？请问，您找谁？
   Wéi? Qǐng wèn, nín zhǎo shéi?
   Hello? Who would you like to speak with?

2. **DONOVAN:** 王大鹏先生在吗？
   Wáng Dàpéng Xiānshēng zài ma?
   Is Mr. Wang Dapeng in?

3. **WANG:** 我就是啊。请问，你是哪位？
   Wǒ jiù shì a. Qǐng wèn, nǐ shi něiwèi?
   Speaking. Excuse me, who is this?

4. **DONOVAN:** 我是小唐。你怎么样？
   Wǒ shi Xiǎo Táng. Nǐ zěmmeyàng?
   I'm Little Tang. How are you?

5. **WANG:** 嗨，别提了！这几天真把我忙坏了。你有什么事儿吗？
   Hài, bié tíle! Zhèjǐtiān zhēn bǎ wǒ mánghuàile. Nǐ yǒu shémme shìr ma?
   Oh, don't mention it! The last few days I've really been incredibly busy. Something up?

6. DONOVAN: 小王，我跟你说，这个星期六晚上国际俱乐部有音乐会。不知道你有没有空儿？

Xiǎo Wáng, wǒ gēn nǐ shuō, zhèige xīngqīliù wǎnshàng Guójì Jùlèbù yǒu yīnyuèhuì. Bù zhīdào nǐ yǒu méiyou kòngr?

Little Wang, listen. This Saturday evening the International Club is having a concert. I wonder if you'd be free?

7. WANG: 有啊。星期六几点钟？

Yǒu a. Xīngqīliù jǐdiǎn zhōng?

I am free. What time on Saturday?

8. DONOVAN: 音乐会是七点钟。咱们提前一刻钟在国际俱乐部门口儿见，行吗？

Yīnyuèhuì shi qīdiǎn zhōng. Zámmen tíqián yíkè zhōng zài Guójì Jùlèbù ménkǒur jiàn, xíng ma?

The concert is at seven o'clock. We'll meet 15 minutes beforehand at the entrance to the International Club, O.K.?

9. WANG: 行，一言为定。哦，对了，你能多搞几张票吗？小刘、小赵他们对音乐也挺感兴趣的。

Xíng, yì-yán-wéi-dìng. Ò, duìle, nǐ néng duō gǎo jǐzhāng piào ma? Xiǎo Liú, Xiǎo Zhào tāmen duì yīnyuè yě tǐng gǎn xìngqude.

O.K., agreed. Oh, yes, could you get a few more tickets? Little Liu and Little Zhao are also quite interested in music.

10. DONOVAN: 这，我估计问题不大。

Zhè, wǒ gūjì wèntí bú dà.

I think there should be no big problem with that

11. WANG: 好，就这样儿吧。到时候儿见！

Hǎo, jiù zhèiyangr ba. Dào shíhour jiàn!

O.K., then that's how it will be. See you when the time comes!

12. DONOVAN: 就这样儿定了。拜拜！

Jiù zhèiyangr dìngle. Báibái!

Then it's settled like this. Bye!

New Vocabulary 🎧

唐	**Táng**	Tang (surname)
嗨	**hài**	(indicates exasperation)
提	**tí**	mention
坏	**huài**	be bad
忙坏	**mánghuài**	extremely busy
国际	**guójì**	international
俱乐部	**jùlèbù**	club
国际俱乐部	**Guójì Jùlèbù**	International Club

会	huì	gathering, meeting
音乐	yīnyuè	music
音乐会	yīnyuèhuì	concert
空	kòng(r)	free time
有空	yǒukòng(r)	have free time
提前	tíqián	move up (a time or date)
一言为定	yì-yán-wéi-dìng	be agreed with one word
刘	Liú	Liu (surname)
感	gǎn	feel
兴趣	xìngqu	interest
对⋯感兴趣	duì...gǎn xìngqu	be interested in...
定	dìng	settle, decide
拜拜	báibái	"bye-bye"

Supplementary Vocabulary 🎧

| 市内电话 | shìnèi diànhuà | local telephone call |

Notes on the Conversation

Extended use of bǎ

Look at the sentence in the conversation **Zhèjǐtiān zhēn bǎ wǒ mánghuàile** "These past few days I've been incredibly busy" (literally "These last few days really have taken me and made me so busy that I'm going to break down"). The coverb **bǎ** can be used in an abstract, extended sense like this. Some more examples of the extended use of **bǎ**: **Nǐ zhēn bǎ wǒ qìsǐle!** "You're making me furious!" (literally "You really have taken me and made me angry to the point where I'm going to die!"), **Tāde huà bǎ wǒmen shuōde yǎnlèi dōu diàoxialaile** "What he said made us shed tears" (literally, "His words took us and talked to such an extent that tears even fell").

Duì...gǎn xìngqu "be interested in"

The pattern **duì...gǎn xìngqu** "be interested in" (literally "toward...feel interest") is very common and useful for expressing what a certain person is interested in. An alternate pattern with the same meaning is **duì...yǒu xìngqu**, literally "toward...have interest." Examples: **Wǒ duì yīnyuè gǎn xìngqu** "I'm interested in music," **Nǐ duì shémme yǒu xìngqu?** "What are you interested in?," **Nǐ duì Zhōngguo wénhuà gǎn xìngqu ma?** "Are you interested in Chinese culture?," **Wǒ duì Zhōngguo wénhuà bù gǎn xìngqu** "I'm not interested in Chinese culture."

Reading

New Characters and Words

433. 坏	**huài**	be bad
坏人	**huài rén**	bad person
坏事	**huài shì**	bad thing, evil deed
忙坏	**mánghuài**	become extremely busy
434. 提	**tí**	mention
别提了	**Bié tíle!**	"Don't mention it!"
提前	**tíqián**	move up (a time or date)
435. 际	**jì**	border, boundary, edge (can't be used alone)
国际	**guójì**	international
国际关系	**guójì guānxi**	international relations
国际学校	**guójì xuéxiào**	international school
国际和平	**guójì hépíng**	international peace
436. 音	**yīn**	sound
音乐	**yīnyuè**	music
音乐会	**yīnyuèhuì**	musical performance, concert
437. 空	**kōng**	empty; air factory
空气	**kōngqì**	air, atmosphere
空	**kòng(r)**	free time
有空	**yǒukòng(r)**	have free time, be free
438. 趣	**qù**	interest; interesting
兴趣	**xìngqu**	interest
对…有兴趣	**duì...yǒu xìngqu**	be interested in
对…感兴趣	**duì...gǎn xìngqu**	be interested in

A. SENTENCES

一、老高对音乐很有兴趣，一个月去听好几次音乐会。

二、最近几年，北京市的空气越来越坏了，一定要想个办法。

三、那位法国文学专家对中国解放后的文学特别感兴趣。

四、下个星期四在北京有一个国际大会，听说有三百多人打算参加。

五、我知道我做错了，可是还是请你不要跟别人提这件事，好吗？

六、今天晚上的音乐会是八点钟开始，我们应该提前一个钟头到比较好。

七、他们的儿子是小留学生，听说在美国交了坏朋友，自己也学坏了。

八、小方，我有一件事想请你替我办，不知道你这个星期日早上有没有空？

九、北京的国际机场叫"首都机场，"离北京市中心大概有三十公里左右。

十、王大海又把我给气坏了，你以后别跟我提他的名字，我真受不了他！

B. CONVERSATIONS

一、

小张：小房！做什么呢？

小房：学习呢。小张，最近怎么样？

小张：还行。小房，你以后要学什么专业呢？已经决定了吗？

小房：还没决定，不过可能要学国际关系。你呢？

小张：我对生物越来越感兴趣。

小房：生物课不是很难吗？

小张：别提了！真是难得要死，我等一下就得去准备明天的作业。

二、

谢老师：林先生，早！

林先生：谢老师，您好啊！最近忙吗？

谢老师：别提了！学校里的事真把我忙坏了。您知道，我们这种国际
学校，虽然工作很有意思，可是总有忙不完的事。

林先生：是吗？您可别把自己忙坏了。这些事，还是慢慢来吧。

谢老师：我知道了。您放心，我早就习惯了这种生活了！

C. NARRATIVE

一、我跟我的同屋小万很不一样。小万学的是国际关系专业，可是我
对国际关系的问题完全不感兴趣。好像每几个月就有一个国际关
系的什么会，从各国来的人随便讲几句话以后，又定在两、三个
月以内再办一次会。但是这样子解决不了什么问题，只是随便说
说话而已。真不知道哪天才可能有真的国际和平！

二、我去年六月到八月在一家国际大饭店工作了三个月。那时候，真
把我给忙坏了！我得把客人的行李拿到他们住的房间，有时候还
得做司机，开饭店的面包车到机场接客人。我不但一个星期七天
都得上班，而且每天还得工作十个到十二个小时。下班以后已经
很晚了，我完全没有空做自己喜欢做的事。我最感兴趣的音乐会
都没时间参加，一点自由时间都没有。今年那家国际大饭店说什
么、给我多少钱，我也一定不会回到那儿去工作了！

Notes

A2. 想办法 "think of a way" (to solve or handle a problem)

A6. 到 "arrive"

A7a. 小留学生 literally, "little study abroad student" refers to school-age children who are sent to the U.S. or Canada by their parents to attend school, learn English, and attain a Western education.

A7b. 学坏 means "learn and become bad" or "learn bad things."

A9. 市中心 **shìzhōngxīn** "downtown, center"

A10. 把我给气坏了 literally, "took me and made me very mad" or "infuriated me."

B1a. 学习呢 "(I'm) studying."

B1b. 不是很难吗? is a rhetorical question meaning "Isn't it hard?"

B2. 总 **zǒng** "always." 总有忙不完的事 literally, "There are always matters that one can't finish being busy with," or in more colloquial English, "There's always so much work that one can never finish."

C2a. 面包车 **miànbāochē** "minibus, passenger van." This word literally means "bread vehicle," referring to a van's oblong shape, which resembles a loaf of bread.

C2b. 接客人 **jiē kèrén** "meet or pick up guests"

PART TWO

Conversation 🎧

Situation: Carl Johnson, an employee at Sino-American Travel Agency in Beijing, tries to call his Chinese business associate He Zhiwen but has trouble getting through to him.

1. JOHNSON: 喂？请您转三七一。

    Wéi? Qǐng nín zhuǎn sān qī yāo.

    Hello? Please transfer me to 371.

2. OPERATOR: 对不起，三七一分机占线。您是等一会儿，还是过一会儿再打？

    Duìbuqǐ, sān qī yāo fēnjī zhànxiàn. Nín shi děng yìhuǐr háishi guò yìhuǐr zài dǎ?

    I'm sorry, extension 371 is busy. Will you wait a while or call back later?

3. JOHNSON: 我等一等。

    Wǒ děng yideng.

    I'll wait.

4. OPERATOR: *(after a while)*

    喂？您可以跟三七一分机讲话了。

    Wéi? Nín kéyi gēn sān qī yāo fēnjī jiǎnghuàle.

    Hello? You can speak with extension 371 now.

5. PERSON ANSWERING THE TELEPHONE: 喂？您找谁？

    Wéi? Nín zhǎo shéi?

    Hello? Who do you want?

6. JOHNSON:

请您给我找一下儿何志文。

Qǐng nín gěi wǒ zhǎo yixiar Hé Zhìwén.

Could you please find He Zhiwen for me?

7. PERSON ANSWERING
THE TELEPHONE:

何志文，是吗？好，请等一下，我去给您找。别挂，啊！

(after a while) 喂？何志文正在开会呢。您要给他留个话儿吗？

Hé Zhìwén, shi ma? Hǎo, qǐng děng yixia, wǒ qù gěi nín zhǎo. Bié guà, à!...
Wéi? Hé Zhìwén zhèng zài kāihuì ne. Nín yào gěi tā liú ge huàr ma?

He Zhiwen? All right, please wait a minute, I'll go find him for you. Don't hang up, O.K.?... Hello? He Zhiwen is in a meeting right now. Do you want to leave him a message?

8. JOHNSON:

他开完会，请您让他给我打个电话。我姓甄森，中美旅行社的。您一提，他就知道了。

Tā kāiwán huì, qǐng nín ràng tā gěi wǒ dǎ ge diànhuà. Wǒ xìng Zhēnsēn, Zhōng-Měi Lǚxíngshède. Nín yì tí, tā jiù zhīdaole.

When he's finished with his meeting, please have him give me a call. My name is Johnson, from Sino-American Travel Agency. As soon as you mention it, he'll know.

9. PERSON ANSWERING
THE TELEPHONE:

好的，我记下来了。等他开完会，我就告诉他。

Hǎode, wǒ jìxialaile. Děng tā kāiwán huì, wǒ jiù gàosu ta.

O.K., I've written it down. As soon as he's finished with his meeting, I'll tell him.

10. JOHNSON:

麻烦您。

Máfan nín.

Much obliged.

New Vocabulary

转	**zhuǎn**	transfer
分机	**fēnjī**	extension
占线	**zhànxiàn**	be busy (of a telephone)
挂	**guà**	hang, hang up
开会	**kāihuì**	hold or attend a meeting
正在	**zhèng zài**	just be in the midst of
留话(r)	**liúhuà(r)**	leave a message
旅行	**lǚxíng**	travel; trip
旅行社	**lǚxíngshè**	travel agency
一…就…	**yī…jiù…**	as soon as…
记	**jì**	record
下来	**xiàlai**	come down
记下来	**jìxialai**	write down, note down
等	**děng**	as soon as, once

Supplementary Vocabulary

传真	chuánzhēn	facsimile, fax
上来	shànglái	come up
拿上来	náshànglái	take up (to speaker)
上去	shàngqu	go up
拿上去	náshàngqu	take up (away from speaker)
下去	xiàqu	go down
拿下去	náxiaqu	take down (away from speaker)

Notes on the Conversation

Reduplicated monosyllabic verbs with -yi-

Consider in line 3 of the conversation the reduplicated verb **děng yideng** "wait a bit." Many one-syllable verbs like **děng** can be reduplicated with an optional **-yī-** "one" in the middle to give a relaxed, casual sense to the verb. The second iteration of the verb is usually neutral tone. Examples: **kàn yikan** or **kànkan** "take a look," **zǒu yizou** or **zóuzou** "take a walk," **tán yitan** or **tántan** "talk a bit." The reduplicated forms can generally be converted to Verb + **yixia**, so that **děng yideng** and **děng yixia** are interchangeable, both meaning "wait a bit" or "wait a second."

....

Zhèng zài + Verb + ne to express progressive aspect

Look at the sentence **Hé Zhìwén zhèng zài kāihuì ne** "He Zhiwen is holding a meeting right now." The pattern **zhèng zài** + Verb + **ne** expresses that an action is in progress and can often be translated into English with Verb + **-ing**. Both the **zhèng** and the **ne** are optional but, when added, strengthen the sense that an action is in progress. More examples: **Nǐ zhèng zài zuò shémme ne?** "What are you doing right now?," **Wǒ zhèng zài liànxí xiě Hànzì ne** "I'm just now practicing writing Chinese characters," **Xiǎo Lǐ zhèng zài chīfàn ne** "Little Li is just eating right now."

....

Yī...jiù... "as soon as"

The paired adverb pattern **yī...jiù...** most commonly expresses an instantaneous response to a certain situation and is often translated as "as soon as" or "the moment that" or "the minute that." The subject of the **yī** clause may be the same as or different from the subject of the **jiù** clause; if the subject is the same, it's often omitted in the **jiù** clause. Examples: **Wǒ yí kàn jiù zhīdao le** "I knew the moment I looked," **Wèishemme yǒude rén yì xué jiù huì ne?** "Why is it that some people master something the minute they start learning it?," **Tā měitiān yí xiàkè jiù huíjiā** "She goes home each day as soon as classes are over," **Tā yì lái, wǒ jiù zǒule** "The minute he came, I left," **Wǒ yì gēn tā shuōhuà, tā jiù shēngqìle** "The moment I spoke with him, he got angry." Both **yī** and **jiù** are adverbs and therefore must be followed by verbs, never by nouns or pronouns; in other words, the **yī** and **jiù** always *follow* the subjects of their clauses. To say "As soon as you left, he came," you'd have to say **Nǐ yì zǒu, tā jiù láile**; you could NEVER say *Yì nǐ zǒu, jiù tā láile.

....

Reading

New Characters and Words

439.	占	zhàn	occupy
	替…占一个位子	tì...zhàn yíge wèizi	hold a seat for
440.	线	xiàn	wire, line, thread
	占线	zhànxiàn	be busy (of a telephone line)
441.	告	gào	tell (can't be used alone)
442.	诉	sù	tell (can't be used alone)
	告诉	gàosu	tell
443.	挂	guà	hang, hang up
	挂电话	guà diànhuà	hang up the phone; make a phone call
	别挂!	Bié guà!	"Don't hang up!"
444.	传	chuán	transmit
	传话	chuánhuà	pass on a message
	传真	chuánzhēn	send a fax message
	传真机	chuánzhēnjī	fax machine

A. SENTENCES

一、小石，请你把这件衣服挂在门上，谢谢。

二、文先生还没有讲完电话，文太太就先挂了。

三、小毛，请你传个话给老张，明天早上公司不开会了。

四、李老师正在上课呢，不能来接电话；你要不要给他留个话？

五、别忘了，上课之前一定要把手机关上，要不然老师会生气的！

六、妹妹，我刚换了手机，我告诉你我的手机号，你快记下来。

七、请问，桌子上的传真机是我自己一个人用，还是大家一起用？

八、我在酒席上给你留了一个好位子，你怎么也不坐下，让别人给占了？

九、"电话占线"这句话的意思就是说那个人正在跟别人"讲话中"。

十、王大海告诉我他一下课就会去饭馆儿替我们占一个好位子，可是怎么现在找不着他了呢？

B. CONVERSATIONS

一、

楼楼：你怎么现在才来啊？我替你占了一个位子，等你等了半天了！

明明：不好意思，这么晚才到。路上车子太多了，公车开得好慢啊！

楼楼： 没关系。

明明： 还有，我正要出门的时候，家里来了一个很要紧的传真，是我
爸爸传给我的，他现在在日本，有些事需要我替他办，所以很
晚才出门。真对不起啊！

二、

王京生： 老文，我刚才给你打电话怎么一直占线？

文中山： 对不起。可能是因为我在跟我的女儿讲话吧。有什么事吗？

王京生： 我只是想问你，你最近买的那台传真机是在哪里买的？

文中山： 我那台传真机，是吗？南京街那家"平安家具店"后头有一家
小店，我是在那儿买的。

王京生： 那种传真机一台差不多要多少钱？

文中山： 好像一千块左右吧。

C. NARRATIVE

一、我今天一天都在给我们公司的高先生打电话。可是，不知道打了
多少次，电话一直占线。真不知道是为什么，根本没有办法打
进去。只有一次打通了，可是那次接电话的人一句话也没说就挂
了！后来电话一直打不进去。最后没法子，只好用传真机了。其
实，我只是想告诉高先生我今天有一点自己的事，不能去上班。
没想到，今天从早到晚一直为了这件事而忙。

二、"您好！这是二四五分机，李国明。对不起，我正在开会，四点钟
才能回到位子上。请留下您的姓名、单位和时间。我一接到您的
留言，就会给您回电话，谢谢！好，现在可以开始留言……"

Notes

A6. 手机号 "cell phone number"

C1. 为了这件事而忙 "be busy on account of this matter"

Calling about an Ad for an Apartment

PART ONE

Conversation 🎧

Situation: Lydia Dunn, a graduate student in art history at National Taiwan University who is looking for an apartment, calls the telephone number listed in a newspaper advertisement.

1. **TAIWANESE LANDLORD:** 喂？
   Wéi?
   Hello?

2. **DUNN:** 喂？我在报上看到你们的广告——
   Wéi? Wǒ zài bàoshang kàndào nǐmende guǎnggào—
   Hello? In the newspaper I saw your advertisement—

3. **TAIWANESE LANDLORD:** 对不起，你的电话杂音太大了，听不清楚。请你说大声一点。
   Duìbuqǐ, nǐde diànhuà záyīn tài dàle, tīngbuqīngchu. Qǐng nǐ shuō dàshēng yìdiǎn.
   I'm sorry, there's too much static on your line, I can't hear clearly. Please speak a little louder.

4. DUNN:

喂? 我说我在报上看到你们的广告（嗯。），有公寓要出租（是的。）。不知道租出去了没有？

Wéi? Wǒ shuō wǒ zài bàoshang kàndào nǐmende guǎnggào (M.), yǒu gōngyù yào chūzū (Shìde.). Bù zhīdào zūchuqule méiyou?

Hello? I said that I saw your advertisement in the newspaper (Yeah.), you have an apartment to rent out (Yes.). I wonder if it has been rented out or not?

5. TAIWANESE LANDLORD:

还没有，但是有人来看过，好像蛮有兴趣的（哦。）。如果你想来看的话，最好早一点。

Hái méiyou, dànshi yǒu rén lái kànguo, hǎoxiàng mán yǒu xìngqude (Ò.). Rúguǒ nǐ xiǎng lái kànde huà, zuìhǎo zǎo yìdiǎn.

Not yet, but somebody came to look at it, and they seem to be quite interested (Oh.). If you want to come look at it, you'd better come soon.

6. DUNN:

请问，公寓有多大？

Qǐng wèn, gōngyù yǒu duō dà?

Excuse me, how big is the apartment?

7. TAIWANESE LANDLORD:

差不多有三十五坪。有客厅、餐厅、三间卧室、浴室跟厨房。

Chàbuduō yǒu sānshiwǔpíng. Yǒu kètīng, cāntīng, sānjiān wòshì, yùshì gēn chúfáng.

It's about 35 *ping*. It has a living room, dining room, three bedrooms, bathroom and kitchen.

New Vocabulary

报	bào	newspaper
广告	guǎnggào	advertisement
杂音	záyīn	noise, static
听清楚	tīngqīngchu	hear clearly
大声	dà shēng	in a loud voice
公寓	gōngyù	apartment
是的	shìde	"yes"
租	zū	rent
租出去	zūchuqu	rent out
最好	zuìhǎo	it would be best, had better
坪	píng	(unit of area, 36 sq. ft.)
间	jiān	(for rooms)
卧室	wòshì	bedroom
浴室	yùshì	bathroom
厨房	chúfáng	kitchen

Supplementary Vocabulary

窗户	**chuānghu**	window
空调	**kōngtiáo**	air conditioning
声音	**shēngyīn**	sound; voice
小声	**xiǎo shēng**	in a low voice, quietly
安静	**ānjìng**	be quiet
吵	**chǎo**	be noisy
立刻	**lìkè**	immediately

Notes on the Conversation

Zuìhǎo "it would be best"

This common movable adverb means "it would be best" or "had better." Since **zuìhǎo** is a movable adverb, it can occur either before or after the subject; but it occurs most frequently after the subject and before the verb. **Zuìhǎo** is frequently used before the negative imperatives **bié** and **búyào** "don't" to express "You better not…" It's true that **zuìhǎo** sometimes can be translated as "it would be best if," but be careful never to add a **rúguǒ** or **yàoshi** in such a sentence. Examples: **Zuìhǎo duō dài yidian qián** "You had best bring a lot of money," **Nǐ qù yǐqián, zuìhǎo xiān gàosu nǐ fùmǔ** "It would be best if you told your parents before you go," **Nǐ zuìhǎo bié wèn ta** "You'd better not ask him," **Nèijiàn shì zuìhǎo xiān bié gàosu biérén** "It would be best if you didn't tell anyone else about that."

Yǒu + quantity expression + Stative Verb to indicate size or distance

In the conversation, look at the question **Gōngyù yǒu duō dà?** "How big is the apartment?" (literally "Apartment has how big?") Then look at the response: **Chàbuduō yǒu sānshiwǔpíng** "It's about 35 *ping*," literally "(It) approximately has 35 *ping*". The verb **yǒu** "have" can be followed by quantity expressions to indicate size, area, distance, years of age, etc. Often the quantity expression is followed by a Stative Verb. More examples: **Yáo Míng yǒu qīchǐ liùcùn gāo** "Yao Ming is 7 feet 6 inches tall," **Tīngshuō zhèitiáo lù yǒu yìqiānduō yīnglǐ cháng** "I heard this road is more than 1,000 miles long."

Reading

New Characters and Words

445.	声	**shēng**	sound; tone
	声音	**shēngyīn**	sound; voice
	大声	**dà shēng**	in a loud voice
	小声	**xiǎo shēng**	in a low voice; quietly
	四声	**sìshēng**	the four tones

第一声	**dìyīshēng**	first tone
第二声	**dì'èrshēng**	second tone
第三声	**dìsānshēng**	third tone
第四声	**dìsìshēng**	fourth tone
轻声	**qīngshēng**	neutral tone
声调	**shēngdiào**	tone

446.	立	**lì**	stand; establish
	立刻	**lìkè**	immediately
447.	红	**hóng**	be red
	红色	**hóngsè**	the color red
	红酒	**hóngjiǔ**	red wine
448.	黄	**huáng**	be yellow; (surname)
	黄色	**huángsè**	the color yellow
	黄河	**Huáng Hé**	Yellow River
	黄海	**Huáng Hǎi**	Yellow Sea
449.	图	**tú**	drawing, map, chart
	地图	**dìtú**	map
	一张地图	**yìzhāng dìtú**	a map
	图书馆	**túshūguǎn**	library
450.	领	**lǐng**	lead; head
	领事	**lǐngshì**	consul
	总领事	**zǒnglǐngshì**	consul general
	领事馆	**lǐngshìguǎn**	consulate
	总领事馆	**zǒnglǐngshìguǎn**	consulate general

A. SENTENCES

一、为什么中国的中国地图和台湾的中国地图不一样？

二、领事告诉她最好两、三天之内回领事馆再办那件事。

三、那位美国领事中国话讲得好极了，他的四声也特别准。

四、广州的广东话有七个声调，不过香港的广东话只有六个声调。

五、我需要买书、报、几百张白纸、两个本子和一张北京市地图。

六、图书馆的空调冷死了；外头一点儿也不热，根本不需要开空调。

七、这个房子只有两个房间；我们是不是应该换一个大一点儿的房子住呢？

八、那是什么声音？你听到了没有？好像是什么小动物的样子，最好小心一点儿！

九、对不起，这儿是图书馆，请您让您的儿子小声一点儿说话，要不然我们就得请你们立刻出去！

十、王大海说晚上要请客，叫我立刻去买汽水、红酒、白酒、水果和一些小吃。

B. CONVERSATIONS

一、

黄美金：我在找房子住。你觉得这个广告怎么样？

林会　：我看……我觉得看起来满不错的。离大学很近，客房特别大，而且还有书房、阳台什么的。带家具跟电话，每个月五千块，其实这也不算贵。

黄美金：那，你觉得我现在应该怎么办？

林会　：你应该立刻打电话问还有没有。要是还有的话，最好早一点去看，然后再决定。如果房东说还有的话，我愿意跟你一起去看。

二、

毛小姐：你觉得我穿黄色的鞋好看还是穿红色的好看？

简小姐：我觉得黄色的、红色的都不太好看。

毛小姐：是吗？那你说我应当穿什么鞋呢？

简小姐：我看你还不如买一双黑色的鞋。

毛小姐：好吧，我就听你的了。（对鞋店的店员）先生，我需要买一双黑色的高跟鞋，我穿三七号，不知道你们有没有？

店员：有，这双刚上市，您穿穿看。

C. NARRATIVES

一、中国北方有一条很大的河叫黄河。黄河是中国第二长河，有五千四百六十四公里长。黄河的水，因为里头有很多黄色的土，就成了黄色，所以叫黄河。

二、黄国明老先生是成都人，住在成都市小天北街382号，离美国总领事馆不太远。他年轻的时候在美国留学过，对美国的语言和文学都很感兴趣，所以他常常到美国总领事馆的图书馆去看美国的书、报、地图什么的。黄先生差不多每个星期都会去一、两次。因为图书馆就在总领事馆里面，所以天天都能看到那些美国领事进进出出，有时候还能看到总领事司米先生。有一次黄先生还跟总领事说了几句话。黄先生在图书馆里常看到他的朋友老何，也会跟他说说话。不过他们得小声地说话，因为有些人在看书，有些人在学习。黄老先生今天在图书馆已经看完了两本书和一些报纸了。

Notes

A3.   准 **zhǔn** "be accurate or precise," "standard"

B1a.   带 **dài** "include, come with"

B1b.   房东 **fángdōng** "house owner, landlord, landlady"

B2.   店员 **diànyuán** "sales clerk, shop assistant"

C2a.   进进出出 **jìnjìnchūchū** "enter and go out, come and go"

C2b.   小声地说话 "speak quietly"

PART TWO

Conversation 🎧

Situation: Dunn asks more questions about the apartment and makes an appointment to view it (continued from the previous lesson).

1. DUNN:	有没有家具、电话？
	Yǒu méiyou jiājù, diànhuà?
	Does it have furniture and a telephone?
2. TAIWANESE LANDLORD:	有一些简单的家具像沙发、餐桌、书桌、床、衣柜什么的，没有电话。
	Yǒu yìxiē jiǎndānde jiājù xiàng shāfā, cānzhuō, shūzhuō, chuáng, yīguì shemmede. Méiyou diànhuà.
	It has some simple furniture like a sofa, dining table, desk, bed, clothes closet and so on. There's no phone.
3. DUNN:	房租一个月大概是多少？
	Fángzū yíge yuè dàgài shi duōshǎo?
	About how much would the rent per month be?
4. TAIWANESE LANDLORD:	一个月三万块，水电费另外算。
	Yíge yuè sānwànkuài, shuǐdiànfèi lìngwài suàn.
	30,000 NT per month, with water and electricity not included.
5. DUNN:	那我什么时候来比较方便？
	Nà wǒ shémme shíhou lái bǐjiào fāngbian?
	So when would it be convenient for me to come?

6. TAIWANESE LANDLORD: 你可以今天下午过来，明天上午也可以。再晚就怕别人已经要签约了。

Nǐ kéyi jīntiān xiàwǔ guòlái, míngtiān shàngwǔ yě kéyi. Zài wǎn jiù pà biérén yǐjīng yào qiānyuē le.

You could come over this afternoon or tomorrow morning. Any later and I'm afraid somebody else might already want to sign a lease.

7. DUNN: 我今天下午四点左右到，方不方便？

Wǒ jīntiān xiàwǔ sìdiǎn zuǒyòu dào, fāng bù fāngbian?

If I arrived this afternoon around 4:00, would that be convenient?

8. TAIWANESE LANDLORD: 没问题。贵姓？

Méi wèntí. Guìxìng?

No problem. What's your last name?

9. DUNN: 我姓邓，邓丽。

Wǒ xìng Dèng, Dèng Lì.

My last name is Deng, Deng Li.

10. TAIWANESE LANDLORD: 好的，邓小姐，四点钟见。

Hǎode, Dèng Xiáojie, sìdiǎn zhōng jiàn.

All right, Ms. Deng, see you at four o'clock.

11. DUNN: 拜拜！

Báibái!

Bye.

New Vocabulary

一些	**yìxiē**	some
沙发	**shāfā**	sofa
餐桌	**cānzhuō**	dining table
书桌	**shūzhuō(r)**	desk
床	**chuáng**	bed
衣柜	**yīguì**	clothes closet
房租	**fángzū**	rent
水费	**shuǐfèi**	water fee
电	**diàn**	electricity
电费	**diànfèi**	electricity fee
水电费	**shuǐdiànfèi**	water and electricity fee
另外	**lìngwài**	in addition
方便	**fāngbian**	be convenient
别人	**biérén**	another person, others
签约	**qiānyuē**	sign a lease
邓	**Dèng**	Deng (surname)

Supplementary Vocabulary

押金	**yājīn**	deposit
教室	**jiàoshì**	classroom
墙	**qiáng**	wall
院子	**yuànzi**	courtyard, yard
种	**zhòng**	plant
花	**huā(r)**	flower
剪	**jiǎn**	cut
草	**cǎo**	grass
剪草	**jiǎncǎo**	mow the lawn

Notes on the Conversation

Yìxiē "some, a little"

Note **yìxiē** "some, a little" in **Yǒu yìxiē jiǎndānde jiājù** "It has some simple furniture." You've previously seen **zhèixiē** "these," **nèixiē** "those," and **xiē** "some." **Xiē** is actually an abbreviated form of the full form **yìxiē**, which has the same meaning as **xiē**. **Yìxiē** and **xiē** both indicate a small, indefinite number or amount. When they denote an amount of something, they're often interchangeable with **yìdiǎn(r)**. More examples with **(yì)xiē**: **Wǒ yǒu (yì)xiē dōngxi yào mài** "I have some things I want to sell," **Wǒ yǒu (yì)xiē tóngxué xiànzài zài niàn yīxuéyuàn** "I have some classmates who are now studying in medical school," **Tāde péngyou hěn duō, yǒu xiē shi Zhōngguo rén, yǒu xiē shi wàiguo rén** "She has lots of friends; some are Chinese, some are foreign." **Yìxiē** or **xiē**, in the sense of "a little," can also substitute for **yìdiǎn(r)** in comparative constructions. Examples: **Nǐ màn xiē zǒu** "Walk a little slower," **Zhèizhǒng bǐ nèizhǒng hǎo yìxiē** "This kind is a little better than that kind."

Reading

New Characters and Words

451.	床	**chuáng**	bed
	一张床	**yìzhāng chuáng**	a bed
	起床	**qǐchuáng**	get up from bed
	单人床	**dānrénchuáng**	single bed
	双人床	**shuāngrénchuáng**	double bed
452.	另	**lìng**	in addition; another
	另外	**lìngwài**	in addition; another
	另外算	**lìngwài suàn**	be figured in addition; be extra

另外一个	**lìngwài yíge**	another one
453. 怕	**pà**	be afraid; fear
可怕	**kěpà**	be frightful, terrible, horrible
454. 树	**shù**	tree
茶树	**cháshù**	tea tree, tea plant
树林	**shùlín**	woods, forest
455. 花	**huā(r)**	flower
菜花	**càihuā**	cauliflower
456. 草	**cǎo**	grass
一根草	**yìgēn cǎo**	a blade of grass
花草	**huācǎo**	flowers and grass

A. SENTENCES

一、 学校门口儿最近种了好多红花儿，实在是好看！

二、 你怕不怕晚上一个人在对面的那片树林里走路？我可不敢！

三、 菜单上的菜，每道二十五元，米饭和酒另外算，茶水不要钱。

四、 那个大城不怎么好看，应该在路上多种一些树、花儿跟草。

五、 那个房子好像十年没有人住了，外面的草长得这么高，有一点儿可怕。

六、 有时候有中国人说"不太方便，"其实他的意思是"根本不可能"。

七、 听说在香港有的男人很坏，在家里有太太，在外面还另外有"小太太"。

八、 那个房间只有一张单人床，不过我们需要的是一张双人床，能不能换另外一个房间？

九、 我们家人最喜欢吃的两道家常菜一个是用菜花做的，另外一个是用白菜做的。

十、 王大海的同学小林实在很可怕，他喝酒以后常常大声叫，有时候还会打人。

B. CONVERSATIONS

一、

小李：你平常早上几点钟起床？

小林：差不多六点吧。

小李：六点？怎么那么早？

小林：因为我怕更晚会来不及！

二、

方先生: 客人都来了。你要不要到前边儿来跟大家先说几句话?

何小姐: 不行, 不行, 你知道我是最怕讲话的!

方先生: 没关系! 你随便说几句都可以。

何小姐: 对不起, 我完全没有准备。改天吧, 今天真的不太方便。

C. NARRATIVES

中国热带很多地方, 特别是山上, 都种了茶树。中国茶的品种很多, 大的品种有红茶、绿茶和花茶, 另外还有二、三十种比较小的品种像黑茶、白茶、黄茶、花草茶什么的。不同的茶有不同的特点和香味。我特别喜欢喝花茶。我很喜欢跟几个好朋友到我家对面的一家茶馆儿去喝茶。你也喜欢喝茶吗? 你喜欢喝什么品种的茶呢? 你跟我在一起, 不用怕没有茶喝! 你现在忙不忙? 要不要跟我一块儿上茶馆儿去喝茶? 走吧, 我们是老朋友, 我请客!

Notes

A2.   片 **piàn** "section, stretch, expanse". 那片树林里 "in that expanse of woods"

A3.   茶水 **cháshuǐ** "brewed tea"

A4.   不怎么好看 "not particularly attractive"

C1.   热带 **rèdài** "tropical zone, the tropics"

C2.   品种 **pǐnzhǒng** "variety, species"

C3.   红茶 **hóngchá** "black tea." What people in the West call "black tea" is known as "red tea" in China.

C4.   绿 **lǜ** "be green"

C5.   花茶 **huāchá** "flower-scented green tea." A common example of this would be jasmine tea.

C6.   花草茶 **huācǎo chá** "herbal tea"

C7.   特点 **tèdiǎn** "characteristic, trait"

C8.   香味 **xiāngwèi** "aroma, fragrance, scent"

One of the few remaining Japanese-style houses in downtown Taipei

Visiting a Friend at Home

PART ONE

Conversation 🎧

Situation: John Niu, an American studying Chinese medicine in Beijing, visits the home of his Chinese friend, Li Zhijie. Li's mother opens the door.

1. **NIU:**   伯母好！小李在家吗？
   Bómǔ hǎo! Xiǎo Lǐ zài jiā ma?
   Hello, Mrs. Li! Is Little Li home?

2. **MRS. LI:**   在，在。小牛儿，你进来坐吧！志杰马上就来。你先喝点儿茶!
   Zài, zài. Xiǎo Niúr, nǐ jìnlái zuò ba. Zhìjié mǎshàng jiù lái. Nǐ xiān hē diǎnr chá.
   Yes, he is. Little Niu, come in and sit down. Zhijie will be right here. First have some tea.

3. **LI ZHIJIE:** *(calling from a back room)*

   小牛儿，对不起，我正在刮胡子呢。这就完了。
   Xiǎo Niúr, duìbuqǐ, wǒ zhèng zài guā húzi ne. Zhè jiù wánle.
   Little Niu, I'm sorry, I'm just in the middle of shaving. I'll be finished in a second.

4. **NIU:**   小李，你忙你的，别急。
   Xiǎo Lǐ, nǐ máng nǐde, bié jí.
   Little Li, you take your time, don't rush.

5. CHILD: *(enters room)*

外婆！

Wàipó!

Grandma!

6. MRS. LI: 小牛儿，你见过我的外孙鹏鹏吗？

Xiǎo Niúr, nǐ jiànguo wǒde wàisūn Péngpeng ma?

Little Niu, have you met my grandson Pengpeng before?

7. NIU: 见过，见过。

Jiànguo, jiànguo.

Yes, I have.

8. MRS. LI: 鹏鹏，你问牛叔叔好。

Péngpeng, nǐ wèn Niú Shūshu hǎo.

Pengpeng, say hello to Uncle Niu.

9. CHILD: 牛叔叔好！

Niú Shūshu hǎo!

Hello, Uncle Niu!

10. NIU: 鹏鹏，你好！越长越高了！

Péngpeng, nǐ hǎo! Yuè zhǎng yuè gāole.

Hi, Pengpeng! The more you grow, the taller you get.

11. MRS. LI: 是，挺高的了。 *(to the child)* 鹏鹏，去吧，到外面去和小朋友玩儿去吧。 *(to Niu)* 小孩儿总是在屋子里待不住！

Shì, tǐng gāode la. Péngpeng, qù ba, dào wàimian qù hé xiǎo péngyou wánr qu ba. Xiǎoháir zǒngshi zài wūzili dāibuzhù!

Yes, he is quite tall. Pengpeng, go, go outside and play with your little friends. Kids can never stay indoors for very long!

New Vocabulary

伯母	bómǔ	aunt (wife of father's older brother)
牛	Niú	Niu (surname)
刮	guā	scrape
胡子	húzi	beard, mustache
刮胡子	guā húzi	shave
这	zhè	right away
忙	máng	be busy with (something)
急	jí	be in a hurry
外婆	wàipó	grandmother (maternal)
外孙	wàisūn	grandson (daughter's son)
小朋友	xiǎo péngyou	little friend, child

总是	**zǒngshi**	always
屋子	**wūzi**	room
待	**dāi**	stay
待不住	**dāibuzhù**	not be able to stay

Supplementary Vocabulary

伯父	**bófù**	uncle (father's older brother)
外公	**wàigōng**	grandfather (maternal)
外孙女	**wàisūnnǚ(r)**	granddaughter (daughter's daughter)
留胡子	**liú húzi**	grow a beard or mustache

Notes on the Conversation

Zhè "right away, right now"

The adverb **zhè** "right away, right now" is often followed by **jiù** to stress how soon something will happen, for example, **Zhè jiù wánle** "(I'll) be finished right away." Some more examples: **Bié zháojí, tā zhè jiù lái** "Don't get excited, she'll be here right away," **Nǐ fàngxīn hǎole, wǒ zhè jiù gěi nǐ bàn** "Why don't you just relax; I'll take care of it for you right away."

Nǐ + Verb + nǐde

In this lesson's conversation, note **Nǐ máng nǐde**, which literally means "You be busy with your things." In freer English, this could be translated as "You just go ahead and take care of your own business" or, in the context of this conversation, "You just take your time." In Lesson 5, Part 2, we had already seen a similar sentence: **Nǐ mǎi nǐde, wǒ mǎi wǒde** "You buy your things and I'll buy mine." Also common is **Nǐ zǒu nǐde ba** "Why don't you just go ahead," which can be abbreviated to **Zǒu nǐde ba**. These expressions basically all mean "You take care of your own business and don't concern yourself with me."

Reading

New Characters and Words

457.	孩	**hái**	child (can't be used alone)
	孩子	**háizi**	child
	男孩子	**nánháizi**	boy
	女孩子	**nǚháizi**	girl
	男孩儿	**nánhái**	boy
	女孩儿	**nǚhái**	girl

小孩	**xiǎohái(r)**	child
小孩子	**xiǎo háizi**	small child
坏孩子	**huài háizi**	bad child

458. 马　　　　　**mǎ**　　　　　horse; (surname)

司马　　　　　**Sīmǎ**　　　　Sima (a two-syllable surname)

马上　　　　　**mǎshàng**　　immediately, right away

459. 相　　　　　**xiāng**　　　　mutually

相当　　　　　**xiāngdāng**　　rather, quite

460. 管　　　　　**guǎn**　　　　control, manage; (surname)

别管我!　　　**Bié guǎn wǒ!**　　"Don't bother me!"

461. 严　　　　　**yán**　　　　be stern, severe; (surname)

462. 重　　　　　**zhòng**　　　　be heavy

你有多重?　　**Nǐ yǒu duō zhòng?**　　"How much do you weigh?"

严重　　　　　**yánzhòng**　　be serious, grave

A. SENTENCES

一、司马，你回国请别忘了替我问你爸爸、妈妈好！

二、有的人总是爱管别人，其实他们应该先管好自己。

三、我们往前走了没有几步，就到了一条相当深的河。

四、这件行李怎么这么重啊！好像里头放了很多石头的样子！

五、虽然其他人都把这件事看得很严重，但是司马先生一点儿也不紧张。

六、这么严重的问题需要马上解决！你怎么还先上茶馆跟朋友喝茶去了呢？

七、老白和他爱人住的房子很小，只有两间屋子，他们根本不可能生两、三个孩子。

八、虽然中美关系最近几年好像相当不错，但还有不少问题，有的问题不太要紧，有的相当严重。

九、虽然大多数人总是说生男生女都一样，其实不少人还是觉得如果只能生一个孩子，那么生男孩子比较好。

十、除了王大海之外，其他参加酒席的客人，就是严东山、李想、管二妹、司马红、马立国和牛小花，已经全来了。

B. CONVERSATIONS

一、

小严：小马，我问你，你有多高？

小马：我一米八二。

小严： 你有多重？

小马： 我九十八公斤，可是……你为什么问我这些问题？

二、

严小姐： 你觉得这儿的气候怎么样？

马先生： 这儿的气候啊？我觉得……相当好，还可以吧。

严小姐： 真的吗？我觉得这个地方最近几个星期热得要死，又那么干，我真受不了！

马先生： 没有你说的那么严重吧！

C. NARRATIVES

一、 最近几年，越来越多的孩子不好好儿地在学校里学习，这是不是已经成了相当严重的问题了呢？可能会有人说，这根本不是什么问题，大家都想得太多，管得也太多了。但是我就觉得如果我们这些做爸爸、妈妈的不管自己孩子的事儿，那么还有谁会去管呢？我觉得，孩子学习的问题不能不管。孩子一有问题，就要马上解决！

二、 我的外公六十九岁了，马上就要七十岁了。他老人家住在台湾台南市，离台南火车站不太远。我平常每年六月都回台湾去看他。我最爱我的外公，因为他对我相当好。记得我小时候，外公常常带我去菜市场买菜。他不管有多忙，总是会找时间请我吃一点儿台南的小吃或是给我买一点儿美国没有的小东西。我非常高兴我有那么好的一位外公！

Notes

A3.　 没有几步 "a couple of steps"

A9.　 生男生女都一样 literally, "Giving birth to boys or giving birth to girls is all the same," that is, "It's all the same whether you give birth to a boy or a girl."

C1a.　 不好好儿地在学校里学习 "don't learn well in school."

C1b.　 成 **chéng** "become"

C1c.　 做 **zuò** "be, act as, serve as." 我们这些做爸爸、妈妈的 literally, "We, these who serve as dads and moms," or more colloquially "We, as parents."

C2a.　 老人家 **lǎorenjia** "elderly person"

C2b.　 记得我小时候 "I remember when I was small."

C2c.　 不管 **bùguǎn** "no matter, regardless"

PART TWO

Conversation 🎧

Situation: Li Zhijie finishes shaving and joins his friend John Niu (continued from the previous conversation).

1. **LI ZHIJIE:** 我来了，我来了！小牛儿，对不起，让你久等了。
   Wǒ láile, wǒ láile! Xiǎo Niúr, duìbuqǐ, ràng nǐ jiǔ děngle.
   I'm coming, I'm coming! Little Niu, sorry to keep you waiting so long.

2. **NIU:** 没关系，没关系。
   Méi guānxi, méi guānxi.
   Don't worry about it.

3. **MRS. LI:** 小牛儿，在这儿吃饭吧！
   Xiǎo Niúr, zài zhèr chīfàn ba!
   Little Niu, have dinner here!

4. **NIU:** 不用了。等会儿我跟小李谈完了，就回去。
   Bú yòngle. Děng huǐr wǒ gēn Xiǎo Lǐ tánwánle, jiù huíqu.
   That's not necessary. In a little while when I finish talking with Little Li, I'll go home.

5. **LI ZHIJIE:** 不，小牛儿，你就在这儿吃吧。咱们一边儿吃一边儿谈。
   Bù, Xiǎo Niúr, nǐ jiù zài zhèr chī ba. Zámmen yìbiānr chī yìbiānr tán.
   No, Little Niu, why don't you just have dinner here. We can talk while we eat.

6. **NIU:** 那也好。简单点儿，别太麻烦了！
   Nà yě hǎo. Jiǎndān diǎnr, bié tài máfanle!
   Well, all right. But keep it simple, don't go to too much trouble!

7. MRS. LI: 哦，不麻烦，马上就弄好。
Ò, bù máfan, mǎshàng jiù nònghǎo.
Oh, it's no trouble, it'll be ready in no time.

8. NIU: *(when the meal is over)*
小李，时候不早了，我该走了。
Xiǎo Lǐ, shíhou bù zǎole, wǒ gāi zǒule.
Little Li, it's getting late, I should be going now.

9. LI ZHIJIE: 再坐一会儿吧！
Zài zuò yihuir ba!
Why don't you sit a while longer?

10. NIU: 不了，我还得上街买点儿东西。
Bù le, wǒ hái děi shàngjiē mǎi diǎnr dōngxi.
No, I still have to go out on the street to buy something.

11. LI ZHIJIE: 好吧。既然你还有事，我就不挽留了。以后有空儿再来玩儿。
Hǎo ba. Jìrán nǐ hái yǒu shì, wǒ jiù bù wǎnliúle. Yǐhòu yǒu kòngr zài lái wánr.
O.K. Since you still have things to do, I won't make you stay. Come again when you're free.

12. NIU: 伯母，我走了。小李，明天学校见！
Bómǔ, wǒ zǒule. Xiǎo Lǐ, míngtiān xuéxiào jiàn!
Mrs. Li, I'll be leaving. Little Li, see you at school tomorrow!

13. LI ZHIJIE: 明天见。我不送了，慢走！
Míngtiān jiàn. Wǒ bú sòngle, màn zǒu!
See you tomorrow. I won't see you out, take care!

New Vocabulary 🎧

等会儿	děng huǐr	in a little while
谈	tán	talk
一边	yìbiān(r)	on the one hand
一边A一边B	yìbiān(r) A yìbiān(r) B	do B while doing A
麻烦	máfan	be troublesome
弄	nòng	do, make
弄好	nònghǎo	fix, prepare, finish
街	jiē	street
上街	shàngjiē	go out on the street
既然	jìrán	since
既然…就…	jìrán…jiù…	since
挽留	wǎnliú	urge someone to stay
送	sòng	see someone off or out

Supplementary Vocabulary

| 大使 | dàshǐ | ambassador |
| 谈话 | tánhuà | talk, speak |

Notes on the conversation

Yìbiān(r) A yìbiān(r) B "on the one hand A, on the other hand B"

The paired adverb pattern **yìbiān(r) A yìbiān(r) B** is used to indicate that one action (action B) occurs while another action (action A) is in progress. It often translates into English as "on the one hand… on the other hand…" or "(do B) while (doing A)." Note that with this pattern, the main or longer action (action A) comes first, with the secondary action (action B) coming last. Oftentimes where in English you'd use an "and," you'd in Chinese use **yìbiān(r) A yìbiān(r) B**. For example, for English "Let's eat and talk," the best equivalent would be **Wǒmen yìbiānr chī yìbiānr tán ba**; in this case, you could NOT say *Wǒmen chīfàn gēn tánhuà ba**. More examples: **Tā yìbiānr chī zǎofàn, yìbiānr kàn bào** "He read the newspaper while he ate breakfast," **Zhōngguo rén xǐhuan yìbiān hē chá, yìbiān liáotiān** "Chinese people like to chat while drinking tea," **Zuìhǎo búyào yìbiānr kāichē, yìbiānr kàn dìtú** "Better not look at maps while you're driving."

....

Jìrán...jiù... "since"

The paired adverb pattern **jìrán...jiù...** means "since" or "given the fact that" (not "since" as in "since a certain time"). **Jìrán** is a movable adverb and can stand either before or after the subject of the clause it occurs in. However, **jiù** always follows the subject and stands before the verb. Unlike English, where the "since" clause may come first or last, in Chinese the clause with **jìrán** normally comes first. Examples: **Jìrán nǐ xǐhuan, wǒ jiù sònggei nǐ ba** "Since you like it, I'll give it to you," **Jìrán nǐ bù zhīdào, wǒ jiù gàosu nǐ ba** "Since you don't know, I'll tell you," **Jìrán nǐ shēnti bù shūfu, nǐ jiù huíjiā xiūxi ba** "Since you don't feel well, why don't you just return home and rest." Distinguish carefully between **jìrán...jiù...** and **yīnwei...suóyi...**. With **yīnwei...suóyi...** there is a strong flavor of "cause and effect," whereas with **jìrán...jiù...** the relationship between the first and second clauses is weaker. Also, **jìrán...jiù** is often used to give suggestions for what to do in the future; it's generally not used to describe past events. For example, English "Since it rained yesterday, they didn't meet" would in Chinese be **Yīnwei zuótiān xiàyǔ, suóyi tāmen méiyou kāihuì**. You couldn't use **jìrán** in a sentence like that.

....

Reading

New Characters and Words

463.	谈	tán	chat, talk
	谈话	tánhuà	talk, speak; conversation; statement
464.	既	jì	since
	既然	jìrán	since

既然…就…	jìrán...jiù...	since
465. 送	sòng	give (a present); deliver; see someone out
送给	sònggěi	give someone a present
466. 使	shǐ	send; envoy; use
大使	dàshǐ	ambassador
大使馆	dàshǐguǎn	embassy
使用	shǐyòng	use, employ
467. 希	xī	hope (can't be used alone)
468. 望	wàng	hope; watch
希望	xīwàng	hope

A. SENTENCES

一、我已经把我的爱给你了，你还要我送给你什么呢？

二、我还没去过中国，真希望以后能有机会去中国留学。

三、你既然时间很紧张，那么我们就一边吃饭一边谈话吧。

四、已经下了一个多星期雨了，大家都希望明天能出太阳！

五、下面是习近平主席2013年8月17日和外国记者谈话的全文……

六、你怎么没有早一点儿告诉我，你等会儿还需要上街买东西？

七、张先生打算改天去大使馆找李大使谈话，因为大使是他的老朋友。

八、既然那家饭馆菜不怎么样，而且服务很差，我们这次就换一家饭馆吧。

九、我想学习怎么使用iPhone手机，请问，谁能给我讲一讲iPhone的使用方法？

十、明天是王大海妈妈的五十岁生日，所以大海要送她一些花儿。

B. CONVERSATIONS

一、

小牛：小李，时候不早了，我该走了。

小李：再坐一会儿吧！

小牛：不了，我还得上街买点东西。

小李：好吧。既然你还有事，我就不留你了。以后有空儿再来吧。

小牛：我走了。小李，明天学校见！

小李：明天见。我不送了，慢走！

二、

高大林：小万，我先走了。公司那边还有点儿事我得办。

万小京：好吧。你既然还有事儿，我就不留你了。

高大林：好，再见！明天见！

万小京：好，我们改天再谈吧。我不送你了，慢走！

C. NARRATIVES

上个星期，我在美国南加州大学的同屋司米文从美国到北京来看我。我已经十多年没看见他了，不过他还是老样子，看起来跟二十几岁的时候差不多一样。因为是米文第一次到中国来，所以白天我带他到很多地方去看了看，像天安门、长城、北海公园、后海和北京动物园。因为我女儿美美很想以后到美国去留学，所以米文有一天也到美国大使馆去问了美美应该怎么样准备去美国的事。每天晚上我跟米文都谈到一、两点钟，谈得非常高兴，也喝了不少酒。米文在我们家住了一个多星期才回美国。他既然从这么远的地方来看我们，我们就在他走的时候送了他很多北京的小吃，希望他会喜欢。我们也希望米文以后有空还能再来我们家住。他也请我们全家有时间到美国去看他，还说如果美美去美国留学的话，可以住在他家。他那样说，我跟我太太特别感谢他，因为美美住在他家不但能省钱，而且女儿住在朋友家，我们这些做爸爸、妈妈的当然也比较放心。

Notes

A1.　全文 **quánwén** "complete text, full text"

B1.　我就不留你了 "Then I won't keep you."

Calling on Someone to Request a Favor

PART ONE

Conversation 🎧 LISTEN

Situation: Bill Sanchez, an American graduate student who is conducting research in Taiwan, visits the Taipei home of his friend Cai Yaquan to request a favor.

1. MR. CAI:　宋先生，欢迎，欢迎！
　　　　　　Sòng Xiānsheng, huānyíng, huānyíng!
　　　　　　Mr. Sanchez, welcome, welcome!

2. SANCHEZ:　对不起，我因为临时有点事，所以来晚了。
　　　　　　Duìbuqǐ, wǒ yīnwei línshí yǒu diǎn shì, suóyi láiwǎnle.
　　　　　　I'm sorry, I'm late because something came up at the last minute.

3. MR. CAI:　没关系。 *(sees Sanchez starting to take off his shoes)* 不用脱鞋。
　　　　　　Méi guānxi. Bú yòng tuōxié.
　　　　　　That's O.K. No need to take off your shoes.

4. SANCHEZ: 我还是脱好了，比较舒服。我也喜欢这个习惯。 *(to Mrs. Cai)*

欸，蔡太太，这是一点小意思。

Wǒ hái shi tuō hǎole, bǐjiào shūfu. Wǒ yě xǐhuan zhèige xíguàn. Éi, Cài Tàitai, zhè shi yìdiǎn xiǎo yìsi.

I'll take them off anyway, it's more comfortable. I also like this custom. Uh, Mrs. Cai, this is a little something for you.

5. MRS. CAI: 哎呀！您太客气了。请坐，我去泡茶。

Āiya! Nín tài kèqile. Qǐng zuò, wǒ qù pàochá.

Oh! You're too polite. Please have a seat, I'll go make some tea.

6. MR. CAI *(offers Sanchez a cigarette):*

请抽烟。

Qǐng chōuyān.

Please have a cigarette.

7. SANCHEZ: 哦，我不会抽，谢谢。

Ò, wǒ bú huì chōu, xièxie.

Oh, I don't smoke, thanks.

8. MR. CAI: 您昨天在电话里说有点事要找我。

Nín zuótiān zài diànhuàli shuō yǒu diǎn shì yào zhǎo wǒ.

You said on the phone yesterday you wanted to see me about some matter.

9. SANCHEZ: 欸，不好意思。有点小事情想拜托您帮个忙。

Éi, bù hǎo yìsi. Yǒu diǎn xiǎo shìqing xiǎng bàituō nín bāng ge máng.

Yes, sorry to bother you with this. There is a little matter I'd like to ask for your help with.

10. MRS. CAI: *(brings a cup of tea for Sanchez)*

请喝茶。

Qǐng hē chá.

Please have some tea.

11. SANCHEZ: 谢谢。

Xièxie.

Thank you.

12. MR. CAI: 不要客气，请直说。

Búyào kèqi, qǐng zhí shuō.

Don't be polite, please be frank.

13. SANCHEZ: 欸，这个，这个，哦，事情是这样子的……

Éi, zheige, zheige, e, shìqing shi zhèiyangzide...

Uh, well, well, uh, the matter is like this...

New Vocabulary 🎧

宋	**Sòng**	Song (surname)
临时	**línshí**	when something happens, at the last minute
来晚	**láiwǎn**	come late
脱	**tuō**	take off (shoes, clothes)
脱鞋	**tuōxié**	take off one's shoes
习惯	**xíguàn**	custom, habit
蔡	**Cài**	Cai (surname)
意思	**yìsi**	intention
一点小意思	**yìdiǎn(r) xiǎo yìsi**	"a little something," a gift
泡茶	**pàochá**	steep tea, make tea
烟	**yān**	tobacco, cigarette; smoke
抽烟	**chōuyān**	smoke
事情	**shìqing**	thing, matter
拜托	**bàituō**	ask someone to do something
帮忙	**bāngmáng**	help
直	**zhí**	be straightforward, frank
直说	**zhí shuō**	speak frankly
这个	**zheige**	(pause filler)

Supplementary Vocabulary 🎧

抽空	**chōukòng**	find time (to do something)
看	**kàn**	call on, visit
关系	**guānxi**	relationship, connection
吸	**xī**	inhale, breathe in
吸烟	**xīyān**	smoke
区	**qū**	area, region
吸烟区	**xīyān qū**	smoking section
非吸烟区	**fēixīyān qū**	non-smoking section

Notes on the Conversation

Some help with different ways of saying "help"

You've now been introduced to three ways to say "help": **bāng**, **bāngzhù**, and **bāngmáng**. **Bāng** most commonly takes a following main verb, for example, **Wǒ bāng nǐ zhǎo** "I'll help you look," **Wǒ bāng**

nǐ dǎ diànhuà "I'll make the call for you," **Qǐng nǐ bāng wǒ jiějué zhèige wèntí** "Please help me solve this problem." If a noun or pronoun object follows, use **bāngzhù** as in **Qǐng nǐ bāngzhù tā** "Please help her." If you're saying "help" without a following object or verb, use the verb-object compound **bāngmáng**, for example, **Qǐng nǐ bāngmáng** "Please help." You can insert **(yí)ge** or nouns or pronouns with or without **-de** between the **bāng** and the **máng**. Examples: **Qǐng nín bāng ge máng** "Please help," **Qǐng nín bāng wǒde máng** "Please do me a favor."

....

Pause fillers and hesitation sounds

In line 13 of this conversation, there are four pause fillers: two occurrences of **e**, which you've seen before, and two occurrences of **zheige**, which occurs for the first time in this lesson. As a pause filler, **zheige** is frequently said two or more times: **zheige, zheige**. Pause fillers and hesitation sounds fill in a pause while the speaker thinks of what to say next and also prevent what is being said next from appearing to be too direct or blunt. Pause fillers serve to keep the conversation going and also allow speakers to retain their turn in turn-taking while they search for their next idea or for the "right word." In this conversation, the use of **zheige, zheige** to a certain extent even indicates politeness, since it reflects Mr. Sanchez' reluctance to bring up his request and bother Mr. Cai. Other common pause fillers include **a**, **m**, **neige** (often repeated as **neige, neige**), **nà** "in that case," **nèmme** "in that case," **suóyi shuō** "and therefore," **jiùshi shuō** "that is to say," **Wǒde yìsi shi shuō** "What I mean is," **Zěmme shuō ne?** "How should I put it?"and **Nǐ zhīdao ma?** "You know?"

....

Reading

New Characters and Words

469.	抽	**chōu**	take out, draw out
	抽空	**chōukòng**	find time
470.	烟	**yān**	tobacco; cigarette; smoke
	抽烟	**chōuyān**	smoke (cigarettes, etc.)
	香烟	**xiāngyān**	cigarette
	一根烟	**yìgēn yān**	a cigarette
	一包烟	**yìbāo yān**	a pack of cigarettes
	一条烟	**yìtiáo yān**	a carton of cigarettes
471.	吸	**xī**	inhale, breathe in
	吸烟	**xīyān**	smoke (cigarettes, etc.)
472.	区	**qū**	area, district, region
	吸烟区	**xīyān qū**	smoking section
	非吸烟区	**fēixīyān qū**	non-smoking section
	地区	**dìqū**	area, district, region, zone
	山区	**shānqū**	mountain region
	林区	**línqū**	forest region

473.	情	qíng	sentiment; situation, condition
	事情	shìqing	thing, matter
	一件事情	yíjiàn shìqing	a thing, a matter
	心情	xīnqíng	mood, state of mind
	爱情	àiqíng	love
474.	帮	bāng	help; gang, group
	帮忙	bāngmáng	help
	四人帮	Sìrénbāng	Gang of Four

A. SENTENCES

一、爱情要紧还是面包要紧？不知道大家的看法是什么？

二、你百忙之中还抽空来看我，真是让我感到很不好意思！

三、这儿是非吸烟区，不是吸烟区，那些人为什么还抽烟呢？

四、我们两点开会，现在已经两点四十了，换句话说，他一定不来了。

五、对不起，我不是不愿意帮你的忙，可是这件事情我还真办不到。

六、老张说话很直，心里想什么就说什么，他以后大概不能做大使！

七、中国西北边的山区，交通不方便，很多地区小孩子还是走路去上学。

八、小张，你又来晚了。我们不是说过9:00开会吗？现在已经9:20了。
你这个习惯一定要改！

九、中国有句老话说"笑一笑，十年少，"意思是常常笑、心情好的人可
以比不喜欢笑、心情不好的人活得更长。

十、王大海很难过地问："为什么我觉得自己还行，但是总是找不到爱
情？"

B. CONVERSATIONS

一、

小王：老高，您能帮我一个忙吗？

老高：是什么事情？

小王：我有一个好朋友下星期五要来看我，但是我们家里没有地方让
他住。不知道有没有可能让他住在你们家？只是一个晚上而已。

老高：当然可以，这根本不成问题。我跟你是老同学，这种事情不用
客气。

小王：真是非常感谢你愿意帮我这么大的忙！

老高：没事儿，没事儿。

二、

张明： 小马，你后天忙不忙？

马清： 好像没什么特别的事情。

张明： 我星期六晚上要办酒席，那天是我外公的一百岁生日。你一定
要抽空来参加！

马清： 你外公的一百岁生日？不简单！我怎么敢不来啊？几点？在哪里？

张明： 时间大概是六点钟，饭店还没决定。我明天再给你打电话。

马清： 好，一言为定！

C. NARRATIVE

一、 作者王定和先生在《为什么中国人会这样，外国人会那样?》那本
书上提到，中国人对不可能的事情有时候不好意思直说不可能，
就用"不方便"来代替。他们听说有一个外国人会说中国话，可是
不认识中国字，可能会跟他说："你不认识中国字？那你看中文报
纸不太方便。"可是那个外国人会想，"有什么不方便？不认识中
国字根本不可能看中文报纸！"

二、 我觉得抽烟是最不好的习惯，比喝酒还坏。抽烟不但对自己不好，
而且对其他人也不好。我特别不喜欢的事情就是看见有人在非吸烟
区抽烟，像在饭馆或在图书馆或在办公室，这实在是太不应该了。
他们不认识字吗？你如果一定得抽烟，一定要先看清楚，这里是吸
烟区还是非吸烟区。如果是非吸烟区，那么就不可以抽烟。我有个
同学，小李，他从小学六年级就开始抽烟，当然没让家里人知道。
他刚开始抽烟的时候，抽得不多，大概每天一、两根香烟，后来越
抽越多，现在每天都抽一包香烟，太可怕了！我一直跟他说他得改
这个坏习惯，可是他现在已经改不了了，怎么办？

Notes

A2a.   百忙之中 **bǎimángzhīzhōng** "in the midst of being extremely busy" or "while being very busy"

A2b.   让我感到很不好意思 "makes me feel very embarrassed"

A5.   办不到 "can't do, can't arrange"

A9.   笑一笑，十年少 **Xiào yí xiào, shínián shào** "Smile and you're ten years younger."

A10.   自己还行 "I myself am not too bad."

PART TWO

Conversation 🎧

Situation: After Sanchez has made his request for a favor, Mr. Cai responds (continued from the previous conversation).

1. MR. CAI: 宋先生，这件事，我尽量帮您打听打听。最晚礼拜五给您答复，好吗？

Sòng Xiānsheng, zhèijiàn shì, wǒ jìnliàng bāng nín dǎtīng dǎtīng. Zuì wǎn lǐbàiwǔ gěi nín dáfù, hǎo ma?

Mr. Sanchez, I'll do my best to help you find out about this matter. At the latest I'll give you an answer by Friday, all right?

2. SANCHEZ: 真是太麻烦您了。不过万一不容易打听到，也不要勉强。

Zhēn shi tài máfan nín le. Búguò wànyī bù róngyi dǎtīngdào, yě búyào miǎnqiǎng.

I'm really putting you to too much trouble. But if it's not easy to find out, don't try too hard.

3. MR. CAI: 我知道。我尽力就是。

Wǒ zhīdao. Wǒ jìnlì jiù shì.

I know. I'll just do my best.

4. SANCHEZ: 蔡先生，我看时候也不早了，我就不多打扰了。告辞了。

Cài Xiānsheng, wǒ kàn shíhou yě bù zǎole, wǒ jiù bù duō dǎrǎole. Gàocíle.

Mr. Cai, I think it's getting late, so I won't disturb you anymore. I'll be on my way.

5. MR. CAI: 忙什么？再坐一下嘛。

Máng shémme? Zài zuò yixia ma.

What's the rush? Sit a bit longer.

6. SANCHEZ: 不了，呃，改天再来拜访。

Bù le, e, gǎi tiān zài lái bàifǎng.

No, uh, I'll come again to visit some other day.

7. MR. CAI: 哦，对了，我突然想起一件事来。我这个礼拜五要去新竹看朋友，不在台北。您礼拜六打电话给我也可以。

Ò, duìle, wǒ tūrán xiángqi yíjiàn shì lai. Wǒ zhèige lǐbàiwǔ yào qù Xīnzhú kàn péngyou, bú zài Táiběi. Nín lǐbàiliù dǎ diànhuà gěi wǒ yě kéyi.

Oh, that's right, I just thought of something. This Friday I'm going to go to Xinzhu to see a friend, and I won't be in Taipei. So you could also call me on Saturday.

8. SANCHEZ: 好的。

Hǎode.

All right.

9. MR. CAI: 我送您下楼。

Wǒ sòng nín xiàlóu.

Let me see you downstairs.

10. SANCHEZ: 不用了，请留步。

Bú yòngle, qǐng liúbù.

That's not necessary, please stay inside.

11. MR. CAI: 那好。 *(they shake hands)* 慢走啊！

Nà hǎo. Màn zǒu a.

Well, all right. Take care.

12. SANCHEZ: 再见！

Zàijiàn!

Goodbye!

13. MRS. CAI: 再见！

Zàijiàn!

Goodbye!

New Vocabulary

尽量	**jìnliàng**	to the best of one's ability
打听	**dǎtīng**	inquire
答复	**dáfù**	answer, reply
万一	**wànyī**	if by chance, in case
打听到	**dǎtīngdào**	inquire and find out
勉强	**miǎnqiǎng**	do with great effort, force
尽力	**jìnlì**	do one's best
…就是	**…jiù shì**	just, simply
打扰	**dǎrǎo**	disturb

告辞	**gàocí**	take leave
拜访	**bàifǎng**	pay a formal call on someone
突然	**tūrán**	suddenly
想起来	**xiángqilai**	think of
新竹	**Xīnzhú**	Xinzhu (name of city in Taiwan)
下楼	**xiàlóu**	go downstairs
留步	**liúbù**	"don't bother to see me out"

Supplementary Vocabulary

上楼	**shànglóu**	go upstairs

Notes on the Conversation

Split Resultative Compounds

In line 7 look at the phrase **Wǒ tūrán xiángqi yíjiàn shì lai** "I suddenly thought of a matter" or "I just remembered something." With resultative compounds that end in the directional endings **-lai** or **-qu**, the object of the verb is either placed in front of the verb as the topic or, as here, is inserted into the verb construction, directly before the **-lai** or **-qu**. For example, to express "I just thought of her name," you could say either **Tāde míngzi wǒ xiángqilaile** or **Wǒ xiángqi tāde míngzi laile**. The basic pattern is: Resultative Verb + Object of Verb + Directional Ending. Some more examples of split resultative compounds: **Tā náqi bǐ laile** "He picked up his pen," **Tā pǎohuí jiā qule** "She ran back home," **Wǒ yǐjīng náhuí shūdiàn qule** "I've already taken it back to the bookstore," **Zhèiběn cídiǎn cháqi zì lai hěn fāngbian** "This dictionary is convenient for looking up characters."

Reading

New Characters and Words

475.	容	**róng**	allow; appearance; contain (surname)
476.	易	**yì**	change; easy (surname)
	容易	**róngyi**	be easy
477.	尽	**jìn**	to the very limit; all; to exhaust
	尽量	**jìnliàng**	to the best of one's ability
	尽快	**jìnkuài**	as fast as possible
	尽可能	**jìn kě'néng**	try one's best, exert maximum effort
478.	力	**lì**	strength; force
	尽力	**jìnlì**	do one's best

力量	**lìliang**	strength, force
力氣	**lìqi**	strength, effort
能力	**nénglì**	ability, capability
479. 化	**huà**	change; melt
文化	**wénhuà**	culture
化学	**huàxué**	chemistry
480. 流	**liú**	flow
河流	**héliú**	rivers
交流	**jiāoliú**	exchange, interact; exchange, interaction
文化交流	**wénhuà jiāoliú**	cultural exchange

A. SENTENCES

一、很多事情说起来容易，做起来可就不那么容易了。

二、你放心，我会尽力在下个星期一以前把这些事情做完。

三、有时候我们很容易忘了一句话的力量可能有多大。

四、王力生的专业是化学，但是我真不知道他有没有能力学那么难的一个专业。

五、今天不但非常冷，而且风也很大，你们如果没什么特别的事情，尽量少出门。

六、从地图上看，黄河从中国的西边一直流到东边的黄海里头去，全长有5,464公里。

七、从1949年到1990年左右，中国大陆跟台湾之间的交流很少，可是最近三十年两岸之间的交流越来越多了。

八、"对不起，我现在不在位子上，请留下您的姓名和电话。我听到这个留言以后，会尽快地回您的电话，谢谢！"

九、中国国际文化交流中心在北京东土城路9号，电话是86-10-64489600，传真是86-10-64201641.

十、王大海虽然长得不高，人也不重，可是他的力气可真大！

B. CONVERSATIONS

一、

男生：为什么大多数男人的力气比女人大?

女生：也有女人力气比男人大!

男生：当然，我知道，可是我说的是"大多数男人"。

女生：男人跟女人就是不一样。你有没有想过这个问题，为什么大多数的女人活得比男人久?

二、

中国的包校长： 容校长，我们两个学校是不是以后应该多交流一下？

美国的容校长： 好啊！您这个主意实在太好了！语言交流、文化交流，都可以。我们今年九月就开始吧！

中国的包校长： 好，一言为定！

C. NARRATIVES

一、 大家都说开车很容易，很多孩子十五、六岁就已经会开车了，可是我已经二十一岁了，还不会开车。我觉得开车不但一点儿也不容易，而且是一件很可怕的事情！我学开车学了好几个月了，真的尽了最大的力，但是每一次开车我还是会觉得很紧张。我妈妈叫我多练习，她说开多了，就好了。请问，你现在要到哪里去吗？我做司机，我送你去，怎么样？我应该多练习开车。上车吧！我们马上就走！

二、 我今年21岁，女，大三，在北大学习。我的专业是日文。我从大一开始，就一直很尽力地学习日文。我对日本文化和日本人的日常生活特别感兴趣。虽然多年以来，中日之间有不少相当严重的问题，而且要解决这些问题也不那么容易，需要很长的时间，但是我还是觉得两国之间的文化交流很要紧。我打算明年到日本去留学，所以现在得尽快学好日文。我最近想找一位在北大学习的日本女同学，跟她进行语言交流，我可以帮她学中文，她帮我学日文。我最大的希望就是以后能帮忙解决中日之间的一些问题！

Notes

A6. 全长 **quáncháng** "total length"

A7a. 大陆 **dàlù** "mainland, continent"

A7b. A 跟 B 之间 **A gēn B zhījiān** "between A and B." 中国大陆跟台湾之间的交流 means "interaction between mainland China and Taiwan."

A7c. 两岸 **liǎng'àn** "the two shores" (of the Taiwan Straits). This is a politically neutral way of referring to mainland China and Taiwan.

A8. 留言 **liúyán** "recorded message"

A10a. 长得不高 **zhǎngde bù gāo** literally, "grew up in such a way that he is not tall" or, in better English, simply "is not tall."

A10b. 人也不重 literally, "As a person he is not heavy" or, in more idiomatic English, "He's not heavy."

C1a. 十五、六岁 "15 or 16 years old"

C1b.   The verb 叫, which often means "call," here means "tell (someone to do something)."

C1c.   练习 **liànxí** "practice"

C1d.   她说开多了，就好了 literally, "She says when I have driven more, it'll be better."

C1e.   你现在要到哪里去吗？ "Do you want to go someplace now?" This sentence is already a question on account of the 吗 at the end, so the question word 哪里 does not mean "Where?" but instead means "somewhere" or "someplace."

C2a.   日常 **rìcháng** "daily, everyday, routine." 日常生活 means "daily life."

C2b.   Pay careful attention to the grammatical structure of the long, complex sentence that begins with 虽然. Everything before the 但是 goes with 虽然. An English translation of the kernel of the sentence would be: "Although for many years…, I still feel that…."

C2c.   多年以来 "for many years"

C2d.   中日之间 "between China and Japan"

C2e.   两国之间 "between the two countries"

C2f.   进行 **jìnxíng** "conduct, carry out, do." 进行语言交流 means "conduct a language exchange."

The campus of the Chinese University of Hong Kong

LESSON 17
Visiting a Sick Classmate

PART ONE

Conversation

Situation: Linda Fuentes, a graduate student in art history in Beijing, visits Hu Xiaoling, a classmate of hers who is recovering from an illness. Hu's mother opens the door.

1. **FUENTES:** 伯母，您好！
   Bómǔ, nín hǎo!
   Hello, Mrs. Hu!

2. **MRS. HU:** 进来吧。晓玲在卧房躺着呢。
   Jìnlái ba. Xiǎolíng zài wòfáng tǎngzhe ne.
   Come in. Xiaoling is lying down in the bedroom.

3. **FUENTES:** 晓玲，听说你病了。现在好点儿了吗？
   Xiǎolíng, tīngshuō nǐ bìngle. Xiànzài hǎo diǎnr le ma?
   Xiaoling, I heard you were sick. Are you better now?

4. **HU XIAOLING:** 已经好多了。其实也没什么大病。谢谢你还跑来看我。
   Yǐjīng hǎo duōle. Qíshí yě méi shémme dà bìng. Xièxie nǐ hái pǎolai kàn wǒ.
   I'm already a lot better. Actually, it isn't anything serious. Thanks for coming over to see me.

5. FUENTES: 本来早就应该来看你，只是这几天忙得很，一直没有工夫，所以直到今天才来。哦，对了，给你带了一点儿水果。

Běnlái zǎo jiù yīnggāi lái kàn nǐ, zhǐ shi zhèjǐtiān mángde hěn, yìzhí méiyou gōngfu, suóyi zhí dào jīntiān cái lái. Ò, duìle, gěi nǐ dàile yidianr shuǐguǒ.

Ordinarily, I should have come to see you a long time ago, it's just that the last few days I was always busy and never had time, that's why I didn't come until today. Oh, that's right, I brought you some fruit.

6. HU XIAOLING: 谢谢你。那，你这几天忙什么呢？

Xièxie nǐ. Nà, nǐ zhèjǐtiān máng shémme ne?

Thanks. So, what have you been busy with the last few days?

7. FUENTES: 还不是忙着期末考试。天天都考，都快把我考晕了！

Hái bú shi mángzhe qīmò kǎoshì. Tiāntiān dōu kǎo, dōu kuài bǎ wǒ kǎoyūnle!

I've been busy with final exams, what else? I've been taking tests every day; soon I'm going to get dizzy from all this testing!

New Vocabulary

卧房	wòfáng	bedroom
躺	tǎng	lie down
病	bìng	get sick; illness, disease
跑	pǎo	run
跑来	pǎolai	run over here, come over
工夫	gōngfu	time
直到	zhí dào	straight up to, until
还不是…	hái bú shi…	if it isn't…
考试	kǎoshì	test
期末考试	qīmò kǎoshì	final examination
考	kǎo	take a test
晕	yūn	be dizzy
考晕	kǎoyūn	become dizzy from testing

Supplementary Vocabulary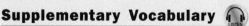

期中考试	qīzhōng kǎoshì	mid-term examination
跑去	pǎoqu	run over there
跑步	pǎobù	run paces, run
赚	zhuàn	earn
赚钱	zhuànqián	earn money
花	huā	spend (money, time)

| 花钱 | huāqián | spend money |
| 有一点… | yǒu yìdiǎn(r)… | be a little… |

Notes on the Conversation

Different ways to express "sick"

In line 3 of the conversation, notice that the word **bìng** is a verb meaning "to get sick" or "to become ill." On the other hand, in line 4 **bìng** is a noun meaning "sickness" or "disease." To say "He/she is sick," say **Tā bìngle** (literally "He/she has gotten sick"; you CANNOT say *Tā shi bìng or *Tā hěn bìng). To say "He/she isn't sick," say **Tā méiyou bìng** (literally "He/she doesn't have an illness"; you CANNOT say *Tā bú bìng.)

Words for "time"

Learn the noun **gōngfu** "free time" as in **Wǒ yìzhí méiyou gōngfu** "I never had free time." The word **gōngfu** is especially colloquial and characteristic of northern Mandarin. You've now had several words that translate as "time": **shíjiān**, **shíhou(r)**, **kòng(r)**, and **gōngfu**. **Gōngfu** and **kòng(r)** refer to "free time." **Shíhou** is usually used for a point or period in time when something happens. The most general of these terms is **shíjiān**, which can be used almost anywhere.

Reduplication of measures and nouns to mean "each" or "every"

As we have seen before, **tiān** "day" when reduplicated as **tiāntiān** gains the meaning "every day." A limited number of measures and monosyllabic nouns can be reduplicated in this way to add emphasis and indicate "each" or "every." These reduplicated forms usually occur only as subjects or topics of sentences; they can't occur as objects after the verb. To say "I like everyone" you couldn't say *Wǒ xǐhuan rénrén; you would have to prepose the **rénrén** and say **Wǒ rénrén dōu xǐhuan**. These reduplicated forms are often followed by the adverb **dōu**, as in the previous example. More examples of reduplicated forms that mean "each" or "every": **niánnián** "every year," **zhāngzhāng** "every one (sheets of paper)," **běnběn** "every volume," **gègè** "every single one (of a group of people)," **jùjù** "each sentence."

Yǒu diǎnr + Stative Verb

Consider the sentence **Wǒ yǒu diǎnr yūn** "I'm a little dizzy." **Yǒu (yi)diǎnr** occurs frequently with Stative Verbs (sometimes also with other verbs) to indicate that something is "a little" something or that something is "somewhat" something. The literal meaning of this pattern is "to have a little." The tones on **yìdiǎnr** are optional and tend to be lost in rapid speech. Examples: **Wǒ yǒu diǎnr è** "I'm a bit hungry," **Wǒ yǒu diǎnr bù shūfu** "I'm a little uncomfortable," **Cài hěn hǎochī kěshi yǒu yìdiǎnr là** "The food is very good but it's a little hot." The meaning of this pattern is usually negative, indicating less than ideal or less than comfortable conditions. For example, you could say **Tāmen màide dōngxi yǒu diǎnr guì** "The things they sell are a little expensive"; but you couldn't say *Tāmen màide dōngxi yǒu diǎnr piányi to mean "The things they sell are a little inexpensive," since "being inexpensive" is normally a desirable quality. When using this pattern, be careful always to include the **yǒu**. You could NEVER say *Wǒ yìdiǎnr máng but should always say **Wǒ yǒu yìdiǎnr máng** "I'm a little busy."

Reading

New Characters and Words

481.	考	**kǎo**	test, take a test
	小考	**xiǎokǎo**	quiz
	大考	**dàkǎo**	final examination
	月考	**yuèkǎo**	monthly test
	期中考	**qīzhōngkǎo**	mid-term examination
482.	试	**shì**	try; test
	试试	**shìshi**	try
	试试看	**shìshi kàn**	try and see
	考试	**kǎoshì**	test, examination; take a test
	期中考试	**qīzhōng kǎoshì**	mid-term examination
483.	病	**bìng**	get sick; illness
	大病	**dà bìng**	major illness
	小病	**xiǎo bìng**	minor illness
	生病	**shēngbìng**	become sick
484.	跑	**pǎo**	run
	跑来	**pǎolái**	run over here, come over
	跑去	**pǎoqù**	run over there
	跑来跑去	**pǎolái pǎoqù**	run all over the place
	跑步	**pǎobù**	run paces, run; running
	慢跑	**mànpǎo**	jog; jogging
485.	飞	**fēi**	fly
	飞机	**fēijī**	airplane
	飞机场	**fēijīchǎng**	airport
	开飞机	**kāi fēijī**	fly an airplane
	坐飞机	**zuò fēijī**	take an airplane, travel by plane
486.	船	**chuán**	boat, ship
	坐船	**zuò chuán**	take a boat, travel by boat

A. SENTENCES

一、老高天天都抽这么多烟，他早晚一定会生病的。

二、学生怕考试，老师喜欢考试，中国、外国都一样。

三、我不能保证一定能解决你的问题，但是我愿意试试看。

四、小林因为明天要坐最早的一班飞机，所以得很早就去飞机场。

五、中国人常说：生、老、病、死是每个人这一生都会走过的路。

六、同学们，快来试试这道菜，我花了好大工夫才做好。你们喜欢吗？

七、我们的中文课天天都有小考，每个月有月考，还有期中考跟大考。

八、坐船去太慢了，得花好多时间；我没有那工夫，还是坐飞机去吧！

九、听说天天跑步的人不太容易生病，所以我决定从明天起，每天早上慢跑半小时。

十、王大海的名字有一个"海"字，可是其实他很怕水，每次坐船都觉得有一点儿受不了。

B. CONVERSATIONS

一、

张阳明：老王，找你找了好久了。你跑到哪里去了？

王明力：我刚到城里去买票去了，因为我最近要到日本去。

张阳明：你要去日本啊？你坐飞机去还是坐船去？

王明力：我平常都坐飞机，所以这次决定坐船。

张阳明：船票现在要多少钱？

王明力：一个人两千五，跟机票差不多一样。

二、

孩子：妈妈，我好像生病了！

妈妈：儿子，你怎么每次学校要考试就会生病？

孩子：我……我……我……

C. NARRATIVES

一、我习惯每天早上去慢跑，可是已经有一个多星期没有跑步了。我这几天真是忙得很！不但学校里有很多考试得准备，而且家里还有很多事情得做。我觉得要是再这样，一定会生病的。我下个星期要坐飞机去香港替"人人公司"开一个很要紧的会，我一定得参加，怎么也不能生病！

二、我去年六月本来要坐飞机去上海，可是去机场的路上有很多车子。我本来应该提前两个小时就到机场，但在路上花了很长时间，好不容易提前半个小时才到。等我从停车场跑到机场的时候，小姐说飞机已经快要飞走了，时间太晚了，她不让我上飞机。所以我现在坐飞机一定会早三个小时到机场，这样不会那么紧张。

Notes

A4.　班 **bān** (for scheduled trips of a plane, bus, or train). 最早的一班飞机 means "the earliest plane."

A5.　这一生 "(in) this life"

A6.　好大工夫 "a lot of time"

A8.　我没有那工夫 "I don't have that/so much time." Here 那工夫 means 那个工夫. In colloquial conversation, the measure 个 is sometimes omitted after 这 and 那.

B1a.　我刚到城里去买票去了 "I just went into town to buy a ticket." The first 去 in this sentence is optional, but such usage is common in Beijing speech.

B1b.　最近 "in the near future, soon." Though 最近 usually means "in the recent past," it can also mean "in the near future." From the Chinese point of view, the meaning is the same: that is, at a time point very close to the present, whether moving back or forward in time.

C2a.　好不容易提前半个小时才到 "barely arrived half an hour in advance"

C2b.　早三个小时 literally, "early by three hours," or in idiomatic English, "three hours early."

PART TWO

Conversation

Situation: Fuentes concludes her conversation with Hu and prepares to leave (continued from the previous conversation).

1. HU XIAOLING: 考得怎么样？
Kǎode zěmmeyàng?
How did you do on your tests?

2. FUENTES: 马马虎虎吧。成绩还没出来呢。晓玲，你好好休息吧。
我不多坐了。过几天再来看你。
Mámahūhū ba. Chéngjī hái méi chūlai ne. Xiǎolíng, nǐ hǎohāo xiūxi ba. Wǒ bù duō zuòle. Guò jǐtiān zài lái kàn nǐ.
So-so, I guess. The grades aren't out yet. Xiaoling, you rest real well. I'll be going on my way. In a few days, I'll come visit you again.

3. HU XIAOLING: 吃了饭再走吧。
Chīle fàn zài zǒu ba.
Why don't you have dinner before you leave?

4. FUENTES: 不了，不了，谢谢你，我得走了。晓玲，你多注意身体，
别太累了。有什么事的话，来个电话，大家都可以帮你。
Bù le, bù le, xièxie nǐ, wǒ děi zǒule. Xiǎolíng, nǐ duō zhùyì shēnti. Bié tài lèile. Yǒu shémme shìde huà, lái ge diànhuà, dàjiā dōu kéyi bāng nǐ.
No, thanks, I must be going now. Xiaoling, you watch your health. Don't tire yourself out. If there should be anything, give us a call, everybody can help you.

5. HU XIAOLING: 太谢谢了。有事我会说的。

Tài xièxie nǐ le. Yǒu shì wǒ huì shuōde.

Thanks so much. If there is anything, I'll be sure to let you know.

6. FUENTES: 伯母，我走了。

Bómǔ, wǒ zǒule.

Mrs. Hu, I'll be going now.

7. MRS. HU: 谢谢你来看晓玲。改天再来玩儿吧。

Xièxie nǐ lái kàn Xiǎolíng. Gǎi tiān zài lái wánr ba.

Thanks for coming to see Xiaoling. Come again to visit some other day.

8. FUENTES: 好，一定来。再见!

Hǎo, yídìng lái. Zàijiàn!

O.K., I'll definitely come. Bye!

9. MRS. HU: 再见!

Zàijiàn!

Goodbye!

New Vocabulary

马马虎虎	**mámahūhū**	so-so, fair; not too bad
成绩	**chéngjī**	grade (on test or in course)
来电话	**lái diànhuà**	call on the telephone

Supplementary Vocabulary

学期	**xuéqī**	semester, term
修	**xiū**	study, take (courses, credits)
学分	**xuéfēn**	credit, credit hour
选	**xuǎn**	choose, select
门	**mén**	(for courses)
篇	**piān**	(for theses, reports, essays)
论文	**lùnwén**	thesis, dissertation
毕业论文	**bìyè lùnwén**	honors thesis
报告	**bàogào**	report
学期报告	**xuéqī bàogào**	term paper
关于	**guānyú**	about, concerning

Notes on the Conversation

Reduplicated Stative Verbs as Adverbs

In line 2, notice the adverb **hǎohāo** "very well" in **Xiǎolíng, nǐ hǎohāo xiūxi ba** "Xiaoling, now you rest up real well." As you might guess, **hǎohāo** derives from **hǎo** "be good." Actually, the idiomatic expression **mànmān lái** "take your time" that you learned earlier also involves this type of reduplication. Monosyllabic stative verbs like **hǎo** or **màn** can be reduplicated, that is, doubled to function as adverbs; they then have a stronger, more vivid effect. In Beijing speech, the second syllable of reduplicated monosyllabic stative verbs is typically changed to Tone 1 and the second syllable is often followed by **-r**. The adverbial marker **-de** can also be added after the **-r**, so that the complete forms would then be **hǎohāorde** "very well" or **mànmānrde** (pronounced as **mànmārde**) "very slowly." Examples: **Nǐmen yào hǎohāor xuéxí!** "You all should do a good job studying!," **Xiǎomèi, kuàikuāirde pǎo!** "Little sister, run quickly!," **Zhōngguo zì yào mànmānrde xiě cái hǎokàn** "Chinese characters should be written slowly, only then do they look good." Reduplicated stative verbs can't be further modified by adverbs of degree such as **hěn** or **fēicháng**, so you couldn't say *hěn hǎohāorde or *fēicháng hǎohāorde. Also, the change to Tone 1 for the second syllable and the addion of **-r** and **-de** are common in Beijing but don't necessarily occur in Mandarin spoken elsewhere.

Reading

New Characters and Words

487.	身	**shēn**	body; oneself (can't be used alone)
488.	体	**tǐ**	body (can't be used alone)
	身体	**shēntǐ**	body; health
	简体字	**jiǎntǐzì**	simplified Chinese character
489.	绩	**jī**	achievement, accomplishment (can't be used alone)
	成绩	**chéngjī**	grade (for test, course); results; achievements
	成绩单	**chéngjīdān(r)**	transcript
490.	注	**zhù**	concentrate on (can't be used alone)
	注意	**zhùyì**	pay attention (to)
	注解	**zhùjiě**	annotation, explanatory note
491.	于	**yú**	be located at, in, on; (surname)
	关于	**guānyú**	about, concerning
492.	论	**lùn**	discuss, debate
	论文	**lùnwén**	thesis, dissertation

A. SENTENCES

一、这位同学，请问，你的学期报告是关于什么的？

二、小李的论文是关于天文的；我的论文是关于语言学的。

三、学中文的学生一定得注意他们的声调，特别是第三声。

四、这本书是关于国际关系的，特别是中美关系，写得非常有意思。

五、小张，你这学期的学期报告得好好儿地准备，这样成绩才会好。

六、你们学校一门课算几个学分？一个学期最多可以上几门课呢？

七、我跟你讲，身体要紧！一定要注意身体，可别把自己的身体忙坏了！

八、要注意看那本书的注解，注解可以帮你很清楚地了解每个句子的意思。

九、我男朋友从前有抽烟的坏习惯，可是因为很多朋友都告诉他抽烟对身体不好，所以他现在不抽了。

十、王大海上学期的成绩很差，所以他不敢让爸爸妈妈看他的成绩单。

B. CONVERSATIONS

一、

金太太：你最近身体怎么样？

马太太：还可以吧，不好也不坏。

金太太：那就好。希望你以后也不会生病。

马太太：是啊，多谢你了！

二、

老师：各位同学请注意，明天的考试请你们好好儿地准备第三课。听到了没有？

学生：可是老师，我们刚上完第二课，还没开始上第三课啊！

三、

小李：小严，你正在写的论文是关于什么的呢？

小严：我的论文是关于中国和西方最近一百五十年的文化交流的。

C. NARRATIVES

一、有的学生愿意考试，可是不喜欢写学期报告，还有的学生比较喜欢用学期报告代替大考。我比较喜欢写学期报告，这样我可以慢慢儿地写，没有太大的压力。当然可能要花比较多的时间，但是不会像考试那么紧张。不过，我这学期的课，四门课里头有三门都有大考！怎么办？那么多考试会给我很大的压力，我怕我要是太紧张，一不注意，身体受不了，最后，这学期的成绩就会不好。

二、中文可以说有两种文字，就是简体字（也叫简化字）和繁体字（也叫正体字）。中国大陆和新加坡使用简体字，台湾和香港使用繁体字。不过，有时候在中国大陆和新加坡也看得到繁体字；同样地，有时候在台湾和香港也看得到简体字。简体字在中国大陆从1956年以后越来越流行，不过，其实中国很早就有简体字。像两千多年前就有"从"这个简体字，而繁体字的"從"是后来才有的。不少简体字是从草书来的，像"東→东"、"為→为"、"樂→乐"。还有的时候，一个简体字代替了两个繁体字，像简体字"面"相当于繁体字的"面"（"side, face"）和"麵"（"flour, noodles"）。当然，很多简体字和繁体字是一样的，例如下面这句话既是简体字，又是繁体字："大家都是好朋友！"有人提出来过，简体字比繁体字容易写，但是繁体字比简体字更容易认识。这是为什么呢？像"说话"的"话"和"生活"的"活,"如果用繁体字来写，差别相当大，所以比较容易分清楚"話、活"这两个字。可是如果写简体字，这两个字只差一点点，很容易看错"话、活"两个字。另外一个例子是"工厂"的"厂"和"广东"的"广,"如果写繁体字是"廠、廣,"如果写简体字是"厂、广,"差不多一样！不过，这都没什么太大的关系，要紧的是现在学习中文的人，简体字、繁体字都得能认。而写呢？我们认为大多数的外国学生会写一种也就够了。

Notes

A7.   把自己的身体忙坏了 literally, "take your own body and make it busy to the extent that it goes bad," or in idiomatic English, "be so busy that you ruin your health"

A8.   了解 **liǎojiě** "understand." Note that the character 了 here represents the syllable **liǎo**, not **le**.

C1.   压力 **yālì** "pressure"

C2a.   繁体字 **fántǐzì** "complex characters, traditional characters"

C2b.   文字 **wénzì** "script, written language"

C2c.   大陆 "mainland." Learn the common expression 中国大陆 "mainland China."

C2d.   新加坡 **Xīnjiāpō** "Singapore"

C2e.   同样地 **tóngyàngde** "in the same way, similarly"

C2f.   流行 **liúxíng** "be prevalent, popular, widespread"

C2g.   草书 **cǎoshū** "cursive script" (in calligraphy)

C2h.   例如 **lìrú** "for instance" or "for example"

C2i.   既···又 **jì...yòu** "both...and"

C2j.   提出来 **tíchūlái** "bring up, mention"

C2k.   差别 **chābié** "difference." Note that 差 is here pronounced **chā** and not **chà**.

C2l.   分清楚 literally, "separate so that something is clear" or "distinguish"

C2m.   只差一点点 "differ by only a very little bit"

C2n.   例子 **lìzi** "example"

C2o.   认 **rèn** "recognize"

C2p.   认为 **rènwéi** "think, be of the opinion, consider"

A Farewell Call on a Favorite Teacher

PART ONE

Conversation 🎧

Situation: After studying in Beijing for a semester, American student Randy Lewis is preparing to return to the U.S. He visits the home of his favorite Chinese teacher, Professor Ding, to say goodbye. Mrs. Ding opens the door.

1. **LEWIS:**
请问，这儿是丁老师家吗？
Qǐng wèn, zhèr shi Dīng Lǎoshī jiā ma?
Excuse me, is this Professor Ding's home?

2. **MRS. DING:**
对，请进。 *(calls to back room)* 老丁，来客人了。
Duì, qǐng jìn. Lǎo Dīng, lái kèrén le.
Yes, please come in. Old Ding, you have a guest.

3. **PROFESSOR DING:** *(as he enters the living room)*
谁啊？唉，是你啊！快请坐。
Shéi a? Ài, shi nǐ a! Kuài qǐng zuò.
Who is it? Oh, it's you! Come, sit down.

4. LEWIS:

老师，我向您告别来了。

Lǎoshī, wǒ xiàng nín gàobié laile.

Professor, I've come to bid you farewell.

5. PROFESSOR DING:

你什么时候走啊？

Nǐ shémme shíhou zǒu a?

When are you leaving?

6. LEWIS:

下星期三。

Xiàxīngqīsān.

Next Wednesday.

7. PROFESSOR DING:

哎呀，时间过得真快！转眼就一年了。记得你刚来的时候，连一句简单的中国话都不会说，现在已经能对答如流了。

Āiya, shíjiān guòde zhēn kuài! Zhuǎnyǎn jiù yìnián le. Jìde nǐ gāng láide shíhou, lián yíjù jiǎndānde Zhōngguo huà dōu bú huì shuō, xiànzài yǐjīng néng duì-dá-rú-liúle.

Gosh, time really passes quickly! In the blink of an eye a year has passed. I remember when you had just come, you couldn't say even a simple phrase in Chinese, and now you can already converse fluently.

8. LEWIS:

多亏老师的帮忙。这一年我可真没少给您添麻烦。

Duō kuī lǎoshīde bāngmáng. Zhèyìnián wǒ kě zhēn méi shǎo gěi nín tiān máfan.

It's all thanks to your help. This past year I really have put you to too much trouble.

New Vocabulary

丁	**Dīng**	Ding (surname)
向	**xiàng**	toward, to
告别	**gàobié**	bid farewell, take leave
哎呀	**āiya**	"gosh"
转眼	**zhuǎnyǎn**	blink the eyes, glance
连	**lián**	even
连···都···	**lián...dōu...**	even
对答如流	**duì-dá-rú-liú**	reply to questions fluently
多亏	**duō kuī**	be thanks to
添	**tiān**	add
麻烦	**máfan**	trouble

Supplementary Vocabulary

发音	**fāyīn**	pronunciation
语法	**yǔfǎ**	grammar

词汇	**cíhuì**	vocabulary
标准	**biāozhǔn**	be standard
流利	**liúlì**	be fluent
生产	**shēngchǎn**	produce

Notes on the Conversation

Inverted Subject and Verb

Consider the sentence **Lái kèrén le** "There has come a guest" or "A guest has come." In Chinese, unspecified, indefinite subjects sometimes follow rather than precede the verb. While the sentence **Kèrén láile** would also be correct, the meaning would be a little different; the latter sentence would mean "The guest has come," in other words, specific guests that the speaker knows about. More examples: **Nàr sǐle bù shǎo rén** "A lot of people died there," **Láile yíwèi Zhāng Xiānsheng** "A Mr. Zhang has come," **Nàr xīn kāile yìjiā Rìběn guǎnzi** "A Japanese restaurant has newly opened there," **Yòu zǒule yíge** "Another one has departed" (another old friend has died).

....

Lián...dōu... and lián...yě... "even"

The paired adverb pattern **lián...dōu...** and its synonym **lián...yě...** both mean "even." **Lián** is placed before the element to be emphasized (which can be the subject, object, or some other element) and **dōu** or **yě** is placed before the verb. Examples: **Lián wǒ dōu huì** "Even I know how," **Lián Wáng Lǎoshī dōu bú rènshi zhèige zì** "Even Professor Wang doesn't recognize this character," **Xiǎo Zhāng fēicháng xǐhuan kàn diànshì, lián chīfànde shíhou dōu kàn** "Little Zhang loves watching TV, he watches even while eating," **Zhèige wèntí lián tā dōu jiějuébuliǎo** "Even she can't solve this problem," **Tā lián yíkuài qián yě méiyou** "He doesn't even have one dollar," **Zěmme lián yíge rén yě méi lái ne?** "How come not even a single person has come?"

....

READING

New Characters and Words

493.	向	**xiàng**	toward, to
	向…告别	**xiàng...gàobié**	bid farewell to
	内向	**nèixiàng**	be introverted
	外向	**wàixiàng**	be extroverted
494.	眼	**yǎn**	eye
	左眼	**zuǒyǎn**	left eye
	右眼	**yòuyǎn**	right eye
	转眼	**zhuǎnyǎn**	blink the eyes; glance; in the blink of an eye
495.	连	**lián**	even; link, connect; (surname)
	连…都…	**lián...dōu...**	even

连…也…	**lián...yě...**	even
大连	**Dàlián**	Dalian (city in Liaoning Province)
496. 利	**lì**	sharp (e.g., a knife); benefit
流利	**liúlì**	be fluent
意大利	**Yìdàlì**	Italy
意大利语	**Yìdàlìyǔ**	Italian language
497. 产	**chǎn**	produce
生产	**shēngchǎn**	produce, manufacture
出产	**chūchǎn**	produce, manufacture
产品	**chǎnpǐn**	product
498. 义	**yì**	righteousness (can't be used alone)
主义	**zhǔyì**	doctrine
共产主义	**Gòngchǎn Zhǔyì**	Communism

A. SENTENCES

一、请问，你们的工厂生产一些什么样的产品呢？

二、小马的左眼正常，可是右眼从小就有点儿毛病。

三、现在在中国还有多少人主张毛主席主张的那种共产主义？

四、四川是中国出产米最多的一个省，而成都平原又是四川省内出产米的中心。

五、常州离南京很近，离上海也不太远，人口有差不多四百万，出产的鱼和米特别多。

六、我认为内向的学生可能看书、写作比较好，但是外向的学生可能口语比较流利。

七、有很多种主义；除了共产主义以外，还有爱国主义、和平主义、自由主义、个人主义什么的。

八、最好把不如意的事情给忘了，一个人不可能完全没有问题，但是我们还是得向前走，对不对？

九、饭馆儿的那位中国服务员告诉我，她一转眼已经来美国二十年了，在这二十年里头，连一次国也没回过。

十、王大海的中文说得很流利，可是他的语法还有一些小错。

B. CONVERSATIONS

一、

连一心同学：老师好！我来向您告别了。我下星期要回大连了。

李老师　　　：你下星期就回去啊？时间过得太快了！一转眼就四年了。

连一心同学：对啊。非常感谢老师这四年以来教了我很多东西。老师去过大连吗？

李老师　　　：没有。我连北京都没去过。不过，如果有机会，我到大连去看你。

连一心同学：好啊！那，老师，我该走了。谢谢老师！请老师多注意身体！

李老师　　　：好，我会的。慢走，再见！

二、

意大利人　　：请问，去意大利大使馆怎么走？

北京的行人：意大利大使馆，是吗？离这儿不远。我告诉您，您再向前走差不多五分钟就到了。

意大利人　　：谢谢您！

北京的行人：不客气。请问，您是意大利人吗？

意大利人　　：是的。

北京的行人：Piacere di fare la sua conoscenza!

意大利人　　：您会讲意大利语啊！您讲得很流利！

北京的行人：哪里，差得很远。只会几句。

C. NARRATIVES

一、快上大学前，我高中的男朋友告诉我他交了别的女朋友，不爱我了。讲完以后，他连看都没看我一眼就走了。我听了又难过又生气，可是又有什么办法呢？现在我上了大学，交了另一个男朋友，他是从中国来的留学生，长得很好看，也很可爱，而且我们在一起非常快乐。所以说，什么事情都应该向前看，一直想以前的事情没有用。

二、我小的时候很坏，经常做坏事，考试也考不好，成绩非常差。在学校里不听老师的话，在家里更不听爸爸妈妈的话。所以爸爸没少打我，妈妈也没少骂我。现在我长大了，才了解爸妈都是为我好，我非常感谢他们。

三、最近几年在中国，很多人讲的一个笑话是，年轻人应该"向前看"还是"向钱看"？我觉得"向前看"虽然好，但要是没有钱，就什么事都做不了，所以我认为最好"向前"，也"向钱"，同时进行。人没有钱活不下去，但人也不是为钱而活。你说对吧？

Notes

A2a. 正常 **zhèngcháng** "be normal"

A2b. 毛病 **máobìng** "disease, illness, defect"

A4a. 平原 **píngyuán** "a plain" (i.e., large area of flat land)

A4b. 四川省内 "within the province of Sichuan"

A6. 口语 **kǒuyǔ** "spoken language"

A7a. 爱国主义 **àiguó zhǔyì** "patriotism"

A7b. 和平主义 **hépíng zhǔyì** "pacifism"

A7c. 自由主义 **zìyóu zhǔyì** "liberalism"

A7d. 个人主义 **gèrén zhǔyì** "individualism"

A8. 如意 **rúyì** "be as one likes or as one wishes"

A9. 连一次国也没回过 "hasn't been back to her native country even once"

C1. 快上大学前 "before I went to college" or "when I was about to go to college"

C2a. 经常 **jīngcháng** "frequently, constantly"

C2b. 骂 **mà** "scold, curse." Notice the structure of the character: two mouths, which give a sense of the meaning, plus the phonetic 马.

C3a. 活不下去 "can't keep on living." The verb ending 下去 sometimes means "continue" or "keep on."

C3b. 为A而B **wèi A ér B** "to B for A." The example here is 为钱而活 "to live for money."

PART TWO

Conversation 🎧

Situation: Lewis continues his conversation with Professor Ding (continued from the previous conversation).

1. **LEWIS:**

说实在的，要不是您教学有方，我也不可能进步得这么快。

Shuō shízàide, yào bú shi nín jiào-xué-yǒu-fāng, wǒ yě bù kěnéng jìnbùde zhèmme kuài.

To tell the truth, if it hadn't been for your excellent teaching, I wouldn't have been able to progress so quickly.

2. **PROFESSOR DING:**

哪儿的话。这是老师应尽的责任嘛。其实，主要还是你自己努力的结果。

Nǎrde huà. Zhè shi lǎoshī yīng jìnde zérèn ma. Qíshí, zhǔyào hái shi nǐ zìjǐ nǔlìde jiéguǒ.

Not at all. This is what a teacher is supposed to do! Actually, this is mostly the result of your own hard work.

3. **LEWIS:**

(after conversing for a while):

老师，时间不早了，我该回去了。

Lǎoshī, shíjiān bù zǎole, wǒ gāi huíqule.

Professor, it's getting late, I should be going back now.

4. **PROFESSOR DING:**

再待会儿吧！

Zài dāi huǐr ba!

Stay for a while longer!

5. LEWIS:
不了，我还有点儿事。
Bù le, wǒ hái yǒu diǎnr shì.
No, I have something else I have to do.

6. PROFESSOR DING:
好，那我就不留你了。回美国后，代我向你的父母问好。别忘了有空给我们来信。
Hǎo, nà wǒ jiù bù liú nǐ le. Huí Měiguo hòu, dài wǒ xiàng nǐde fùmǔ wènhǎo. Bié wàngle yǒukòng gěi wǒmen láixìn.
O.K., then I won't keep you. When you get back to America, give my best to your parents. Don't forget to send us a letter when you have time.

7. LEWIS:
老师，再见！ (to Mrs. Ding) 师母，再见！
Lǎoshī, zàijiàn! Shīmǔ, zàijiàn!
Goodbye, Professor! Goodbye, Mrs. Ding!

8. PROFESSOR DING:
再见！
Zàijiàn.
Goodbye.

9. MRS. DING:
再见！
Zàijiàn.
Goodbye.

New Vocabulary

说实在的	shuō shízàide	to tell the truth
要不是	yào bú shi	if not, if it weren't for
教学有方	jiào-xué-yǒu-fāng	have an effective method in one's teaching
进步	jìnbù	progress
哪儿的话	nǎrde huà	"not at all"
应	yīng	should
尽	jìn	carry out, fulfill
责任	zérèn	responsibility
结果	jiéguǒ	result
留	liú	ask someone to stay
…后	...hòu	after...
代	dài	for, on behalf of
代A向B问好	dài A xiàng B wènhǎo	on A's behalf convey regards to B
信	xìn	letter
来信	láixìn	send a letter
师母	shīmǔ	wife of one's teacher

Supplementary Vocabulary

寄	jì	send
包裹	bāoguǒ	package, parcel
明信片	míngxìnpiàn	picture postcard
贴	tiē	stick
邮票	yóupiào	stamp

Notes on the Conversation

Yào bú shi... "if not..."

In the conversation, look at this line: **Yào bú shi nín jiào-xué-yǒu-fāng, wǒ yě bù kěnéng jìnbùde zhèmme kuài** "If it hadn't been for your excellent teaching, I wouldn't have been able to progress so quickly." The pattern **yào bú shi...** means "if it isn't...," "if not...," or "if it weren't for...." **Yào bú shi** may precede or follow the subject of the first clause; in the second clause there is almost always an adverb like **jiù** "then," **yě** "also," **hái** "still," or **yídìng** "definitely." More examples: **Yào bú shi nǐ gàosu wǒ, wǒ yě bú huì zhīdao** "If you hadn't told me, I wouldn't know," **Yào bú shi nǐ sòng wǒ qù yīyuàn, wǒde bìng yídìng hǎobuliǎo** "If you hadn't taken me to the hospital, I'm sure I wouldn't have gotten better," **Nèixiē rén yào bú shi Rìběn rén jiù shi Hánguo rén, yídìng bú shi Zhōngguo rén** "If those people aren't Japanese then they're Korean, they're definitely not Chinese."

....

Dài A xiàng B wènhǎo "convey A's regards to B"

The pattern **dài A xiàng B wènhǎo** literally means "on behalf of A convey regards to B." In freer English, it often translates as "convey someone's regards to someone else." Observe the sentence in the conversation **Dài wǒ xiàng nǐde fùmǔ wènhǎo**, literally "Represent me toward your parents greet," or in more idiomatic English, "Convey greetings to your parents on my behalf." This is rather formal usage. Another example: **Qǐng nín dài wǒmen xiàng Lín Xiàozhǎng wènhǎo** "Please convey our regards to President Lin."

....

READING

New Characters and Words

499.	责	zé	duty, responsibility (can't be used alone)
500.	任	rèn	duty; bear (can't be used alone)
	任	Rén	(surname)
	责任	zérèn	responsibility
	尽责任	jìn zérèn	fulfill a responsibility
	应尽的责任	yīngjìnde zérèn	a responsibility that one should carry out
501.	父	fù	father (can't be used alone)

502.	母	**mǔ**	mother; female (can't be used alone)
	父母	**fùmǔ**	parents
	师母	**shīmǔ**	wife of one's teacher
503.	教	**jiào**	teach; teaching; religion
	教	**jiāo**	teach
	教学有方	**jiào-xué-yǒu-fāng**	have an especially effective method for teaching
	教员	**jiàoyuán**	instructor
	教书	**jiāoshū**	teach
504.	信	**xìn**	letter; have faith in, believe; (surname)
	来信	**láixìn**	send a letter (to where the speaker is)
	明信片	**míngxìnpiàn**	picture postcard
	回信	**huíxìn**	respond with a letter
	信用	**xìnyòng**	credit; trustworthiness
	相信	**xiāngxìn**	believe, believe in

A. SENTENCES

一、父母对孩子有责任，当然孩子对父母也有责任，是不是？

二、小牛长得好看，可是说话不算话，是一个完全没有信用的人。

三、王老师已经死了，可是师母还在，不过她年纪已经很大了。

四、小金很难过，因为她常给父母写信，可是父母很少给她回信。

五、我星期六、星期日有空的时候，最喜欢给朋友们写信或者明信片。

六、我父母都是高中教员，他们是很多年前在高中教书的时候认识的。

七、最近你的中文进步得很快，相信你到了中国以后，还会进步得更快！

八、说实在的，我不是什么"语言教学专家，"只不过是一个小教员而已。

九、这种工作责任很重，不知道我能不能尽那么大的责任，不过我愿意试一下。

十、王大海说他二十岁以前相信的很多东西，现在已经不相信了。

B. CONVERSATIONS

石文美：老师，好久不见了！我是石文美。您最近好吗？老师看起来跟十年前没什么两样！

包老师：不，老了！你是石文美，我记得你！

石文美：对，对，石文美。老师还在学校教书吗？

包老师：对！我还在北一女教书，不过今年可能是最后一年了。

石文美：当年向老师学到了很多很多东西。要不是老师教学有方，我那时候也不会进步得那么快。

包老师：哪儿的话，这是老师应尽的责任。
石文美：老师多保重！代我向师母问好！
包老师：好，谢谢你，我会的。再见！
石文美：再见，老师！

C. NARRATIVE

一、我姓任，任万里，今年十九岁。家在中国湖北省应城市。父母都是在湖北的一个小镇出生长大的。那里人口不多，只有几百人。城里没什么大公司或饭店，只有一所小学和几家小店。我父母是高中教员，在应城市一所中学教书。他们每天从早忙到晚。说实在的，很多人不知道老师有多忙，他们拿的钱不多，可是工作量和责任好重啊！

二、我的父母很爱我，但是说实在的，他们可能有点儿太爱我了！我妈妈每个星期六都给我写信，爸爸每个星期天都给我打电话，管我管得很严。虽然我的父母一直对我很好，也尽了父母应尽的责任，而且要不是因为他们，我今天也不可能上这么好的大学，可是他们为什么那么喜欢管我？我妈妈今天又来信了，叫我不要抽烟、不要喝酒。我爸爸还加上了一句："别忘了，上大学不可以交男朋友"。那，我在大学除了学习以外还能做什么？那种生活太没意思了！

Notes

A8.　只不过 zhǐbúguò "only, merely"

B1.　A跟B没什么两样 A gēn B méi shénme liǎngyàng "A is no different from B." The sentence 老师看起来跟十年前没什么两样 means "Teacher, you look no different from ten years ago."

B2.　北一女 Běiyī'nǚ "Taipei Municipal First Girls' Senior High School." This is an abbreviation for 台北市立第一女子高级中学.

B3.　当年 dāngnián "at that time, in those days"

B4.　向A学到B xiàng A xuédào B "to learn B from A"

B5.　多保重 duō bǎozhòng "take good care of yourself"

C1a.　应城 Yìngchéng (a city of about 600,000 in eastern Hubei province)

C1b.　小镇 xiǎozhèn "small town"

C1c.　很多人不知道老师有多忙 "Lots of people don't know how busy a teacher is."

C1d.　工作量 gōngzuòliàng "amount of work, workload"

C2.　管我管得很严 "(They) control me very strictly."

LESSON 19
Hobbies

PART ONE

Conversation 🎧 LISTEN

Situation: Sally Lee, who is spending her junior year in Beijing, has been invited to the home of a Chinese classmate. After dinner the two young women ask about each other's hobbies.

1. CHINESE CLASSMATE: 李文，你有什么嗜好吗？
   Lǐ Wén, nǐ yǒu shémme shìhào ma?
   Sally, do you have any hobbies?

2. LEE: 我喜欢音乐。从小在美国学钢琴。
   Wǒ xǐhuan yīnyuè. Cóng xiǎo zài Měiguo xué gāngqín.
   I like music. From the time I was little, I've been studying piano in America.

3. CHINESE CLASSMATE: 怪不得我常看你一边走一边哼调子。
   Guàibudé cháng kàn nǐ yìbiān zǒu yìbiān hēng diàozi.
   No wonder I often see you humming a tune while you walk.

4. LEE: 是吗？
   Shì ma?
   Really?

5. **CHINESE CLASSMATE:** 除了音乐，你还有其他的爱好吗？

Chúle yīnyuè, nǐ hái yǒu qítāde àihào ma?

Besides music, do you have any other hobbies?

6. **LEE:** 还喜欢看小说儿或是参观博物馆。你呢？你的嗜好是什么？

Hái xǐhuan kàn xiǎoshuōr huòshi cānguān bówùguǎn. Nǐ ne? Nǐde shìhào shi shémme?

I also like to read novels or visit museums. And you? What are your hobbies?

7. **CHINESE CLASSMATE:** 画画儿，特别是国画儿。还有下棋。围棋、象棋、跳棋我都下。

Huàhuàr, tèbié shi guóhuàr, hái yǒu xiàqí. Wéiqí, Xiàngqí, Tiàoqí, wǒ dōu xià.

Painting, especially Chinese painting, also playing Chinese chess. Go, Chinese chess, Chinese checkers, I play them all.

New Vocabulary 🎧

嗜好	shìhào	hobby; addiction
钢琴	gāngqín	piano
怪不得	guàibudé	no wonder
哼	hēng	hum
调子	diàozi	tune, melody
是吗	shì ma	"really?"
爱好	àihào	interest, hobby
小说	xiǎoshuō(r)	novel
参观	cānguān	visit
博物馆	bówùguǎn	museum
画	huà	paint
画	huà(r)	painting
画画	huàhuà(r)	paint paintings
国画	guóhuà(r)	Chinese painting
下	xià	play (chess or checkers)
下棋	xiàqí	play chess
围棋	Wéiqí	Go (a kind of chess)
象棋	Xiàngqí	Chinese chess
跳棋	Tiàoqí	Chinese checkers

Supplementary Vocabulary

唱	chàng	sing
歌	gē(r)	song
唱歌	chànggē(r)	sing a song
看书	kànshū	read
照	zhào	take (photographs)
照相	zhàoxiàng	take photographs
好听	hǎotīng	be nice-sounding, pretty

Notes on the Conversation

Guàibudé "no wonder"

Guàibudé "no wonder" or "no wonder that…" is gramatically composed of the verb **guài** "find strange," **-bù-** "not," and **dé** "can," that is, "cannot find something to be strange." **Guàibudé** expresses a sudden awareness of the reason why something is as it is. **Guàibudé** can function as an independent comment, for example, **Guàibudé!** "No wonder!"; or it can be followed by a sentence. The meaning and use of **guàibudé** are similar to **nánguài** that you had earlier. Examples: **Tā hěn ài chī, guàibudé tā nèmme pàng!** "He loves to eat, no wonder he's so fat!," **Nǐ shuō tāmen chūqu lǚxíngle? Guàibudé wǒ zuìjìn méi kànjian tāmen** "You say they went traveling? No wonder I haven't seen them recently," **Jiāzhōude tiānqi nèmme hǎo, guàibudé Zhōngguo rén dōu xǐhuan bāndao Jiāzhōu qù** "The climate in California is so good, no wonder Chinese all like to move to California."

READING

New Characters and Words

505.	唱	chàng	sing
506.	歌	gē(r)	song
	一首歌	yìshǒu gē	a song
	唱歌	chànggē(r)	sing songs
507.	怪	guài	blame; be strange
	难怪	nánguài	no wonder
	怪不得	guàibudé	no wonder that
508.	观	guān	look at (can't be used alone)
	参观	cānguān	visit (as a tourist or observer)
509.	画	huà	paint; painting

一张画	**yìzhāng huà(r)**	a painting
画画	**huàhuà(r)**	paint a painting
国画	**guóhuà(r)**	traditional Chinese painting
山水画	**shānshuǐ huà(r)**	landscape painting
510. 照	**zhào**	shine; illuminate; take (photographs)
照相	**zhàoxiàng**	take a photograph
照相机	**zhàoxiàngjī**	camera
照相馆	**zhàoxiàngguǎn**	photo studio, photo shop

A. SENTENCES

一、 我的爱好是画画儿、照相、以及看小说儿。

二、 这个照相机是在哪儿买的？价钱怎么这么贵？

三、 白老太太不但喜欢画画儿，而且也很喜欢唱歌儿。

四、 这首歌的调子太高了，我唱不了这么高的调子！

五、 我们今天要参观的第一家工厂做鞋子，第二家工厂做手表。

六、 老张从小只喜欢一个人在家看书，怪不得他没有什么朋友。

七、 中国人非常喜欢天安门，每天都有好几万人到那里去参观。

八、 那个意大利人从小就住在北京，难怪他的中国话讲得那么流利。

九、 你说你的专业是音乐，是吗？怪不得我常看你一边儿走，一边儿
唱歌儿！

十、 王大海告诉大家他的爱好是唱歌儿，可是大家都觉得他唱得很难听。

B. CONVERSATIONS

一、

中国同学： 好，现在请每位同学给我们唱一首歌儿！

美国同学： 要唱歌儿啊？我们在美国很少唱歌儿，我不太会唱。一定
得唱吗？

中国同学： 你随便唱一首，大家都是好朋友，没关系。

美国同学： 这样子。好吧，可是我真的不太会唱。如果唱得不好听，
你们可别笑我！

中国同学： 不会的。

美国同学： 好，一、二、三、唱："王老先生有块地"。对不起，这个
调子太高了！我再来一次吧……

二、

美国人：您好！对不起，不好意思，请您帮我们照一张相，好吗？

中国人：好，没问题。不过，等一下，这个照相机怎么用？

美国人：我教您……奇怪，好像坏了。怎么办？
中国人：离这儿不远有一家照相馆，我带您去。

C. NARRATIVES

我听过这样一个笑话。有一个男的外国大学生到中国去学中文。他很想多找机会讲中国话。有一天，他的中文老师的一个朋友请客，老师就带他一块儿去吃饭。去以前，老师提醒他，看见其他的中国客人，可以说一句："你好吗？"老师和学生到了饭店，坐下了。外国学生左手边坐着一位中国老太太。他就开口问老太太："你妈好？"老太太觉得很奇怪，就问那位老师："我妈已经死了很多年了，这个老外为什么会问我的妈怎么样？"外国男生右手边坐着一位年轻小姐，年纪跟他差不多。他想再试一次，就跟那位小姐说："妈，你好！"小姐听他这样说，很不高兴，就对他说："我不是你妈！"说完站起来就走了。这个外国大学生觉得中文实在是太难了，决定回国去，不再学中文了。从这个笑话，我们可以知道，在中文里，语法特别要紧："你好吗？"、"你妈好？"、"妈，你好！"这三句话的意思太不一样！所以外国人要学好中文，一定得注意中文的语法。

Notes

B1.　王老先生有块地 "Old Mr. Wang had a plot of land." This is the first line of the Chinese translation of the American song "Old MacDonald Had a Farm." Note that the noun 地 "land, ground" takes the measure 块 "piece of, plot of." Also note that 地 is pronounced **dì** to represent the word for "land, ground" but it is pronounced **de** when it represents the adverbial modifier, as in 简单地说 "say simply."

B2.　奇怪 **qíguài** "be strange." The character 怪 is one of the new characters for this lesson. Note that the word 奇怪 reoccurs in the Narrative for this lesson.

C1.　提醒 **tíxǐng** "remind." The character 醒 by itself is how one writes the verb **xǐng** "awaken, wake up."

Students practicing oil painting on the campus of National Taiwan Normal University

PART TWO

Conversation 🎧 LISTEN

Situation: Lee is invited by her classmate to view a performance of Peking opera (continued from the previous conversation).

1. **CHINESE CLASSMATE**: 对了，你对京剧感兴趣吗？
   Duìle, nǐ duì Jīngjù gǎn xìngqu ma?
   Oh, yes, are you interested in Peking opera?

2. **LEE**: 京剧啊？我虽然不太懂，但是挺爱看。
   Jīngjù a? Wǒ suīrán bú tài dǒng, dànshi tǐng ài kàn.
   Peking opera? Though I don't understand it very well, I do love to watch it.

3. **CHINESE CLASSMATE**: 这个星期六晚上我要跟父母一起去人民剧场看《白蛇传》。正好多一张票，你愿意跟我一起去吗？
   Zhèige xīngqīliù wǎnshang wǒ yào gēn fùmǔ yìqǐ qù Rénmín Jùchǎng kàn "Bái Shé Zhuàn." Zhènghǎo duō yìzhāng piào. Nǐ yuànyi gēn wǒ yìqǐ qù ma?
   This Saturday evening I'm going to People's Theater with my parents to see *Chronicle of the White Snake*. I just happen to have an extra ticket. Would you like to go together with me?

4. **LEE**: 太好了！几点开始？
   Tài hǎole! Jǐdiǎn kāishǐ?
   Great! What time does it begin?

5. **CHINESE CLASSMATE**: 八点。我星期六晚上七点一刻来找你。
   Bādiǎn. Wǒ xīngqīliù wǎnshang qīdiǎn yíkè lái zhǎo nǐ.
   At 8:00. I'll come looking for you Saturday night at 7:15.

6. LEE:	好，真谢谢你！

Hǎo, zhēn xièxie nǐ!
O.K., thanks so much!

7. CHINESE CLASSMATE:	这还用谢？星期六见！

Zhè hái yòng xiè? Xīngqīliù jiàn!
No need to thank me. See you Saturday!

New Vocabulary

京剧	Jīngjù	Peking opera
人民	rénmín	people
剧场	jùchǎng	theater
人民剧场	Rénmín Jùchǎng	People's Theater (in Beijing)
蛇	shé	snake
传	zhuàn	chronicle, biography
白蛇传	Bái Shé Zhuàn	"Chronicle of the White Snake"
正好	zhènghǎo(r)	just, as it happens

Supplementary Vocabulary

分	fēn	part, fraction
…分之…	…fēnzhī…	(for fractions)
百分之…	bǎifēnzhī…	…percent
…点…	…diǎn…	(pattern for decimals)
有用	yǒuyòng	be useful
没有用	méiyou yòng	not have any use
中华	Zhōnghuá	(literary name for "China")
共和国	gònghéguó	republic
中华人民共和国	Zhōnghuá Rénmín Gònghéguó	People's Republic of China
中华民国	Zhōnghuá Mínguó	Republic of China

Notes on the Conversation

Fractions, percent, and decimals

Fractions are created on the pattern: Denominator + **fēn** + **zhī** + Numerator. Examples: **sānfēnzhīyī** "one-third," **sìfēnzhīsān** "three-fourths," **wǔfēnzhīyī** "one-fifth." More complicated fractions work the same way, for example, **shíbāfēnzhīwǔ** "5/18." Percentage is expressed with the same pattern as for fractions using **bǎifēnzhī**, literally, "of a hundred parts." Examples: **bǎifēnzhīyī** "1%," **bǎifēnzhīshí** "10%," **bǎifēnzhīwǔshí** "50%," **bǎifēnzhībǎi** "100%." As regards decimals, the word for the decimal point is **diǎn**. The number before the decimal point is pronounced like any other number, but the numbers after the decimal point are simply read off one digit at a time. Examples: **yī diǎn èr sì** "1.24," **sìshijiǔ diǎn bā liù** "49.86," **liǎngbǎi èrshisān diǎn liù wǔ** "223.65."

....

Reading

New Characters and Words

511.	研	**yán**	grind; study (can't be used alone)
512.	究	**jiū**	study (can't be used alone)
	研究	**yánjiū**	study, research
	中国研究	**Zhōngguo Yánjiū**	Chinese Studies
	美国研究	**Měiguo Yánjiū**	American Studies
	近东研究	**Jìndōng Yánjiū**	Near Eastern Studies
	对···有研究	**duì...yǒu yánjiū**	be an expert in, have expertise in
	研究生	**yánjiūshēng**	graduate student
	研究所	**yánjiūsuǒ**	graduate school
513.	懂	**dǒng**	understand
	听懂	**tīngdǒng**	understand by hearing
	看懂	**kàndǒng**	understand by reading
514.	民	**mín**	people (can't be used alone)
	人民	**rénmín**	people
	人民日报	**Rénmín Rìbào**	*People's Daily* (name of a newspaper)
	民国···年	**Mínguó...nián**	in the...year of the Republic
	原住民	**yuánzhùmín**	native people
	三民主义	**Sān Mín Zhǔyì**	"The Three Principles of the People"
515.	华	**huá**	China
	华	**Huà**	Hua (surname)
	华人	**Huárén**	Chinese person; Chinese people
	中华人民共和国	**Zhōnghuá Rénmín Gònghéguó**	People's Republic of China
	中华民国	**Zhōnghuá Mínguó**	Republic of China
516.	亲	**qīn**	parent, relative; to kiss
	父亲	**fùqīn**	father
	母亲	**mǔqīn**	mother
	父母亲	**fùmǔqīn**	parents
	亲人	**qīnrén**	family member

A. SENTENCES

一、《人民日报》是中华人民共和国的第一大报。

二、华国树的父亲对天文很有研究，他的母亲对数学很有研究。

三、母亲大声地叫："孩子们！晚饭预备好了，快下来吃饭吧！"

四、"王爱华，女，民国三十七年出生于中华民国台湾省台东市。"

五、这个研究报告说美国的原住民占美国总人口的百分之一点七。

六、对不起，我没有完全听懂您刚才说的话，您能不能再讲一次？

七、听说在马来西亚，华人占总人口的四分之一，马来人占总人口的
四分之三。

八、一个外国人如果认识差不多两千个中国字，就应该可以看懂《人
民日报》了。

九、中华人民共和国的首都是北京，中华民国的首都是台北，不过也
有人说中华民国的首都是南京。

十、大海，我们今天一共是五个人，所以米饭你只能拿五分之一，懂
不懂？

B. CONVERSATIONS

李天乐：请问，你是华人吗？

高利民：是啊，我是华人。你呢？

李天乐：我也是华人。你在哪里出生的？

高利民：我在马来西亚出生的。你呢？

李天乐：我在新加坡出生的。

C. NARRATIVES

一、我的同学们都是研究生物和化学的，只有我一个人是研究文学
的。他们常常笑我说文学没有什么用。可是没办法，我真的只对
文学感兴趣。

二、从前，可能是民国二十年左右吧，我们家对面住着一个老头姓
何，大家都叫他何老头。何老头很喜欢唱歌儿。记得有一天早
上，何老头走到街上，站在一张桌子上，跟很多人说："我想人人
都知道我很会唱歌儿。我也知道有很多朋友都喜欢听我唱。现在
我要给你们唱几首最好听的歌儿，你们听一听！"他还说了很多别
的话，说了半天。何老头说话，听的人真不少，大概有一百多个
人。何老头就开始唱了。唱了一会儿，人就都走了，只有我跟我
父亲没走。何老头跟我父亲说："先生，我唱的歌儿就是您和您的
女儿懂。他们都不懂，所以都走了。"我父亲说："先生，您唱的歌

儿我们也不懂。我们没走，是因为那张桌子是我们的，我们还需
要用!"

Notes

A1.   第一大报 "biggest newspaper"

A4.   This sentence is in formal written register or style. The word 于 corresponds to 在 in spoken
register.

A7a.   马来西亚 **Mǎláixīyà** "Malaysia" (reoccurs in Conversation in Part B)

A7b.   总人口 **zǒngrénkǒu** "total population"

A7c.   马来人 **Mǎlái rén** "Malay" (person)

A9.   Though the majority of people in Taiwan consider Taipei to be the capital of Taiwan, Republic
of China, there are some who argue that, for historical and legal reasons, Nanjing is still the
de jure capital of the Republic of China.

B.   新加坡 **Xīnjiāpō** "Singapore"

C2a.   老头 **lǎotóu(r)** "old man"

C2b.   住着一个老头姓何 "there lived an old man with the last name of He"

A scene from Beijing Opera about **Sūn Wùkōng** "The Monkey King"

Going to the Movies

PART ONE

Conversation 🎧

Situation: In the male dorm at Capital Normal University in Beijing, Li Xiaodong asks his American friend John Niu if he would like to watch a movie with him.

1. AMERICAN: 进来。
   Jìnlái.
   Come in.

2. CHINESE: 嗨！
   Hài!
   Hi!

3. AMERICAN: 欸，晓东！
   Èi, Xiǎodōng!
   Hey, Xiaodong!

4. CHINESE: 干什么呢？
   Gàn shémme ne?
   What are you up to?

5. AMERICAN: 学习呢。
   Xuéxí ne.
   Studying.

6. CHINESE: 是吗？呃，下午你有空吗？想不想去看场电影儿？
Shì ma? E, xiàwǔ nǐ yǒukòng ma? Xiǎng bu xiǎng qù kàn chǎng diànyǐngr?
Really? Uh, are you free this afternoon? Would you like to go see a movie?

7. AMERICAN: 可以啊。有什么好片子吗？
Kéyi a. Yǒu shémme hǎo piānzi ma?
Sure. Are there any good films?

8. CHINESE: 最近有一部新片子，刚上演，名叫《月的主人》，听说不错。讲的是三十年代中国一个著名音乐家的故事。
Zuìjìn yǒu yíbù xīn piānzi, gāng shàngyǎn, míng jiào "Yuède Zhǔrén." Tīngshuō bú cuò. Jiǎngde shi sānshí niándài Zhōngguo yíge zhùmíng yīnyuèjiāde gùshi.
Recently there's a new film that just began playing titled "Moon Master." I've heard it's pretty good. It's the story of a famous musician in China in the 1930s.

New Vocabulary

干	**gàn**	do
场	**chǎng**	(for a showing of a movie)
电影	**diànyǐng(r)**	movie
片子	**piānzi**	film, movie
部	**bù**	(measure for films)
上演	**shàngyǎn**	begin to play (of a film at a theater)
名叫	**míng jiào**	be named
月	**yuè**	moon
讲	**jiǎng**	tell the story of, be about
故事	**gùshi**	story
讲故事	**jiǎng gùshi**	tell a story
年代	**niándài**	decade
著名	**zhùmíng**	be famous, well-known
音乐家	**yīnyuèjiā**	musician

Supplementary Vocabulary

电影院	**diànyǐngyuàn**	movie theater
说故事	**shuō gùshi**	tell a story
将来	**jiānglái**	in the future
计划	**jìhua**	plan
当	**dāng**	serve as, work as, act as
医生	**yīshēng**	medical doctor

画家	**huàjiā**	painter (artist)
钢琴家	**gāngqínjiā**	pianist
小说家	**xiǎoshuōjiā**	novelist
银行家	**yínhángjiā**	banker

Notes on the Conversation

-Jiā as a suffix indicating professions

Note the suffix **-jiā** in the noun **yīnyuèjiā** "musician." The suffix **-jiā** is attached to nouns (and less frequently to verbs) to form a noun relating to a certain profession. It often corresponds to the English suffixes "-ist" or "-er." Examples: **gāngqín** "piano" + **jiā** → **gāngqínjiā** "pianist," **xiǎoshuō** "novel" + **jiā** → **xiǎoshuōjiā** "novelist," **yǔyánxué** "linguistics" + **jiā** → **yǔyánxuéjiā** "linguist," **yínháng** "bank" + **jiā** → **yínhángjiā** "banker," **huà** "painting" + **jiā** → **huàjiā** "painter," **yīnyuè** "music" + **jiā** → **yīnyuèjiā** "musician." The term **zhuānjiā** "expert, specialist" which was introduced earlier also contains this suffix. Names of professions ending in **-jiā** are normally not used to refer to oneself, since that would be considered immodest. For example, to say "I'm a painter," you might say **Wǒ xǐhuan huàhuàr** "I like to paint." To say "I'm a linguist," you might say **Wǒ gǎo yǔyánxué gōngzuò** "I do linguistics work."

Niándài "decade"

In line 8 of the conversation, note the noun **niándài** "decade" in **sānshí niándài** "the decade of the 1930s." Some more examples: **liùshí niándài** "the sixties," **qīshí niándài** "the seventies," **bāshí niándài** "the eighties." Some speakers prefer to use **líng** "zero" instead of **shí**, so you'll also sometimes hear **sānlíng niándài** "the 1930s," **wǔlíng niándài** "the 50s," and so forth.

Reading

New Characters and Words

517.	影	**yǐng**	shadow; image; film (can't be used alone)
	电影	**diànyǐng(r)**	movie
	看电影	**kàn diànyǐng(r)**	see a movie
518.	新	**xīn**	be new, fresh
	新年	**xīn nián**	New Year
	新年快乐！	**Xīn nián kuàilè!**	"Happy New Year!"
519.	故	**gù**	cause, reason; therefore
	故事	**gùshi**	story
	说故事	**shuō gùshi**	tell a story
	讲故事	**jiǎng gùshi**	tell a story

520.	将	**jiāng**	will, be about to; take
	将来	**jiānglái**	in the future
521.	计	**jì**	calculate; plan; (surname)
	计算机	**jìsuànjī**	computer; calculator
522.	划	**huà**	plan (can't be used alone)
	计划	**jìhua**	plan

A. SENTENCES

一、最近有一个新片子，讲的是五十年代法国一个画家的故事。

二、一九七六年，毛主席死了以后，中国走上了一条全新的道路。

三、中国的新年不是一月一号，有的时候在一月，有的时候在二月。

四、今晚的电影名叫《活着》，是关于中国人民五十年代生活的电影。

五、五十、六十年代在中国，大人、小孩儿、男人、女人穿的衣服都一样。

六、听说王先生以前是小说家；他每次到我们家都会讲很多有意思的故事。

七、我的同屋差不多每天晚上都看一场电影，我真不懂他什么时候做作业！

八、白小姐在一家新开的进出口公司做事，听说那家公司的生意做得很不错。

九、张新民的老大是画家，老二是音乐家，老三做生意；所以做爸爸的他现在可以放心了。

十、王大海最怕有人问他"你将来有什么计划？，"因为他还没有计划，也不知道将来要做什么。

B. CONVERSATIONS

一、

班立新：小计，我不会用这个计算机。你可不可以教我怎么用？

计国明：我看看。这个计算机好像坏了。你最好换一个新的吧！

二、

女生：你将来有什么计划？

男生：我喜欢小孩子，所以将来想当小学老师。你呢？

女生：我从小就对音乐感兴趣，所以将来打算当音乐家。

男生：你这个计划不错！

C. NARRATIVES

一、我小的时候非常喜欢看故事书，我什么样的故事都喜欢看。我也很喜欢画画儿，可是画得不太好。很多人常问我将来有什么计划，我告诉他们长大了以后想做小说家或画家。现在我已经长大了，可是如果有人问我将来打算做什么，我会有一点儿紧张，也不知道该说什么，因为说真的，我还没决定我将来的计划。

二、王大川先生是一位非常好的画家，人人都听过他的名字。他最近画了一张新画儿叫"牛吃草，"所以我跟我父亲、母亲都去看了。我们看他的这张画儿看了很久，是一大张白纸，上面什么都没有。所以我就问王先生："这张画儿为什么叫'牛吃草'？草在哪儿呢？"王先生告诉我们说牛把草吃完了，所以没有草了。后来别人问王先生："那，牛呢？牛在哪儿？"王先生先看了画儿，然后看了那个人，就告诉他因为没有草了，所以牛也走了。

Notes

A1. 今晚 is an abbreviation of 今天晚上.

A8. 新开的进出口公司 "a newly opened import-export company"

A9. 做爸爸的他 "he, who is the father"

PART TWO

Conversation 🎧

Situation: Niu agrees to go to the movie with Li. After watching the movie, the two young men come out of the movie theater (continued from the previous conversation).

1. AMERICAN: 哦，太好了！我还从来没看过这类的电影儿呢。在什么地方？几点开演？
   Ò, tài hǎole! Wǒ hái cónglái méi kànguo zhèilèide diànyǐngr ne. Zài shémme dìfang? Jǐdiǎn kāiyǎn?
   Oh, great! I've never before seen this kind of movie. Where is it? What time does it start?

2. CHINESE: 北京图书馆，三点半。三点我来找你，怎么样？
   Běijīng Túshūguǎn, sāndiǎn bàn. Sāndiǎn wǒ lái zhǎo nǐ, zěmmeyàng?
   At the Beijing Library at 3:30. I'll come looking for you at 3:00, O.K.?

3. AMERICAN: 好啊。
   Hǎo a.
   O.K.

4. CHINESE: 好，再见。
   Hǎo, zàijiàn.
   All right, bye.

5. AMERICAN: 再见。 *(that afternoon, after his Chinese friend has purchased the tickets)* 几排的？
   Zàijiàn... Jǐpáide?
   Bye...Which row?

6. CHINESE: 位子不错，楼下十五排，十六、十八号儿。我们进去吧。
(when they come out of the theater) 你觉得这个电影儿怎么样？
Wèizi bú cuò, lóuxià shíwǔpái, shíliù, shíbāhàor. Wǒmen jìnqu ba... Nǐ juéde zhèige diànyǐngr zěmmeyàng?
The seats are pretty good. Downstairs, row 15, numbers 16 and 18. Let's go in... What do you think of this movie?

7. AMERICAN: 太棒了！很感人。
Tài bàngle! Hěn gǎn rén.
It was fantastic! Very touching.

8. CHINESE: 他们说的话，你都能听懂吗？
Tāmen shuōde huà, nǐ dōu néng tīngdǒng ma?
Could you understand everything they said?

9. AMERICAN: 大部分都懂，有的地方说得太快，听不太明白。不过电影的主要内容我都能理解。
Dà bùfen dōu dǒng. Yǒude dìfang shuōde tài kuài, tīngbutàimíngbai. Búguò diànyǐngde zhǔyào nèiróng wǒ dōu néng lǐjiě.
I understood most of it. In some places they spoke too fast and I couldn't understand very well. But I was able to understand the gist of the film.

New Vocabulary

从来	**cónglái**	all along, always
从来没⋯过	**cónglái méi...-guo**	have never ever...before
类	**lèi**	kind, type, category
开演	**kāiyǎn**	begin to be shown (of a film)
北京图书馆	**Běijīng Túshūguǎn**	Beijing Library
排	**pái**	row
楼下	**lóuxià**	downstairs
感	**gǎn**	touch, move (emotionally)
部分	**bùfen**	part, portion
大部分	**dà bùfen**	greater part, majority, most
明白	**míngbai**	understand
听不太明白	**tīngbutàimíngbai**	can't understand very well
主要	**zhǔyào**	essential, main
内容	**nèiróng**	content
理解	**lǐjiě**	understand

Supplementary Vocabulary

楼上	**lóushàng**	upstairs
演员	**yǎnyuán**	actor
导演	**dǎoyǎn**	director
电影明星	**diànyǐng míngxīng**	movie star

Notes on the Conversation

Cónglái méi(you)...guo "have never ever...before"

In this pattern, **cónglái méi(you)** precedes the verb and **-guo** is suffixed to the verb. While it's of course possible to use only **méi(you)...-guo**, the addition of the **cónglái** strengthens the meaning, much like English "never ever...before." Examples: **Wǒ cónglái méi jiànguo ta** "I've never ever seen him before," **Wǒ cónglái méiyou chīguo zhèmme hǎochīde Zhōngguo cài** "I've never eaten Chinese food as delicious as this before," **Wǒ cónglái méi tīngshuōguo nèizhǒng shìqing** "I've never ever heard of something like that before," **Wǒ cónglái méi zhèmme qīngsōngguo** "I've never ever felt so relaxed before."

Reading

New Characters and Words

523.	类	**lèi**	kind, type, category
	人类	**rénlèi**	mankind, humanity
	人类学	**rénlèixué**	anthropology
524.	排	**pái**	row, line
	排行	**páiháng**	(refers to one's rank or order in a family)
525.	楼	**lóu**	building; floor
	上楼	**shànglóu**	go upstairs
	下楼	**xiàlóu**	go downstairs
	楼上	**lóushàng**	upstairs
	楼下	**lóuxià**	downstairs
	专家楼	**zhuānjiā lóu**	(foreign) experts building
526.	部	**bù**	part, section; (measure for films)
	部分	**bùfen**	part, portion
	大部分	**dà bùfen**	majority, greater part, most
	外交部	**Wàijiāo Bù**	Foreign Ministry
	东部	**dōngbù**	eastern part (of an area)

南部	*nánbù*	southern part (of an area)
西部	*xībù*	western part (of an area)
北部	*běibù*	northern part (of an area)
中部	*zhōngbù*	central part (of an area)

527. 理	*lǐ*	pay attention to
理解	*lǐjiě*	understand; understanding
经理	*jīnglǐ*	manager
总经理	*zǒngjīnglǐ*	general manager
地理	*dìlǐ*	geography
物理	*wùlǐ*	physics
心理学	*xīnlǐxué*	psychology
心理学家	*xīnlǐxuéjiā*	psychologist

| 528. 它 | *tā* | it |

A. SENTENCES

一、我今天到书店买了书和地图，可是已经忘了把它放在什么地方了！

二、长白山的林区是中国东北边的主要林区，大概有28万平方公里。

三、我的中国同屋有一次告诉我他希望将来在中国外交部工作。

四、美国老一代的华人，大部分是从广东省来的，他们的母语是台山话。

五、我们的司机老何告诉我他从来没有在大城市开过车，但是他愿意试一试。

六、我在我们家排行老四，我上面有一个哥哥、两个姐姐，下面还有一个弟弟、三个妹妹。

七、我们大二得决定专业，我准备学人类学，我的一个同屋要学心理学，另一个同屋要学物理。

八、美国的中国饭馆，相当一部分都叫"北京楼，"不过他们卖的菜不一定是北京风味儿的菜！

九、北京市西部、北部和东北部都有山，西部的山叫西山，各位听说过的香山也就是西山的一部分。

十、那部爱情片王大海已经看了十多次了，可是主要内容他还是不太理解。

B. CONVERSATIONS

林美华：京京，早！好久不见了！听说你最近换工作了，是吗？你现在在哪儿工作啊？

管京京：对，我现在在第十五街的"北京楼"饭馆做经理。

林美华： 经理？不简单！你喜欢这个工作吗？

管京京： 喜欢，只是我们工作实在太忙了。

林美华： "北京楼"我早就听说过，可是从来没去过。

管京京： 那么，这样好了。今晚你跟你爱人过来看看，你们是我的客
人，我请你们吃饭。楼上有包间，大部分人不知道。你们五
点半过来吧，那个时候客人还不是太多。

C. NARRATIVES

一、 我觉得爱情片根本不好看！每个爱情片的主要内容都差不多一
样：一个人爱上另外一个人，可是另外那个人不爱他。中间还加
上很多别的小故事。过了一、两个小时以后，那两个人又爱上了
别人。我真是觉得像爱情片这类的电影一点儿意思也没有！

二、 在台湾说得最多的一种语言就是台湾话，也叫台语。说台语的人
口大概有一千五百多万，占台湾总人口的三分之二。不过，台
湾其他人大部分多少也听得懂一点儿台语。台语这种方言相当难
学，比北京话要难得多。台语一共有七个声调，它的字也很特
别，跟北京话或广东话不太一样。你如果住在台湾会讲台湾话真
的很有用，这样很多事情办起来比较方便。

Notes

A1.   老一代 **lǎo yídài** "the older generation"

A8.   相当一部分 "quite a number of, a considerable portion of"

B.   包间 **bāojiān** "private room, separate room" (in a restaurant)

Talking About Sports

PART ONE

Conversation 🎧

Situation: Tom Ryan, an American who is teaching English in Taiwan, is talking with his Taiwanese friend Huang Jikuan about their favorite sports.

1. HUANG: 汤姆，你喜欢哪些运动？
   Tāngmǔ, nǐ xǐhuan něixiē yùndòng?
   Tom, which sports do you like?

2. RYAN: 我喜欢网球和游泳。以前在美国的时候也常晨跑。你呢？
   Wǒ xǐhuan wǎngqiú hàn yóuyǒng. Yǐqián zài Měiguode shíhou yě cháng chénpǎo. Nǐ ne?
   I like tennis and swimming. Before, when I was in the States, I also often jogged in the morning. And you?

3. HUANG: 我喜欢打棒球、乒乓球，偶尔也打羽毛球。欸，你个子这么高，篮球应该打得不错吧？
   Wǒ xǐhuan dǎ bàngqiú, pīngpāngqiú, ǒu'ěr yě dǎ yǔmáoqiú. Éi, nǐ gèzi zèmme gāo, lánqiú yīnggāi dǎde bú cuò ba?
   I like to play baseball and Ping-Pong, and occasionally I also play badminton. Hey, you're so tall, you ought to be pretty good at basketball!

4. **RYAN:** 其实，我以前在高中的时候是篮球校队，不过现在已经很久没打了。

Qíshí, wǒ yǐqián zài gāozhōngde shíhou shi lánqiú xiàoduì, búguò xiànzài yǐjīng hěn jiǔ méi dǎle.

Actually, in the past when I was in high school, I was on the school basketball team, but now I haven't played for a long time.

5. **HUANG:** 不简单！那你来台湾这么久，有没有学一些不一样的运动，比如说，中国武术、功夫什么的？

Bù jiǎndān! Nà nǐ lái Táiwān zèmme jiǔ, yǒu méiyou xué yìxiē bù yíyàngde yùndòng, bǐrú shuō, Zhōngguo wǔshù, gōngfū shemmede?

Wow! So, having been in Taiwan so long, have you learned some different sports, for example, Chinese martial arts, kung fu, and so forth?

6. **RYAN:** 我自己没有，不过住我隔壁的室友倒是每个星期天早上都会到附近的公园去学打太极拳。

Wǒ zìjǐ méiyou, búguò zhù wǒ gébìde shìyǒu dàoshi měige xīngqītiān zǎoshàng dōu huì dào fùjìnde gōngyuán qù xué dǎ tàijíquán.

I myself haven't, but the dormmate who lives next to me, every Sunday morning he'll go to the park nearby to learn how to shadow box.

New Vocabulary 🎧

哪些	**něixiē**	which ones, which
运动	**yùndòng**	sport, athletics, exercise
网	**wǎng**	net
球	**qiú**	ball
网球	**wǎngqiú**	tennis
和	**hàn**	and (Taiwan Mandarin pronunciation)
游泳	**yóuyǒng**	swimming; swim
晨跑	**chénpǎo**	jog in the morning
打	**dǎ**	play (a sport)
打球	**dǎqiú**	play a ball game
棒球	**bàngqiú**	baseball
乒乓球	**pīngpāngqiú**	Ping-Pong
偶尔	**ǒu'ěr**	once in a while, occasionally
毛	**máo**	feather, hair (on body), fur
羽毛	**yǔmáo**	feather, plumage
羽毛球	**yǔmáoqiú**	badminton
个子	**gèzi**	height, stature, build

篮球	lánqiú	basketball
队	duì	team
校队	xiàoduì	school team
比如	bǐrú	for example
比如说	bǐrú shuō	for example
武术	wǔshù	martial art
功夫	gōngfū	kung fu
室友	shìyǒu	roommate
倒是	dàoshi	actually, to the contrary
公园	gōngyuán	park
太极拳	tàijíquán	taiji
打太极拳	dǎ tàijíquán	practice taiji

Supplementary Vocabulary 🎧

成功	chénggōng	succeed
比方说	bǐfang shuō	for example

Notes on the Conversation

Yǒu méiyou + Verb to indicate questions

Take a sentence with a completed action verb with -le such as Tā qùle "She went." To transform this into a question, we could add ma (Tā qùle ma? "Did she go?") or use the affirmative-negative question form, which ends in Verb + -le + méiyou (Tā qùle méiyou? "Did she go?"). Now, in southern Mandarin and sometimes even in the Mandarin spoken in the North, you will hear yǒu méiyou placed before the verb, rather than having -le méiyou follow after the verb. Thus, in place of the question pattern Nǐ qùle méiyou? "Did you go?" you will frequently hear Nǐ yǒu méiyou qù? "Did you go?" More examples: Tā yǒu méiyou lái? "Has he come?," Nǐ yǒu méiyou mǎi? "Did you buy it?" Either of these alternatives is fine for you to use, but be aware the pattern with Verb + -le + méiyou will make you sound more "northern" in your speech, while the pattern with yǒu méiyou + Verb will make you sound more "southern."

Dàoshi "on the contrary"

In line 5, the Taiwanese student asks the American student if he has learned any Chinese martial arts. Notice how the American answers and pay special attention to the adverb dàoshi: Wǒ zìjǐ méiyou, búguò zhù wǒ gébìde shìyǒu dàoshi měige xīngqītiān zǎoshàng dōu huì dào fùjìnde gōngyuán qù xué dǎ tàijíquán. An expanded translation of this might be: "I myself haven't but the dormmate who lives next to me, he, on the contrary (unlike me), every Sunday morning he'll go to the park nearby to learn how to shadow box." The adverb dàoshi means "contrary to expectations," "on the contrary," "actually," or "but." Dàoshi, which can be shortened to dào, is sometimes best expressed by stress or intonation. More examples: **Nǐ jiào biérén qù, nǐ zìjǐ dàoshi bú qù!** "You told others to go but you yourself, on the contrary, you didn't go!," **Qíguài, dàde piányi, xiǎode dào guì** "That's strange, the large ones are cheaper, but the small ones on the contrary are more expensive," **Shí'èr yuè méi xiàxuě, shíyuè dào xiàle yìchǎng dà xuě** "In December it didn't snow, but in October, on the contrary, there was a big snow."

Reading

New Characters and Words

529. 球	**qiú**	ball, globe
打球	**dǎqiú**	play a ball game
排球	**páiqiú**	volleyball
球鞋	**qiúxié**	sneakers, athletic shoes
530. 队	**duì**	team, group
校队	**xiàoduì**	school team
球队	**qiúduì**	ball-playing team
531. 运	**yùn**	move, transport
运气	**yùnqi**	luck
运动	**yùndòng**	sport, exercise, athletics
运动鞋	**yùndòng xié**	athletic shoes
532. 功	**gōng**	merit; achievement (can't be used alone)
成功	**chénggōng**	succeed
功夫	**gōngfū**	kung fu (type of martial art)
中国功夫	**Zhōngguo gōngfū**	Chinese kung fu (type of martial art)
用功	**yònggōng**	be hardworking, studious
功课	**gōngkè**	homework; schoolwork
533. 室	**shì**	room (can't be used alone)
室友	**shìyǒu**	roommate, dorm mate
办公室	**bàngōngshì**	office
教室	**jiàoshì**	classroom
地下室	**dìxiàshì**	basement
534. 倒	**dào**	on the contrary, and yet
倒是	**dàoshi**	actually; to the contrary

A. SENTENCES

一、各位同学，现在请你们把今天的功课交给老师！
二、我的运气常常不太好；我室友的运气倒是不错。
三、我的室友参加校队以后，都没有时间和我去看电影了。
四、你早上可以去人民公园学中国功夫、打太极或者做其他的运动。
五、"容力为先生，容力为先生，请您尽快到办公室来接电话！"
六、我虽然没有参加什么球队，但是我还是很喜欢跟朋友随便打打球。
七、各地吃饭的习惯都不一样，比方说中国人吧，北方人喜欢吃面，南方人爱吃米饭。
八、中国人觉得好的开始很要紧，比如说，有一句老话说："好的开始是成功的一半儿。"
九、我们中文课的教室在楼上，可是老师的办公室在地下室，这样跑来跑去对大家都不太方便。
十、王大海不怎么用功，他妹妹倒是很用功，也上了很多很难的课，比方说，化学、物理、心理学什么的。

B. CONVERSATIONS

一、

马川：明天去哪里打球？
王可：要不要去加油站后面的那个小公园？
马川：我觉得我们应该换一个地方，比方说领事馆后面那一大块空地或者食品店前面的那个公园都行。
王可：随便你，去哪里都行。

二、

妈妈：你手里拿着什么呢？
儿子：是个球，我等一下要到公园去跟同学打球。对了，妈，我的运动鞋放在哪里了？我找不着了！
妈妈：今天不能打球，会下雨的！
儿子：这么干的天气，下什么雨？
妈妈：我刚才听天气预报说会下雨的。再说，你的功课还没做完呢！
儿子：好吧，好吧，不去就不去！

C. NARRATIVES

一、我这个人个子长得比较高，跑步跑得也不慢。以前在成功大学学习的时候，我很喜欢运动。比如说跟室友们一起打球或是到公园去打太极、学中国功夫什么的。可是现在我已经参加工作了，每天从早到晚得在办公室里头上班，实在太忙了，根本没有空到外头去运动。

二、金金小妹妹今年六岁了，今天是她上小学一年级的第一天。她的老师王老师开始教班上的小朋友写中国字了。老师告诉他们，开始总是最难，只要用功学习，写第二张就容易得多了。"那么，老师，"金金说，"我一开始就写第二张吧！"

Notes

A1.　交给 **jiāogěi** "hand over to," "give to"

A4.　人民公园 **Rénmín Gōngyuán** "People's Park." There are public parks with this name in many mainland Chinese cities, the most famous of which are in Shanghai, Tianjin, Guangzhou, and Chengdu.

B1.　空地 **kòngdì** "empty land, vacant land"

B2a.　再说 **zài shuō** "furthermore, besides, moreover"

B2b.　好吧，好吧，不去就不去！ "O.K., O.K., then I just won't go!"

C1.　参加工作 "participate in work, work"

People playing baseball on the campus of National Taiwan Normal University

PART TWO

Conversation

Situation: Ryan and Huang continue their conversation about sports and agree to go jogging together (continued from the previous lesson).

1. **RYAN:** 他说跟他一起学的人差不多都是中老年人。难道年轻人都不喜欢打太极拳吗？

   Tā shuō gēn tā yìqǐ xuéde rén chàbuduō dōu shi zhōnglǎonián rén. Nándào niánqīng rén dōu bù xǐhuan dǎ tàijíquán ma?

   He says the people learning with him are mostly middle-aged or older people. Don't tell me that young people all dislike practicing shadow boxing?

2. **HUANG:** 年轻人比较喜欢晚上去跳舞，或是假日的时候到郊外走走。打太极拳得四、五点钟就出门，对他们来说太早了，起不来。

   Niánqīng rén bǐjiào xǐhuan wǎnshang qù tiàowǔ, huòshi jiàride shíhou dào jiāowài zóuzou. Dǎ tàijíquán děi sìwǔdiǎn zhōng jiù chūmén, duì tāmen lái shuō tài zǎole, qǐbulái.

   Young people prefer going dancing in the evening, or during holidays going walking in the countryside. To shadow box you have to go out at 4:00 or 5:00; as far as they're concerned, that's too early, they can't get up.

3. **RYAN:** 原来是这样。

   Yuánlái shi zhèiyang.

   So that's how it is.

4. HUANG: 你刚才说你以前喜欢晨跑。我倒是每天早上六点到六点半跑半
个钟头。怎么样？有没有兴趣和我一起跑？

Nǐ gāngcái shuō nǐ yǐqián xǐhuan chénpǎo. Wǒ dàoshi měitiān zǎoshang liùdiǎn dào liù diǎn bàn pǎo bàn'ge zhōngtóu. Zěmmeyàng? Yǒu méiyou xìngqu hé wǒ yìqǐ pǎo?

You just said you used to like jogging. Actually, every morning from 6:00 to 6:30, I run for half an hour. How about it? Would you be interested in running with me?

5. RYAN: 好啊！我也好久没跑了。明天我们在哪里碰面？

Hǎo a! Wǒ yě hǎo jiǔ méi pǎole. Míngtiān wǒmen zài náli pèngmiàn?

Sure! I haven't run for a long time. Where shall we meet tomorrow?

6. HUANG: 我六点整在体育馆前面等你，怎么样？

Wǒ liùdiǎn zhěng zài tǐyùguǎn qiánmiàn děng nǐ, zěmmeyàng?

At six o'clock sharp I'll wait for you in front of the gym, O.K.?

7. RYAN: 好，一言为定！

Hǎo, yì-yán-wéi-dìng!

O.K., agreed!

New Vocabulary

中年	**zhōngnián**	middle age
中年人	**zhōngnián rén**	middle-aged people
老年	**lǎonián**	old age
老年人	**lǎonián rén**	old people
难道···吗	**nándào...ma**	don't tell me that...
年轻人	**niánqīng rén**	young people
跳舞	**tiàowǔ**	dance
假	**jià**	vacation, leave
假日	**jiàrì**	holiday, day off
郊外	**jiāowài**	the countryside around a city
对···来说	**duì...lái shuō**	as regards..., for..., to...
起来	**qǐlái**	get up
原来	**yuánlái**	actually, so
碰面	**pèngmiàn**	meet (face-to-face)
整	**zhěng**	exact, sharp (of clock times)
体育	**tǐyù**	physical education
体育馆	**tǐyùguǎn**	gymnasium

Supplementary Vocabulary

社会	**shèhuì**	society
团体	**tuántǐ**	group
社团	**shètuán**	organization, club
加入	**jiārù**	join
放假	**fàngjià**	take a vacation
请假	**qǐngjià**	request leave
春假	**chūnjià**	spring vacation, spring break
暑假	**shǔjià**	summer vacation
寒假	**hánjià**	winter vacation
教育	**jiàoyù**	education

Notes on the Conversation

Nándào...ma "don't tell me that..."

The pattern **nándào...ma** is common and useful. It indicates surprise or incredulity and can be translated as "don't tell me that…," "you don't mean to say that…," or "could it be that…." **Nándào** itself is a movable adverb, so it can occur at the beginning of a sentence or before a verb or adverb. Sometimes the final **ma** is omitted and sometimes there is a **shuō** right after **nándào**. Examples: **Nándào tā lián yíkuài qián dōu méiyou ma?** "Could it be that he doesn't have even a dollar?," **Nǐ nándào shuō bú rènshi wǒ ma?** "You don't mean you don't recognize me?!," **Zhèmme zhòngyàode shìqing, nándào nǐ hái bù zhīdào ma?** "Such an important matter, don't tell me you don't even know yet?," **Nèmme guìde jiāju, nándào yǒu rén yuànyi mǎi ma?** "Such expensive furniture, you mean there are people willing to buy it?"

....

Duì...lái shuō "as regards"

The pattern **duì...lái shuō** "as regards," "as far as…is concerned," or "for" is very common and useful. It expresses that, as regards a certain person or persons, a given situation is a certain way. Especially common is the expression **duì wǒ lái shuō** "as far as I'm concerned." Other examples: **Duì Zhōngguo rén lái shuō, Chūnjié shi zuì zhòngyàode jiérì** "For Chinese people, the Chinese New Year is the most important festival," **Duì tā lái shuō, xiànzài zuì zhòngyàode shìqing shi zhuànqián** "As far as she's concerned, the most important thing now is to make money," **Duì niánqīng rén lái shuō, dǎ tàijíquán méiyou tiàowǔ yǒu yìsi** "For young people, shadow boxing is not as much fun as dancing."

....

Reading

New Characters and Words

535. 假	jià	vacation, leave
假	jiǎ	false; if
假日	jiàrì	holiday, day off
放假	fàngjià	take a vacation
请假	qǐngjià	request leave
假如	jiǎrú	if
假如…的话	jiǎrú...-de huà	if
536. 春	chūn	spring
春假	chūnjià	spring vacation
春天	chūntiān	spring
春节	Chūnjié	"Spring Festival," Chinese New Year
537. 整	zhěng	exact, sharp (of clock times)
六点整	liùdiǎn zhěng	six o'clock sharp
调整	tiáozhěng	adjust
538. 育	yù	education (can't be used alone)
教育	jiàoyù	education (can't be used alone)
体育	tǐyù	physical education
体育馆	tǐyùguǎn	gymnasium
539. 社	shè	society, organization (can't be used alone)
社会	shèhuì	society
社会学	shèhuìxué	sociology
社会主义	shèhuì zhǔyì	socialism
手球社	shǒuqiú shè	handball club
国乐社	Guóyuè shè	Chinese music club
服务社	fúwù shè	service club
540. 团	tuán	group; organization
社团	shètuán	organization; club
记者团	jìzhě tuán	reporters group
团体	tuántǐ	group

A. SENTENCES

一、老师，我假如需要请假的话，应该跟谁说？跟老师请假就可以了吗？

二、老李刚告诉我大学的体育馆春假也开；他是学体育的，他应该知道。

三、春天快到了，也快要放春假了；难道春假的时候，你哪儿都不去吗？

四、你放心，假如那天是法定假日，公司一定放假，你也就不需要请假了。

五、马可虽然是一位相当爱国的美国人，但是他觉得社会主义也有它好的地方。

六、中国的新年也叫"春节，"春节的时候，中国人都放三天的假。

七、明天是假日，而且听说从后天起，油价又要调整了，难怪今天加油的车特别多。

八、对我来说，这道菜调料还不够，我看最好叫他们调整一下，要不然味道就不对了。

九、我的室友大一那年加入了九个社团，有手球社、歌唱队、国乐社、数学社、物理社、化学社、记者团、国际问题研究会还有山地服务社，当然他最后忙得根本没有时间学习！

十、"王大海，原来你是学社会学的，同学们都告诉我你的专业是教育！"

B. CONVERSATIONS

一、

李春生：你今天什么时候下班？

于津平：五点，跟平常一样。

李春生：好，那我五点在体育馆的入口等你。你一定要五点整到！

于津平：放心吧，我不会像上次那样让你久等，这次一定会准时到。

二、

妈妈：女儿，你怎么最近每天都早上十点才起来？

女儿：妈妈，难道你忘了吗？这星期放假！其实，我们年轻人都很晚才起来。十点起床对年轻人来说已经算很早的了。

C. NARRATIVES

一、我记得有一次放假，跟爸爸妈妈一起参加了一个团体，大家一起坐船去日本。我那时候还是一个孩子，才七岁。可是团里大部分人都是一些中老年人。他们每天七点整就起来吃早饭，中午吃了饭一定要休息一、两个钟头。他们讲的话也非常没意思。我一个礼拜后差一点受不了，不过正好我们也要回家了。

二、台湾可以说是有两个社会：一个是台北市，另一个是台湾的中南部。在台北市，大多数人讲国语，而且觉得台湾是中国的一部分。可是在中南部，多数人在家里讲台语或客家话，那儿的文化和社会习惯也跟台北不太一样。对很多住在台湾中南部的人来说，中国根本是外国，所以假如有人问他们"你觉得自己是台湾人还是中国人?，"他们大概会说自己是台湾人，不是中国人。

Notes

A4.   法定假日 **fǎdìng jiàrì** "legal holiday"

A9.   Distinguish the different tones and meanings of 加入 **jiārù** in this sentence and of 假如 **jiǎrú** in A1.

B1a. 像上次那样 literally, "resembling last time that way" or, in idiomatic English, "like last time"

B1b. 准时 **zhǔnshí** "be on time, punctual"

C1a. 中午 **zhōngwǔ** "noon, at noon"

C1b. 休息 **xiūxi** "rest"

C1c. 礼拜 **lǐbài** "week"

LESSON 22

Soccer and an Excursion to the Great Wall

PART ONE

Conversation 🎧

Situation: Kevin Johnson is visiting the home of his Beijing University classmate Cao Jianhua. The two young men are discussing what television program to watch.

1. JOHNSON: 现在有什么好节目？

   Xiànzài yǒu shémme hǎo jiémù?

   What good programs are on now?

2. CAO: 一频道有世界杯足球赛，二频道有文艺晚会。你想看哪个？

   Yī píndào yǒu Shìjiè Bēi zúqiúsài, èr píndào yǒu wényì wǎnhuì. Nǐ xiǎng kàn něige?

   On channel one there is the World Cup Soccer match, and on channel two there is a variety show. Which one do you want to see?

3. JOHNSON: 还是看足球吧！哪个队对哪个队？

   Hái shi kàn zúqiú ba. Nǎge duì duì nǎge duì?

   Let's watch the soccer. Which team is playing against which team?

4. CAO: 英格兰对巴西。

   Yīnggélán duì Bāxī.

   England against Brazil.

5. JOHNSON: 那快开电视吧。 *(he turns on the TV set)* 哎呀，比赛已经开始了！
Nà kuài kāi diànshì ba. Āiya, bǐsài yǐjīng kāishǐle!.
So hurry up and turn on the TV. Oh, no, the game has already begun!

6. CAO: 还好，刚开始。哟！已经一比零啦！
Hái hǎo, gāng kāishǐ. Yò! Yǐjīng yī bǐ líng la.
At least it only just started. Wow! It's already one to zero.

7. JOHNSON: 哦，好球！真棒！小曹，你说谁能赢？
Ò, hǎo qiú, zhēn bàng! Xiǎo Cáo, nǐ shuō shéi néng yíng?
Oh, good ball, fantastic! Little Cao, who do you think will win?

8. CAO: 难说。这两个队都是世界有名的强队。谁运气好，谁就赢。
Nán shuō. Zhèiliǎngge duì dōu shi shìjiè yǒumíngde qiáng duì. Shéi yùnqi hǎo, shéi jiù yíng.
Hard to say. These two teams are both world-famous strong teams. Whoever is lucky will win.

New Vocabulary 🎧

节目	jiémù	program
频道	píndào	channel
世界	shìjiè	world
世界杯	Shìjiè Bēi	World Cup
足球	zúqiú	soccer
足球赛	zúqiúsài	soccer competition
文艺	wényì	literature and art
晚会	wǎnhuì	evening party
文艺晚会	wényì wǎnhuì	variety show
对	duì	pair off against; versus
英格兰	Yīnggélán	England
巴西	Bāxī	Brazil
开	kāi	turn on (a machine, light, etc.)
电视	diànshì	television
比赛	bǐsài	competition
比	bǐ	compare; to (in comparing scores)
曹	Cáo	Cao (surname)
赢	yíng	win
有名	yǒumíng	be famous
强	qiáng	be strong

Supplementary Vocabulary

看电视	**kàn diànshì**	watch television
电视节目	**diànshì jiémù**	television program
电视台	**diànshìtái**	television station
新闻	**xīnwén**	news
喜剧	**xǐjù**	comedy
连续剧	**liánxùjù**	soap opera, serial
弱	**ruò**	be weak
赢	**shū**	lose (i.e., not win)
平	**píng**	be flat, even; tied (score)

Notes on the Conversation

Comparing sports scores with the verb bǐ "compare"

In line 6 of the conversation, note the expression **yī bǐ líng** "one to zero" (referring to a score in a sport or other competition). As in English, the higher score is usually placed first. In the case of a tie score, the number of points is stated followed by the word **píng** "tied" (literally "level"). The corresponding question would be **Jǐ bǐ jǐ?** "How many points to how many points?" Examples: **sān bǐ yī** "three to one," **èrshiliù bǐ shíbā** "26 to 18," **bā píng** "eight tied."

Question words used in pairs

In line 8, look at **Shéi yùnqi hǎo, shéi jiù yíng** "Whoever is lucky will win." When question words like **shéi** are used in pairs, they take on an indefinite sense that can be translated into English by the corresponding question word plus "-ever." The clause in which the second question word occurs often contains a **jiù** "then." Question words in pairs can function as topic or subject, object, place word, or adverb. Examples: **Nǐ chī shémme, wǒ jiù chī shémme** "I'll eat whatever you eat," **Nǐ dào nǎr qù, wǒ jiù dào nǎr qù** "I'll go wherever you go," **Nǐ jǐdiǎn qù, wǒ jiù jǐdiǎn qù** "Whatever time you go, I'll go." If the subject of the first clause is the same as the subject of the second clause, the subject in the second clause can be deleted, for example, **Nǐ xiǎng gàn shémme jiù gàn shémme ba** "Do whatever you like." Sometimes the question word in the second clause has a different function from the question word in the first clause, for example, **Shéi yào, wǒ jiù sònggěi shéi** "Whoever wants it, I'll give it to them."

Reading

New Characters and Words

541.	世	**shì**	generation; world (can't occur alone)
542.	界	**jiè**	boundary; circles (can't occur alone)

世界	shìjiè	world
世界第一	shìjiè dìyī	number one in the world
全世界	quán shìjiè	the whole world
世界上	shìjièshang	in the world
世界有名	shìjiè yǒumíng	be world-famous
世界和平	shìjiè hépíng	world peace

543. 目　mù　eye (can't occur alone)

| 节目 | jiémù | program |
| 价目表 | jiàmùbiǎo | price list |

544. 视　shì　look at, regard, inspect (can't occur alone)

电视	diànshì	television
看电视	kàn diànshì	watch television
电视台	diànshìtái	television station
电视节目	diànshì jiémù	television program
电视机	diànshìjī	television set, TV set
电视记者	diànshì jìzhě	television reporter, television journalist

545. 强　qiáng　be strong, powerful; superior; (surname)

| 强队 | qiáng duì | strong team |

546. 足　zú　foot; enough (can't occur alone)

足球	zúqiú	soccer
足球队	zúqiú duì	soccer team
足球社	zúqiú shè	soccer club

A. SENTENCES

一、这么多有名的足球队，哪个队最强真的很难说。
二、听说法国香水是世界上最好的香水，当然价钱也不低。
三、我们学校的足球队强是强，可是我想另外那个队可能更强。
四、"台北101"从2004年一直到2010年算是全世界最高的楼。
五、张大千是中国非常有名的画家，你看，这是他画过的一些画儿的价目表。
六、何先生是电视台的总经理，不过他自己倒是很少看电视，他说好的节目实在太少了。
七、黄河从中国的西边流到东边，一共有五千四百六十四公里长，是世界第六长河。
八、明天的晚会有很多有名的人要参加，听说也会有电视记者在场，你最好穿好一点儿的衣服。

九、马友友是一位非常有名的音乐家，他的父母是中国人，不过他是在法国出生，在美国长大的。

十、王大海说他最近跟他女朋友一起看了两部很有名的中国电影，一个叫《黄土地》，另一个叫《人到中年》。

B. CONVERSATIONS

一、

李国强：老关，你在看什么？

关先明：我在看电视。

李国强：我的意思是说，你在看什么节目呢？

关先明：我在看足球。很好笑！

李国强：你为什么说很好笑？

关先明：因为这两个足球队实在太差了。

李国强：现在几比几？

关先明：我已经看了半个小时了，还是〇比〇！

二、

张三：小李，你觉得小王、小白他们，谁将来会比较有名？

李四：这实在很难说。小王、小白他们两个人都是很强的音乐家。我看以后两个都会相当有名！

三、

强文星：姐姐，你跟我看一会儿电视，好吗？北京台的节目看起来不错！

强文美：不行，我现在没时间看电视。我们学校晚上要开晚会，他们请我帮忙准备，我十分钟之内就得出门了。

C. NARRATIVES

一、大部分的美国小孩，每天都看好几个钟头的电视节目，而且想看什么就看什么，没人管。虽然我也是美国人，但是我们家不是那样。我们家只有一台小小的电视机，放在爸爸妈妈的房间里。爸爸从来不让我跟哥哥看电视，每次我们想看的时候，他就叫我们去做作业。有时候父母不在家，我们就会到他们的房间打开电视机，站在那儿看几分钟。一听见爸爸妈妈开车回来的声音，就马上把电视机关上，跑回自己的房间去学习。我刚上大学的时候，觉得很自由，没人管，要做什么都可以，当然也可以随时看电视。不过后来才知道，根本没有什么好看的节目，还不如不看。这样不但可以节省时间，还能省电！

二、 从前有几个人得到一壶酒。这壶酒只够一个人喝。应该给谁喝呢？有一个人提议说：“我们每个人都在地上画一条蛇吧。谁先画完，这壶酒就给谁喝。”大家都同意这个办法，就开始在地上画。有一个人很快就把蛇画完了。他看别人都还没画完，就很得意地说：“你们实在画得太慢了！你们看，我的蛇已经画完了，我现在再给它添上几只脚吧！”当他正在给蛇画脚的时候，另一个人已经把他的蛇画完了，就把酒壶拿过去，说：“蛇是没有脚的，你现在给它添上了脚，就不是蛇了。所以第一个画完蛇的人应该算是我而不是你！”说完了这句话，他就把酒喝完了。这个故事叫“画蛇添足，”一直到现在，如果有人做了什么完全不需要做的事情，中国人可能会说：“你这真是画蛇添足！”

Notes

A3. 强是强 "as for being strong, it's strong all right" or, in idiomatic English, "is pretty strong"

A8. 在场 **zài chǎng** "be present, be on the scene"

A10. The film 黄土地, known in English as *Yellow Earth*, appeared in 1984. The director was Chen Kaige and the cinematographer was Zhang Yimou. The film 人到中年 is known in English as *At Middle Age* and appeared in 1982; it was directed by Qiming Wang.

B1. 我的意思是说 "what I mean is"

B2. The Chinese names 张三 and 李四 are used much like English "John Doe" and "Jane Roe" as placeholder names to stand for Chinese people who are unnamed.

B3. 北京台 "the Beijing (television broadcasting) station"

C1. 省电 **shěngdiàn** "conserve electrical power"

C2a. 蛇 **shé** "snake." The measure used with 蛇 is 条, so to say "this snake," one would say 这条蛇.

C2b. 添 **tiān** "add"

C2c. The character 足, as you learned in this lesson, means "foot." The well-known four-character expression 画蛇添足, which is the title of this story, literally means "draw a snake and add feet." It refers to ruining an effect by adding something superfluous.

C2d. 得到 **dédào** "obtain, get"

C2e. 壶 **hú** "flask, jar, pot"

C2f. 提议 **tíyì** "propose, suggest"

C2g. 得意 **déyì** "be pleased with oneself, complacent, self-satisfied"

C2h. 只 **zhī** (measure for feet). The phrase 给它添上几只脚 means "add several feet to it."

C2i. 脚 **jiǎo** "foot"

C2j. 当···的时候 **dāng...-de shíhou** "when" or "while"

PART TWO

Conversation 🎧

Situation: American Professor Peter McCoy's good friend Mei Tingsheng takes him to see the Great Wall of China at Badaling.

1. **McCOY:** 小梅，我终于登上长城了！
   Xiǎo Méi, wǒ zhōngyú dēngshang Cháng Chéng le!
   Little Mei, I've finally climbed onto the Great Wall!

2. **MEI:** 是啊。中国人常说："不到长城非好汉"。现在你也算得上是"好汉"了！
   Shì a. Zhōngguo rén cháng shuō: "Bú dào Cháng Chéng fēi hǎohàn." Xiànzài nǐ yě suàndeshang shi "hǎohàn" le!
   Yes. Chinese people often say: "If you don't go to the Great Wall, you're not a brave man." Now you, too, can be regarded as a "brave man"!

3. **McCOY:** 啊，真是名不虚传。小梅，长城到底有多长？
   À, zhēn shi míng-bù-xū-chuán. Xiǎo Méi, Cháng Chéng dàodǐ yǒu duō cháng?
   Wow, it really lives up to its reputation. Little Mei, how long really is the Great Wall?

4. **MEI:** 好像有六千多公里长。
   Hǎoxiàng yǒu liùqiānduōgōnglǐ cháng.
   I think it's over 6,000 kilometers long.

5. **McCOY:** 长城是什么时候建的？
   Cháng Chéng shi shémme shíhou jiànde?
   When was the Great Wall built?

6. MEI: 大约是在两千多年前，战国时代就开始建了。后来历代不断地扩建。不过这里的这一段是明朝的时候修的。

Dàyuē shi zài liǎngqiānduōnián qián, Zhànguó Shídài jiù kāishǐ jiànle. Hòulái lìdài búduànde kuòjiàn. Búguò zhèlide zhèiyíduàn shi Míngcháode shíhou xiūde.

More than 2,000 years ago, during the Warring States Period, they began building it. Later in successive dynasties it kept being expanded. But this section here was built during the Ming.

7. McCOY: 那个时候修起来可真够不容易的。

Nèige shíhou xiūqilai kě zhēn gòu bu róngyide.

At that time to build it must have really been quite difficult.

8. MEI: 可不是！这些材料儿全得靠人工搬运，死了不知道有多少人！

Kě bú shì! Zhèixiē cáiliàor quán děi kào réngōng bānyùn, sǐle bù zhīdào yǒu duōshǎo rén!

That's for sure! The material all had to be transported by hand. No one knows how many people died!

New Vocabulary 🎧

梅	**Méi**	Mei (surname)
终于	**zhōngyú**	finally, at last
登	**dēng**	climb
登上	**dēngshang**	climb onto
好汉	**hǎohàn**	brave man
算上	**suànshang**	include, count
名不虚传	**míng-bù-xū-chuán**	have a well deserved reputation
到底	**dàodǐ**	after all, really
公里	**gōnglǐ**	kilometer
建	**jiàn**	build
时代	**shídài**	period
战国时代	**Zhànguó Shídài**	Warring States Period
历代	**lìdài**	successive dynasties
不断地	**búduànde**	unceasingly, continuously
扩建	**kuòjiàn**	expand
明朝	**Míngcháo**	Ming Dynasty
修	**xiū**	build
够…的	**gòu...-de**	quite... , rather...
可不是	**kě bú shì**	"that's for sure"
材料	**cáiliào(r)**	material
靠	**kào**	depend on
人工	**réngōng**	human labor, manual labor
搬运	**bānyùn**	transport

Supplementary Vocabulary

英里	**yīnglǐ**	mile
战争	**zhànzhēng**	war
宽	**kuān**	be wide

Notes on the Conversation

Use of <u>zài</u> in time expressions

Although **zài** "be located at" most commonly describes physical location, it can also describe location in time. Line 6 of the conversation contains an example of this usage of **zài: zài liǎngqiānduōniánqián** "more than 2,000 years ago." This type of **zài** is optional.

Gòu + Stative Verb + <u>-de</u> "quite"

The word **gòu** followed by a Stative Verb plus **-de** can mean "quite," "pretty," or "rather." This is informal, colloquial usage. The **gòu**, which here functions as an adverb, is the same **gòu** that elsewhere means "be enough" (cf. colloquial English "Today it sure is cold enough," in which "enough" has a meaning similar to **gòu**). In line 7 of the conversation, **Kě zhēn gòu bu róngyide** means "It really wasn't easy at all" or "It was really quite difficult." **Kě zhēn** "really" is sometimes added for emphasis. More examples: **Nǐ yě gòu mángde** "You're pretty busy yourself," **Zhèjǐtiān kě zhēn gòu lěngde** "These last few days sure have been cold enough."

Reading

New Characters and Words

547. 底	**dǐ**	bottom, base; ground
到底	**dàodǐ(r)**	after all, really
底下	**dǐxia**	underneath
桌子底下	**zhuōzi dǐxia**	underneath the table
年底	**niándǐ**	end of the year
月底	**yuèdǐ**	end of the month
548. 建	**jiàn**	establish, build
建成	**jiànchéng**	build to completion, construct
549. 修	**xiū**	build, repair; study, take (a course)
修起来	**xiūqilai**	in the building of something
主修	**zhǔxiū**	major in; major

修建	**xiūjiàn**	build, construct
550. 靠	**kào**	depend on, lean on
可靠	**kěkào**	be reliable, dependable
551. 战	**zhàn**	battle, war
战国时代	**Zhànguó Shídài**	Warring States Period
第一次世界大战	**Dì'yīcì Shìjiè Dàzhàn**	World War I
第二次世界大战	**Dì'èrcì Shìjiè**	Dàzhàn World War II
552. 争	**zhēng**	compete; fight
战争	**zhànzhēng**	war
战争片	**zhànzhēngpiàn**	war film

A. SENTENCES

一、中国的万里长城是战国时代修建的。
二、中国人常说："在家靠父母，出门靠朋友。"
三、今天天气很热，牛和马都在树底下吃草。
四、桌子底下到底是什么东西啊？好像是什么小动物的样子！
五、我们生活在这个时代，特别需要世界和平，战争对谁都不好。
六、希望我今年年底之前能修完人类学专业的四十五个学分。
七、听说最近在中国，越来越多的女人觉得爱情不可靠，房子比男人更可靠。
八、那部电影是战争片，是关于第二次世界大战的时候美国和日本之间的战争。
九、现在中国哪儿都在建新房子，可是因为人口太多，可能十年以内房子还是不够住。
十、那天王大海问我："什么样的朋友才算得上是一生的朋友呢？"

B. CONVERSATIONS

张建树：小王，我刚看了一部新电影，战争片，是关于第二次世界大战的。战争实在太可怕了！
王建中：对啊。我最近看了一本书，是关于第一次世界大战的，也是够可怕的。
张建树：世界各国人民都要和平，谁都不要战争。
王建中：可不是。
张建树：所以大家都应该学习外国的语言和文化！
王建中：一点儿也不错。

C. NARRATIVES

一、从前的楼和房子都是靠人工修建的。虽然建起来很慢，但是建成了以后都是很可靠的好房子，很多年都不会坏。现在随便要在哪儿建房子，只要几个月就建好了。现在的新房子好看是好看，可是不一定比老房子好。因为房子应该要慢慢儿地建，几个月建好的房子常常这里坏，那里坏，你可能还得花很多钱去修。虽然很多人喜欢买新房子，可是以后我买房子还是比较愿意买老一点儿的房子。所以很多人说："鞋子是新的好，房子跟朋友是老的好!"

二、中国大陆东西有差不多五千两百公里长，南北有差不多五千五百公里长。中国的海岸线有一万八千多公里。海南东西有一百六十九公里长，南北有一百五十五公里长。海南的海岸线有一千五百多公里。台湾东西有一百四十四公里长，南北有三百九十四公里长。台湾的海岸线也有一千五百多公里。

Notes

A4.   好像是什么小动物的样子 "It seems like it's some kind of little animal."

A5.   生活在这个时代 "live in this period." 在 here functions as a postverb.

A10.   一生 **yìshēng** "whole life long, life-long"

C2a.   大陆 **dàlù** "continent, mainland." The common collocation 中国大陆 means "mainland China."

C2b.   东西 **dōng xī** "east and west" or "from east to west." Be careful to distinguish this from the noun 东西 **dōngxi** "thing."

C2c.   海岸线 **hǎi'ànxiàn** "coastline"

The Great Wall near Badaling

Emergencies (I)

PART ONE

Conversation

Situation: Ruth Guerriera has been chatting with her friend Ma Cihui in the student coffee shop at Capital University of Economics and Business in Beijing when she suddenly feels ill.

1. GUERRIERA: 慈辉，我觉得很不舒服。

   Cíhuī, wǒ juéde hěn bù shūfu.

   Cihui, I don't feel very good.

2. MA: 什么地方不舒服？你是不是生病了？要不要去医院看看？

   Shémme dìfang bù shūfu? Nǐ shì bu shi shēngbìng le? Yào bu yao qù yīyuàn kànkan?

   Where does it hurt? Are you sick? Do you want to go to a hospital to see a doctor?

3. GUERRIERA: 头疼，恶心，想吐，浑身没劲儿，好像还有点儿发烧。也许是感冒了。我想用不着去医院，休息两天就会好的。

   Tóu téng, ěxin, xiǎng tù. Húnshēn méi jìnr, hǎoxiàng hái yǒu diǎnr fāshāo. Yěxǔ shi gǎnmàole. Wǒ xiǎng yòngbuzháo qù yīyuàn. Xiūxi liǎngtiān jiù huì hǎode.

   My head hurts, I'm nauseous, and I feel like throwing up. I'm weak all over and I may have a fever. Maybe I caught a cold. I don't think I need to go to a hospital. If I rest for two days then I should be all right.

4. MA:　现在早晚气温变化挺大的。一不注意就容易着凉，闹不好还
会转成肺炎。我想你最好还是去医院看看。

(to nurse, after they arrive at the hospital)

同志，我这位朋友病了。她不大会说汉语，能不能给她找一
位懂英语的大夫？

**Xiànzài zǎowǎn qìwēn biànhuà tǐng dàde. Yī bú zhùyì jiù róngyi zháoliáng.
Nàobuhǎo hái huì zhuǎnchéng fèiyán. Wǒ xiǎng nǐ zuìhǎo hái shi qù yīyuàn
kànkan... Tóngzhì, wǒ zhèiwèi péngyou bìngle. Tā bú dà huì shuō Hànyǔ. Néng bu
néng gěi tā zhǎo yíwèi dǒng Yīngyǔde dàifu?**

There's now a huge change in temperature from morning to evening. The minute
you're not careful, it's easy to catch cold. If you don't get better, it could even turn
into pneumonia. I think you had best go to a hospital to see a doctor... Comrade, this
friend of mine is ill. She can't speak Chinese very well. Could you find her a doctor
who understands English?

5. NURSE:　您等一下儿。那位大夫正忙着呢。

Nín děng yíxiàr. Nèiwèi dàifu zhèng mángzhe ne.

Wait just a moment. That doctor is busy right now.

New Vocabulary 🎧

生病	**shēngbìng**	become sick
医院	**yīyuàn**	hospital
头	**tóu**	head
疼	**téng**	be painful, hurt
恶心	**ěxin**	be nauseous, feel like vomiting
吐	**tù**	spit, throw up
浑身	**húnshēn**	entire body
劲	**jìn(r)**	energy
发烧	**fāshāo**	have a fever
也许	**yěxǔ**	perhaps, maybe
感冒	**gǎnmào**	catch cold
用不着	**yòngbuzháo**	not need to
早晚	**zǎowǎn**	morning and evening
气温	**qìwēn**	temperature
变化	**biànhuà**	change
着凉	**zháoliáng**	catch cold
闹	**nào**	suffer (from an illness)
闹不好	**nàobuhǎo**	suffer from an illness and not get better
转成	**zhuǎnchéng**	turn into

肺	fèi	lung
肺炎	fèiyán	pneumonia
不大	bú dà	not very much
大夫	dàifu	doctor

Supplementary Vocabulary

看病	kànbìng	see a doctor

Notes on the Conversation

How to say you're sick

For "I got sick," you can say either **Wǒ bìngle** or **Wǒ shēngbìngle. Shēngbìng** "get sick" is a verb-object compound, so the two syllables can be separated. Examples: **Wǒ cónglái méi shēngguo bìng** "I've never been sick," **Tā shēngle yìchǎng dà bìng** "He had a serious illness," **Tīngshuō tā shēngle yìzhǒng hěn qíguàide bìng** "I heard she came down with a strange illness."

Talking about various maladies and pains

To say "I have a headache," use the double topic-comment construction **Wǒ tóu téng**, literally "As for me, the head is painful." The same pattern is used for "I have a stomachache": **Wǒ dùzi téng**. Note that in all these expressions, there is no verb **yǒu** "to have"; you could never say *Wǒ yǒu tóu téng. To say "It really hurts," say **Hǎo téng ó!** In Southern China, instead of **téng**, many speakers use the verb **tòng**, which has the same meaning as **téng**.

Staying in a hospital

As regards the use of the word **yīyuàn** "hospital," in English we say "stay" in a hospital, but in Chinese one says "live" in a hospital, using the verb **zhù**. Example: **Tā zhùle sān'ge xīngqīde yīyuàn** "He stayed in the hospital for three weeks."

Reading

New Characters and Words

553.	医	yī	medical doctor; heal (can't be used alone)
	医生	yīshēng	medical doctor
	西医	Xīyī	Western medicine; doctor of Western medicine
	中医	Zhōngyī	Chinese medicine; doctor of Chinese medicine
	医学	yīxué	medicine, medical science
554.	院	yuàn	courtyard; institute (can't be used alone)

院子	**yuànzi**	courtyard, yard
医院	**yīyuàn**	hospital
住院	**zhùyuàn**	be in a hospital, be hospitalized
电影院	**diànyǐngyuàn**	movie theater
研究院	**yánjiūyuàn**	research institute; graduate school
医学院	**yīxuéyuàn**	medical school

555.	变	**biàn**	change; be transformed
	变成	**biànchéng**	turn into, become
	变化	**biànhuà**	change
556.	许	**xǔ**	permit; (surname)
	也许	**yěxǔ**	perhaps, maybe
557.	志	**zhì**	aspiration; ideal (can't be used alone)
	同志	**tóngzhì**	comrade (politically); fellow gay person
558.	英	**yīng**	hero; England, English; (surname)
	英国	**Yīngguo**	Britain, England
	英国人	**Yīngguo rén**	Englishman, Englishwoman
	英文	**Yīngwén**	English language
	英语	**Yīngyǔ**	English language
	英里	**yīnglǐ**	mile

A. SENTENCES

一、小许，别动，我正在画你的头，快画完了。

二、那家医院有中医也有西医，看病非常方便。

三、先生在屋子里修家具，太太在院子里种花儿。

四、最近几十年，气候变化是全世界一个很严重的问题。

五、医院的人都说那位大夫是好人，他是怎么变成坏人的呢？

六、你们用不着叫我"许志明同志，"叫我"小许"就行了。

七、你可不可以帮我一个忙？可不可以教我怎么样把JPG转成PDF？

八、那位外国医生好像不大会说中国话，也许我们应该跟他说英语。

九、世界各国早就使用公里了，只有美国和英国还在用英里，实在很难理解。

十、王大海跟他女朋友常去学校后头那家电影院看电影。

B. CONVERSATIONS

一、

高英华夫人：您上次是什么时候来广州的？

马爱华夫人：七、八年前吧。

高英华夫人：难怪您说什么都不认识了。最近几年广州的变化很大！

马爱华夫人：是啊，今天的广州跟我上次来的时候比，很不一样。

高英华夫人：过几年，广州也许还有更大的变化。

马爱华夫人：有可能。

二、

孩子：妈妈，人真的是从猴子变来的吗？

妈妈：可以这么说。

孩子：（想了一下）怪不得猴子越来越少了！

C. NARRATIVES

一、许志明同志从英国回来了。他瘦多了，变得我们都认不出来了。当《人民早报》记者问到他这次英国之行的时候，他说："还好，该办的事情都办完了，不过这次运气不太好，在英国的几个月也过得不太如意。"原来许同志刚去英国的第二个星期就病了，住了两个多星期的医院。他觉得虽然英国的医生还不错，但是医院里的饭太难吃了。他也说虽然学了很多年的英文，可是英国英文的口音特别难懂，有时候他根本听不懂大家在说什么。他还说英国的天气不大好，常常下雨。最后他告诉记者："现在回家了，我非常高兴！"

Jiùhùzhàn

二、有一个小学老师想考考他的学生，看看他们的英语能力到底怎么样。他把"How are you?"三个字写在黑板上，问学生谁能说说这句英文的意思？没有人敢说话，所以他就随便点了一个学生。那个学生想，这几个单字他都认识，只是连在一起是什么意思，他真的不太清楚，只好猜猜看。他说，"这句话的意思是不是'怎么是你'?"老师听后，笑了一下说："不对，再来一句试试"。他就写了"How old are you?,"问另一个学生。那个学生说："'How old are you?'的意思应该是'怎么老是你?'，对不对，老师?"

Notes

A3.   修 "build"

B2.   猴子 **hóuzi** "monkey"

C1a.   瘦 **shòu** "be thin"

C1b.   变得我们都认不出来了 "He had changed so that we weren't able to recognize him."

C1c.   The word 当 at the beginning of the third sentence means 当…的时候 "when…" In this usage, 当 can be pronounced either **dāng** or **dàng**.

C1d.   英国之行 "trip to England"

C1e.   口音 **kǒuyīn** "accent" (in speaking a language or dialect)

C2a.   黑板 **hēibǎn** "blackboard"

C2b.   点 **diǎn** "select, choose, call on"

C2c.   单字 **dānzì** "individual vocabulary word"

C2d.   连 **lián** "join, link." 连在一起 means "joined together, linked together."

C2e.   猜 **cāi** "guess." 猜猜看 means "try and guess."

C2f.   老是 **lǎoshi** "always"

C2g.   There are numerous versions of this story, some involving high-level Chinese political leaders testing each other's English. In that case, the incorrect Chinese translations of the English expressions "How come it's you?" 怎么是你 and "How come it's always you?" 怎么老是你 carry a subtext of veiled criticism of the other person, i.e., "How come it's always you (who causes me political problems)?" Many Chinese speakers delight in this type of double entendre.

PART TWO

Conversation

Situation: While walking on a street in downtown Taipei, Susan Everett suddenly realizes her purse has been stolen.

1. EVERETT: 小偷！有人偷了我的皮包！

Xiǎotōu! Yǒu rén tōule wǒde píbāo!

Thief! Somebody stole my purse!

2. PASSERBY: 什么？怎么回事？

Shémme? Zěmme huí shì?

What? What happened?

3. EVERETT: 就是那个人！赶快抓住他，不要让他跑掉！这附近有没有警察？

Jiù shi nèige rén! Gǎnkuài zhuāzhù tā, búyào ràng tā pǎodiào. Zhè fùjìn yǒu méiyou jǐngchá?

It's that guy! Hurry up and catch him, don't let him run away. Is there a policeman nearby?

4. PASSERBY: 我去叫一位警察来。

Wǒ qù jiào yíwèi jǐngchá lái.

I'll go call a policeman.

5. EVERETT: *(speaking to a policeman who has arrived)*

我是美国人，在师大国语中心读书。我的皮包、护照、各种证件都被偷了。不知道那个人跑到哪里去了。现在怎么办？我那些东西非找回来不可！

Wǒ shi Měiguo rén, zài Shīdà Guóyǔ Zhōngxīn dúshū. Wǒde píbāo, hùzhào, gèzhǒng zhèngjiàn dōu bèi tōule. Bù zhīdào nèige rén pǎodào náli qùle. Xiànzài zěmme bàn? Wǒ nèixiē dōngxi fēi zhǎohuílai bù kě!

I'm an American, I'm studying at the NTNU Mandarin Training Center. My purse, passport, and all kinds of IDs were stolen. I don't know where that man ran to. What should I do now? I've got to get those things of mine back!

6. POLICEMAN: 别急，别急！我们一定尽力帮你找。请你先跟我到警察局去一趟。

Bié jí, bié jí! Wǒmen yídìng jìnlì bāng nǐ zhǎo. Qǐng nǐ xiān gēn wǒ dào jǐngchájú qù yitang.

Don't worry! We'll definitely do our best to help you find them. Please first go to the police station with me.

7. EVERETT: 好吧。

Hǎo ba.

Well, O.K.

New Vocabulary

小偷	xiǎotōu	thief
偷	tōu	steal
皮包	píbāo	purse
怎么回事	zěmme huí shì(r)	"what's the matter?"
赶快	gǎnkuài	quickly
抓住	zhuāzhù	catch hold of
跑掉	pǎodiào	run away
师大	Shīdà	National Taiwan Normal University (NTNU)
国语中心	Guóyǔ Zhōngxīn	Mandarin Center
护照	hùzhào	passport
证件	zhèngjiàn	identification paper
被	bèi	(indicates passive)
跑到	pǎodào	run to
那些	nèixiē	those
非…不可	fēi...bù kě	must
找回来	zhǎohuílai	find and get back
急	jí	be worried, anxious
警察局	jǐngchájú	police station

Supplementary Vocabulary

钱包	qiánbāo	wallet
骂	mà	scold, curse
骗	piàn	trick, deceive

Notes on the Conversation

Passive voice with bèi

In line 5 of the conversation, examine the coverb **bèi** in the sentence **Wǒde píbāo, hùzhào, gèzhǒng zhèngjiàn dōu bèi tōule** "My purse, passport, and all kinds of IDs were stolen." The pattern Subject + **bèi** + Verb + Complement expresses passive voice, for example, **Tā bèi màle** "She was scolded." If the agent—that is, the part that tells by whom the action of the verb is performed—is expressed, then the pattern is Subject + **bèi** + Agent + Verb + Complement, for example, **Tā bèi lǎoshī màle** "She was scolded by the teacher." More examples: **Nǐ bèi piànle!** "You got tricked!," **Wǒde xiāngzi bèi názǒule** "My suitcase was taken away," **Xìn dàgài bèi yóujú nòngdiūle** "The letter was probably lost by the post office," **Wǒmen shuōde huà dōu bèi tāmen tīngjiànle** "Everything we said was heard by them." In a Chinese passive sentence, the main verb must be capable of having an object and has to have a verb suffix such as **-le** or some other complement attached to it. If there is a negative or auxiliary verb, it must precede the **bèi**, so to say "Your things were *not* taken away" you'd say **Nǐde dōngxi méi bèi názǒu**. Traditionally, the Chinese passive is used for infelicitous events such as "be killed," "be hurt," or "be stolen," but due to influence from Western languages, **bèi** is now sometimes used even for happy events. Chinese uses passive voice less than English, so don't overuse the Chinese passive. Depending on the context, some Chinese verbs may be interpreted in a passive sense without the need for any overt passive marking, for example, **Chēzi yǐjīng màile** "The car has already been sold."

Fēi...bù kě "must"

Also in line 5, look at **Wǒ nèixiē dōngxi fēi zhǎohuílai bù kě** "Those things of mine must be found." **Fēi** is a Classical Chinese word that means "not"; **bù kě** is also Classical Chinese and means "cannot." The pattern **fēi...bù kě** involves a double negative that literally means "cannot not," in other words, "must" or "have to." The two parts of the pattern surround the verb phrase of the sentence. Examples: **Nǐ fēi qù bù kě** "You've got to go!" **Wǒ fēi cānjiā zhèicì huódòng bù kě** "I have to take part in this activity," **Wǎnfàn yǐqián, fēi bǎ nǐde fángjiān shōushi gānjìng bù kě!** "You must clean up your room before dinner!" Sometimes **fēi...bù kě** can also indicate strong likelihood, for example, **Nǐ yàoshi bù duō chuān diǎnr yīfu, fēi gǎnmào bù kě** "If you don't wear more clothes, you're sure to catch cold."

Reading

New Characters and Words

559.	偷	tōu	steal; stealthily, secretly
	小偷	xiǎotōu	thief
	偷看	tōukàn	secretly look at, steal a glance at, peek at
560.	赶	gǎn	rush, hurry, make a dash for
	赶到	gǎndào	rush to a place
	尽快赶到	jìnkuài gǎndào	rush as quickly as possible to a place
	赶快	gǎnkuài	quickly
561.	读	dú	read, read aloud; study

读书	**dúshū**	study
读者	**dúzhě**	reader
读研究生	**dú yánjiūshēng**	study as a graduate student
562. 护	**hù**	protect, guard (can't be used alone)
护照	**hùzhào**	passport
保护	**bǎohù**	protect
563. 皮	**pí**	skin; leather
皮包	**píbāo**	purse
皮带	**pídài**	belt
皮鞋	**píxié**	leather shoes
皮鞋厂	**píxié chǎng**	leather shoe factory
564. 被	**bèi**	quilt; by (indicates passive)
被打了	**bèi dǎle**	was hit
被偷了	**bèi tōule**	was stolen
被她拿走了	**bèi tā názǒule**	was taken away by her
被子	**bèizi**	quilt

A. SENTENCES

一、我将来要读医，我男朋友决定读人类学。

二、我的行李被别人拿走了，我非赶快找回来不可。

三、考试的时候，那个同学偷看手机，被老师看见了。

四、他新买的皮鞋和皮带都是意大利进口的，好看极了。

五、小谢在校时，不用功读书，现在只好在一家皮鞋厂工作。

六、我刚才放在桌子上的土司不见了，是不是被你吃了？说实话！

七、虽然有人说过"偷来的水果最香，"不过最好还是不要偷水果！

八、十二点的那班公车快要开了，我们得快一点儿赶到车站，要不然就来不及了。

九、清代的时候很多孩子一开始读书，都从《三字经》、《千字文》和《百家姓》读起。

十、王大海的护照被偷了，他非找回来不可，要不然怎么回国呢？

B. CONVERSATIONS

一、

男生：我的钱包不见了！好像被偷了！

女生：真的吗？是什么时候被偷的？你看见小偷了吗？

男生： 我没看见，可是我非找回来不可。里头除了五千多块钱以外，
 还有我的护照和别的证件。怎么办？

女生： 你先别急，让我帮你想个办法……

二、

小许： 你下班以后怎么不赶快回家？在这儿等什么呢？

老张： 我非得在这里等一会儿不可。你不知道，我和我爱人说好了，
 下班后谁先到家谁做饭。

小许： 怪不得你爱人也在前面等着呢！

老张： 什么？！

C. NARRATIVES

一、 我有个男同学，他的女朋友叫李文英。他有一次送了她一本英文
 书，前面写了他的名字和日期，还加了一句"我爱说英文"。请注
 意，"我爱说英文"这句话从左往右读也通，从右往左读也通。你
 们想这位男同学大概希望他的女朋友怎么读这个句子？为什么？

二、 在北京城外头住着一个白老头儿。他的太太早死了。他有一个儿
 子，叫白二。这时候白二也有二十多岁了。白二的朋友给他介绍了
 一位张小姐做他的太太。不到一年她就生了一个男孩子，他们叫
 他"小三儿"。小三儿从小就不爱读书，到了十几岁，认识的字也不
 多。他不大会讲话，也不大会做事，大家都说小三儿是个笨孩子。
 有一天，白老头儿给了小三儿两块钱和两个碗，对他说："这一块
 钱买酒，这一块钱买糖。快去，我等着喝呢。"小三儿说："我这就
 去！"他拿着钱走了。没有多大工夫，就见小三儿跑回来了，很
 急的样子对白老头儿说："忘了问您，哪个碗买酒用，哪个碗买糖
 用？"白老头儿很不高兴地说："你真是个笨孩子！哪个碗不都一样
 吗？"小三儿听了这句话，又走了。过了一会儿小三儿又回来了，对
 白老头儿说："我忘了哪块钱是买酒的，哪块钱是买糖的？"白老头
 儿听见这句话很生气，就打小三儿，小三儿被他打得大哭。正在这
 个时候，白二从饭馆儿回家来了。一进门儿就看见他父亲打他的孩
 子小三儿。白二一句话也没说，就用手打他自己的头。白老头儿觉
 得很奇怪，就问他："你这是怎么回事？"白二说："你不是打我的儿
 子吗？现在我也打你的儿子！"

Notes

A1.   读医 **dúyī** "study medicine"

A5. 时 at the end of a clause is an abbreviated, more formal equivalent of ……的时候 "when." Thus, 在校时 means, "When he/she was in school… ."

A6. 说实话 **shuō shíhuà** "speak the truth, tell the truth"

A8. 班 **bān** (measure for scheduled runs of a bus, train, or airplane). 十二点的那班公车 means "the twelve o'clock bus."

A9a. 清代 **Qīngdài** "Qing period." The dates for the Qing are 1644–1911.

A9b. 从……读起 "start studying from"

A9c. 三字经 **Sān Zì Jīng** *Three Character Classic*

A9d. 千字文 **Qiān Zì Wén** *Thousand Character Primer*. Literally, this means "The Thousand Character Writing."

A9e. 百家姓 **Bǎi Jiā Xìng** *Book of One Hundred Family Names* and the two preceding books were all textbooks widely used in imperial China to teach Chinese children classical Chinese language and culture.

B2. 说好 **shuōhǎo** "agree"

C1a. 日期 **rìqī** "date"

C1b. 从左往右读 "read from left to right"

C1c. 通 **tōng** "make sense, be logical, be coherent"

C2a. 笨 **bèn** "be stupid"

C2b. 在北京城外头住着一个白老头儿 "Outside of Beijing city, there lived an old man with the last name of Bai."

C2c. 介绍 **jièshao** "introduce." The pattern A给B介绍C is used to convey "A introduces C to B."

C2d. 不到一年 "before a year was up"

C2e. 碗 **wǎn** "bowl"

C2f. 糖 **táng** "sugar"

C2g. The 这 in 我这就去 means "immediately" or "right away"

C2h. 没有多大工夫 "before very long" (literally, "there was not very much time")

C2i. 哪个碗不是都一样吗？ "Isn't it all the same which bowl it is?" or "It makes no difference which bowl it is!"

C2j. 过了一会儿 **guòle yìhuǐr** "after a while"

C2k. 哭 **kū** "cry"

C2l. 进门儿 **jìnménr** "enter a door or gate, come in"

C2m. 奇怪 **qíguài** "be strange"

C2n. 你不是打我的儿子吗？ "Aren't you hitting my son?" This is a rhetorical question; the speaker really means, "You are hitting my son!"

LESSON 24
Emergencies (II)

PART ONE

Conversation 🎧 LISTEN

Situation: Nancy Yates has lost her bag. She asks at the security guard station at the entrance to National Taiwan Normal University if anyone has found it.

1. **YATES:** 先生，我今天早上掉了一个袋子。不知道有没有人捡到？

   Xiānsheng, wǒ jīntiān zǎoshang diàole yíge dàizi. Bù zhīdào yǒu méiyou rén jiǎndào?

   Sir, I lost a bag this morning. I wonder if anybody picked it up?

2. **SECURITY GUARD:** 你的袋子有什么特征吗？

   Nǐde dàizi yǒu shémme tèzhēng ma?

   Does your bag have any special characteristics?

3. **YATES:** 白色跟黑色的，大概比我这个袋子大一倍，上面写着"Williams"。里面除了一千多块台币以外，还有我的学生证跟借书证。

   Báisè gēn hēisède, dàgài bǐ wǒ zhèige dàizi dà yíbèi. Shàngmian xiězhe "Williams." Lǐmiàn chúle yìqiānduōkuài Táibì yǐwài, hái yǒu wǒde xuéshēngzhèng gēn jièshūzhèng.

   It's white and black, probably twice as big as this bag of mine. It has "Williams" written on it. Inside, in addition to over a thousand NT, there are also my student ID and library card.

4. SECURITY GUARD: 你是哪个国家的？叫什么名字？
Nǐ shi něige guójiāde? Jiào shémme míngzi?
What country are you from? What's your name?

5. YATES: 我是美国人，叫叶南喜。
Wǒ shi Měiguo rén, jiào Yè Nánxǐ.
I'm American, my name is Nancy Yates.

6. SECURITY GUARD: *(checks in back of booth and returns with a bag):*
你看，这是不是你的袋子？
Nǐ kàn, zhè shì bu shi nǐde dàizi?
Take a look, is this your bag?

7. YATES: 没错，没错，就是我的！
Méi cuò, méi cuò, jiù shi wǒde!
Yes, it is; that's mine!

8. SECURITY GUARD: 请你检查一下东西是不是都在？
Qǐng nǐ jiǎnchá yixia dōngxi shì bu shi dōu zài?
Please examine it to see if everything is there.

9. YATES: *(examines the purse and its contents)*
我看看。钱、学生证、借书证都在。真谢谢你！
Wǒ kànkan. Qián, xuéshēngzhèng, jièshūzhèng dōu zài. Zhēn xièxie nǐ!
Let me see. The money, my student ID, library card, they're all there. Thanks so much!

10. SECURITY GUARD: 没什么，应该的。以后小心一点！麻烦你在这里签个名。
Méi shémme, yīnggāide. Yǐhòu xiǎoxīn yidian! Máfan nǐ zài zhèli qiān ge míng.
You're welcome, that's my job. In the future, be more careful! Please sign your name here.

New Vocabulary

掉	**diào**	lose
捡到	**jiǎndào**	pick up
特征	**tèzhēng**	special characteristic
倍	**bèi**	time(s)
台币	**Táibì**	NT (Taiwan currency)
学生证	**xuéshēngzhèng**	student I.D.
借	**jiè**	borrow; lend
借书证	**jièshūzhèng**	library card
国家	**guójiā**	country
叶	**Yè**	Ye (surname)
错	**cuò**	error, mistake

没错	méi cuò	"that's right"
检查	jiǎnchá	inspect, examine
没什么	méi shémme	"you're welcome"
应该的	yīnggāide	something one ought to do
签名	qiānmíng	sign one's name

Supplementary Vocabulary

丢	diū	lose
人民币	Rénmínbì	RMB (PRC currency)
救命	jiùmìng	"help!"
失火	shīhuǒ	fire breaks out

Notes on the Conversation

Bèi to express "times"

Look at this sentence in the conversation: **(Wǒ diàode dàizi) dàgài bǐ wǒ zhèige dàizi dà yíbèi** "(The bag I lost) is probably once again as big as this bag of mine" or, in smoother English, "…is probably twice as big as this bag of mine." **Bèi** is a measure meaning "times" or "-fold"; note that this **bèi** is a completely different word from the **bèi** that indicates passive that you learned in the previous lesson. More examples: **Tā kāichē kāide bǐ wǒ kuài yíbèi** "He drives twice as fast as I do," **Wǒmen bānde xuésheng bǐ tāmen bānde duō yíbèi** "Our class has twice as many students as theirs," **Zhōngguo bǐ Rìběn dà hǎojǐbèi** "China is many times bigger than Japan." **Bèi** can also be used with the verb **shì**, for example, **Nǐde gōngzī shi wǒde gōngzīde liǎng bèi** "Your pay is twice my pay." Sometimes **bèi** is used alone, for example, **Zuìjìn shínián nàrde rénkǒu zēngjiāle wǔbèi** "In the last 10 years the population there has increased by 500%."

Jiè as "borrow" and "lend"

Jièshūzhèng "library card" literally means "borrow book certificate." The verb **jiè** is common and useful; depending on the context and how it's used, it can mean either "borrow" or "lend." To say "borrow something from someone," the pattern is **gēn…jiè**. Examples: **Wǒ gēn tā jièle shíkuài qián** "I borrowed ten dollars from her," **Wǒ kě bu kéyi gēn nǐ jiè yìzhī bǐ?** "Could I borrow a pen from you?," **Bù hǎo yìsi, wǒ zuìjìn shǒutóu bǐjiào jǐn, néng bu néng gēn nǐ jiè yidianr qián?** "I'm embarrassed to ask but recently I've been kind of short on money; could I borrow some money from you?" Depending on the context, **jiè** can also mean "lend," for example, **Jīntiān shi xīngqītiān, suóyi túshūguǎn bú jiè shū** "Today is Sunday, so the library doesn't lend out books." To say "lend something to someone," use the pattern **bǎ** + Item + **jiègěi** + Person. Examples: **Tā bǎ chēzi jiègěi wǒ le** "He lent me his car," **Wǒ bǎ yǔsǎn jiègěi tā le** "I lent her my umbrella," **Qǐng nǐ bié bǎ zhèixiē dōngxi jiègěi biérén!** "Please don't lend these things to others!"

Reading

New Characters and Words

565.	掉	**diào**	fall, drop; lose, misplace
	跑掉	**pǎodiào**	run off, run away
	死掉	**sǐdiào**	die
	忘掉	**wàngdiào**	forget
	卖掉	**màidiào**	sell off
566.	火	**huǒ**	fire
	火车	**huǒchē**	train
	火山	**huǒshān**	volcano
	火山口	**huǒshānkǒu**	crater of a volcano
567.	检	**jiǎn**	examine (can't be used alone)
	体检	**tǐjiǎn**	physical examination
568.	查	**chá**	examine, check
	查	**Zhā**	Zha (surname)
	查字	**cházì**	look up characters
	检查	**jiǎnchá**	inspect, examine; inspection
	查号台	**cháhàotái**	information, directory assistance
569.	危	**wēi**	danger (can't be used alone); (surname)
570.	险	**xiǎn**	danger (can't be used alone)
	危险	**wēixiǎn**	be dangerous; danger

A. SENTENCES

一、从上海到南京，你看最好是坐飞机，火车，还是汽车？

二、火虽然有用，但也很危险，大人、小孩儿都应该特别小心。

三、这个火山很有名，每年有成千上万的人从世界各地来看它。

四、他越是想早一点儿把他的房子卖掉，就越是卖不掉，真着急！

五、今天天气不好，开车太危险了，还是坐火车吧，又省事又安全。

六、那个地方很危险，小偷特别多，你要随时注意自己的皮包或钱包。

七、这个字我不认识，我查过可是查不到，你能不能告诉我是什么意思？

八、你运气不错，钱包找回来了！快检查一下，看里面的东西是不是都还在。

九、美国人常说中国是共产主义国家，但是中国人自己说中国是社会主义国家。

十、王大海小时候学的法语，现在全忘掉了！

B. CONVERSATIONS

许先生：你比较喜欢坐飞机，火车，还是汽车？

何小姐：坐火车或是汽车都可以，可是我不喜欢坐飞机。

许先生：为什么？

何小姐：安全检查越来越麻烦。什么都得检查，而且很多东西不准带。

许先生：没错！

何小姐：还有，我总怕飞机会掉下来。每一、两年都有飞机掉下来，每次都有好多人死掉。

许先生：其实，你不用怕这个。现在的飞机都很安全。我在哪儿读过，坐飞机比坐汽车还安全！当然坐火车也很安全。

C. NARRATIVES

一、我是加拿大的华人，在广州出生，十一岁的时候跟着父母来到加拿大。记得我刚开始学英文的时候，觉得很难。差不多每个字都看不懂，所以刚查完一个字马上又得查另外一个字。经过了十几年，虽然现在有时候还有生字得查，但现在，我英文读得、说得就跟加拿大人差不多一样，而且我很高兴我也没忘掉我的母语中文。我在大学的时候还学了一点日文，不过因为一直没有机会用，所以我的日文早就"还给"老师了！

二、不少外国留学生在美国读完研究生，拿到学位以后，都不想回国。他们想尽了办法要留在美国工作，因为美国的生活好，而且也比较自由，比方说言论自由就不是每个国家都有的。所以很多国家都有人才外流的问题，也可以说是人才外"留"。当然，不住在自己的国家，也不应该完全忘掉自己的"根"。所以，如果我们能够把我们的母语传给下一代，是非常好的事情。

A jade window in a traditional house in Penghu

Notes

A3a.   成千上万 **chéng-qiān-shàng-wàn** "tens of thousands (of)"

A3b.   世界各地 "all over the world" (literally, "world each place")

A4.   卖不掉 "can't sell, can't get rid of something by trying to sell it"

A5.   安全 **ānquán** "be safe, secure"

B1.   安全检查 **ānquán jiǎnchá** "safety inspection, security check." This is nowadays often abbreviated to 安检.

B2.   麻烦 "be troublesome, bothersome"

B3.   准 **zhǔn** "allow, permit"

C1a.   跟 **gēn** "follow." 跟着 means "following."

C1b.   经过 **jīngguò** "pass through, go through." The phrase 经过了十几年 literally, means "having gone through more than ten years" or, in idiomatic English, "after more than a dozen years."

C1c.   母语 **mǔyǔ** "mother tongue, native language"

C2a.   人才 **réncái** "capable person, person of talent"

C2b.   外流 **wàiliú** "flow outward" or "outflow"

C2c.   人才外流 **réncái wàiliú** "brain drain"

C2d.   学位 **xuéwèi** "degree"

C2e.   想尽办法 **xiǎngjìn bànfǎ** "try every possible way or means"

C2f.   言论自由 **yánlùn zìyóu** "freedom of speech"

C2g.   人才外留 "people of talent stay abroad." This is a Chinese pun since 人才外流 "brain drain" sounds exactly the same as 人才外留.

C2h.   根 **gēn** "root"

C2i.   能够 **nénggòu** "can"

C2j.   代 **dài** "generation." The common phrase 下一代 means "the next generation."

C2k.   把我们的母语传给下一代 "transmit our mother tongue to the next generation"

PART TWO

Conversation 🎧

Situation: David Hart, an employee of Delta Airlines in Beijing, collides with a Chinese bicyclist while on his way to work. A passerby joins them in their discussion of how to handle the aftermath of the accident.

1. HART: 怎么样? 怎么样? 您受伤了没有?
   Zěmmeyàng? Zěmmeyàng? Nín shòushāngle méiyou?
   How are you? Are you O.K.? Did you get hurt?

2. BICYCLIST: 我倒没什么大事。不过，您瞧，我这裤子破了一个大窟窿，我的自行车成了什么样儿了! 要不是我躲得快，还说不定有多危险啊!
   Wǒ dào méi shémme dà shì. Búguò, nín qiáo, wǒ zhè kùzi pòle yíge dà kūlong, wǒde zìxíngchē chéngle shémme yàngr le? Yào bú shi wǒ duǒde kuài, hái shuōbudìng yǒu duō wēixiǎn a!
   I'm pretty much all right. But, take a look, a big hole got torn in my pants, and what has become of my bicycle? If I hadn't dodged quickly, who knows how dangerous it could have been!

3. HART: 对不起，对不起，实在对不起! 说实在的，这也不全怨我。我也是为了躲一个过马路的，结果才把您撞了。
   Duìbuqǐ, duìbuqǐ, shízài duìbuqǐ! Shuō shízàide, zhè yě bù quán yuàn wǒ. Wǒ yě shi wèile duǒ yíge guò mǎlùde, jiéguǒ cái bǎ nín zhuàngle.
   Sorry, sorry, I'm really sorry! To tell the truth, this isn't entirely my fault either. I, too, did this to avoid a person who was crossing the street, and it was only thus, as a result, that I hit you.

4. PASSERBY: 怎么啦？发生什么事儿了？
Zěmme la? Fāshēng shémme shìr le?
What's going on? What happened?

5. BICYCLIST: 他把我撞了！
Tā bǎ wǒ zhuàngle!
He hit me!

6. HART: 是不是我们去找交通警？
Shì bu shi wǒmen qù zhǎo jiāotōngjǐng?
Should we go look for a traffic policeman?

7. PASSERBY: 要不然这样儿吧。你们私了得了。您赔他一条裤子，再赔他点儿修车费。如果叫警察的话，你得耽误好多时间，怪不合算的。
Yàoburán zhèiyangr ba. Nǐmen sīliǎo déle. Nín péi tā yìtiáo kùzi, zài péi tā dianr xiūchēfèi. Rúguǒ jiào jǐngcháde huà, nǐ děi dānwu hǎo duō shíjiān, guài bù hésuànde.
Or why not handle it like this. Just settle privately. You compensate him for a pair of pants, plus give him a little for repair costs. If you call the police, you'll have to waste a lot of time; it's just not worth it.

8. BICYCLIST: 裤子就算了。您赔我三十块钱修车吧。
Kùzi jiù suànle. Nín péi wǒ sānshikuài qián xiūchē ba.
Forget about the pants. Just give me 30 RMB in compensation to repair my bike.

9. HART: 行，行。算咱俩都倒霉。
Xíng, xíng. Suàn zámliǎ dōu dǎoméi.
O.K. I guess both of us are out of luck.

New Vocabulary 🎧

受伤	**shòushāng**	suffer injury, be hurt
倒	**dào**	on the contrary, but
瞧	**qiáo**	look
破	**pò**	break, tear
窟窿	**kūlong**	hole
自行车	**zìxíngchē**	bicycle
成	**chéng**	become, turn into
样儿	**yàngr**	appearance, shape
躲	**duǒ**	dodge, avoid
说不定	**shuōbudìng**	not be able to say for sure
危险	**wēixiǎn**	be dangerous; danger
怨	**yuàn**	blame
马	**mǎ**	horse
马路	**mǎlù**	road
过马路	**guò mǎlù**	cross the road

结果	jiéguǒ	as a result
撞	zhuàng	bump into, collide with
发生	fāshēng	happen
私了	sīliǎo	settle privately
…得了	…déle	…and that will do
赔	péi	compensate, pay damages
修	xiū	repair
修车	xiūchē	repair a vehicle
修车费	xiūchēfèi	cost of repairing a vehicle
耽误	dānwu	delay, get held up
合算	hésuàn	be worthwhile
怪…的	guài…-de	quite, rather
算了	suànle	"forget about it"
咱俩	zámliǎ	the two of us
倒霉	dǎoméi	be out of luck

Supplementary Vocabulary

车祸	chēhuò	car accident
洞	dòng	hole
一路平安	yílù píng'ān	"have a good trip," "bon voyage"

Notes on the Conversation

Shuōbudìng "can't say for sure"

The negative potential resultative compound **shuōbudìng** here retains its basic meaning of "can't say for sure." It derives from the verb **shuō** "say" plus the resultative ending **-dìng** "settle, decide." In other contexts, **shuōbudìng** can function as an adverb meaning "perhaps" or "maybe." Examples: **Shuōbudìng tāmen yǐjīng zǒule** "Maybe they've already left," **Nǐ qiáo, tiān tūrán hēile, shuōbudìng yào xiàyǔle** "Look, the sky has suddenly darkened, maybe it's going to rain," **Shuōbudìng nǐ bìyè yǐhòu yě néng dào Zhōngguó qù gōngzuò** "Perhaps you, too, can go to China to work after graduation."

....

Sentence + déle

A sentence followed by **déle** means "If such-and-such happens, then it will do" or "If such-and-such is done, then it will be O.K." This structure, which is especially common in northern Mandarin, is often used to make a suggestion for resolving a problem or concluding a matter. Examples: **Nǐ qù déle** "If you go, then it will be O.K.," **Jiù zhèmme bàn déle** "Let's just do it like this," **Xiànzài yǐjīng shíyīdiǎn le, wǒmen jiǎndān zài jiālǐ chī dianr déle, bié chūqu chīle** "It's already 11:00, why don't we just eat something simple at home and not bother going out to eat."

....

Reading

New Characters and Words

571.	伤	**shāng**	wound, injury; injure, hurt
	受伤	**shòushāng**	suffer injury, be hurt
572.	破	**pò**	break, tear, split
	打破	**dǎpò**	break, smash
	破坏	**pòhuài**	destroy, damage
573.	结	**jié**	tie; knot
	结果	**jiéguǒ**	as a result, in the end; result
	打结	**dǎjié**	tie a knot
	打中国结	**dǎ Zhōngguo jié**	tie Chinese-style knots
574.	发	**fā**	put forth, issue, distribute
	发生	**fāshēng**	happen
	发票	**fāpiào**	receipt, itemized bill
	发音	**fāyīn**	pronunciation
	发明	**fāmíng**	invent; invention
	发现	**fāxiàn**	discover; discovery
575.	费	**fèi**	spend; expense; (surname)
	修车费	**xiūchēfèi**	cost of repairing a vehicle
	水费	**shuǐfèi**	water fee
	电费	**diànfèi**	electricity fee
	水电费	**shuǐdiànfèi**	water and electricity fee
	破费	**pòfèi**	go to great expense
	费用	**fèiyòng**	expenses, cost, fee
	小费	**xiǎofèi**	tip, gratuity
	费城	**Fèichéng**	Philadelphia
576.	合	**hé**	be in accord with
	合算	**hésuàn**	be worthwhile; reasonable (in price)
	合身	**héshēn**	be well-fitting (of clothes)
	合作	**hézuò**	cooperate; cooperation

A. SENTENCES

一、虽然车子坏了，老张人倒是没有受伤。

二、我们花了那么多钱吃饭，怪不合算的！

三、不好意思，又让您破费了，改天我做东！

四、要不是她非常用功，考试的结果也不会那么好。

五、要是我不来美国，说不定今天已经成为一名医生了。

六、刚才发生了什么事，马路上这么多人？我没注意。

七、我的衣服破了，我去买一件新的算了，这件就不要了。

八、我们买菜的发票不见了，是你拿走了吗？我们还需要。

九、我要是住校外，得自己做饭，除了房钱还得加水费、电费，结果时间和费用加起来，想想是不太合算的，还是住家里得了。

十、王大海的自行车放在教室外面，结果被偷了。

B. CONVERSATIONS

一、

费国华：结果你去了哪家饭馆儿吃饭？

牛进明：去了那家新开的"北京楼"。

费国华：我还没去过那家。那儿的菜怎么样？

牛进明：我觉得还行，虽然不是很好，但是比我上次去的地方好多了。

二、

小石：你的英语发音不错！

老张：哪里。

小石：你是在哪儿学的？

老张：我因为是在美国上的大学，所以发音大概还可以。

小石：难怪这么好，原来你是在美国上的大学。

三、

老师："发现"和"发明"有什么不同？

学生：我爸爸发现了我妈妈，后来爸爸和妈妈发明了我。

C. NARRATIVES

一、有的中国人读书时，一不小心把"山"读成是"三，"或者把"花生"读成"发生"。读书时还是要注意发音，如果发错了音，别人不但听不懂，而且有时会笑话我们的！

二、有一个老外说他在中国最喜欢做的事情就是讲价。比方说，一块500元的手表，只要你有时间讲价，说不定100元就可以买到。不但节省了钱，而且还有机会练习讲中国话！不过，不知道那个卖手表的怎么想。

三、 因为中国国内的战争，再加上美国加州发现了黄金，所以一八五〇
年左右，有两万多华人离开中国的南方，主要是广东省，来到了美
国。一八六〇年之后，从中国来的工人大部分在铁路公司工作，建
铁路。这种工作是非常危险的，死了不少人。铁路完成后大部分的
工人就留在美国了，在美国各地住了下来。在美国，虽然除了原住
民以外，其他的人都是从外国来的，但是那时候的人们不喜欢中国
人，这不只是因为中国人的语言、文化和衣服和他们的不一样，美
国人更怕新来的中国人会拿走他们的工作。一八七〇年以后，事情
变得更坏了，有不少中国人被打伤，也有人被打死。

Notes

A5.   名 **míng** (for persons of a certain profession or social status)

A8.   不见了 **bú jiànle** "is not to be found, has vanished, is gone"

A9a.   校外 **xiàowài** "outside of school, off campus"

A9b.   房钱 **fángqián** "room or house rent"

A9c.   加起来 "add up"

C1.   花生 **huāshēng** "peanut"

C2a.   块 **kuài** (measure for watches). The phrase 一块500元的手表 means "a 500-dollar watch."
Another possible measure for 手表 is 只 **zhī**.

C2b.   只要 **zhǐ yào** "so long as, provided that"

C2c.   练习 **liànxí** "practice"

C3a.   国内 **guónèi** "domestic, internal"

C3b.   再加上 could here be translated as "and added to that, in addition, plus."

C3c.   黄金 **huángjīn** "gold"

C3d.   离开 **líkāi** "leave, depart"

C3e.   来到 **láidào** "come to, arrive at"

C3f.   铁路 **tiělù** "railroad." 铁 is the word for "iron," so 铁路 literally means "iron road."

C3g.   完成 **wánchéng** "complete, accomplish"

C3h.   走 **zǒu** "away." The compound 拿走 means "take away."

C3i.   事情变得更坏了 "the situation became even worse" (literally, "the thing changed so that
it became even worse")

C3j.   被打伤 "be injured, be wounded"

C3k.   被打死 "be beaten to death, be killed"

Chinese-English Vocabulary

This Chinese-English Vocabulary contains all the new Chinese words introduced in the 24 lessons of *Continuing Mandarin Chinese* with Pinyin, characters, English equivalents, and indication of where the word was introduced. The first number in parentheses after each entry refers to the lesson where the word was introduced and the second number refers to the part within the lesson; the letter "R" for some of the entries refers to the reading section in the lessons. The entries are arranged in alphabetical order of the Pinyin spellings, spelled one syllable at a time with the vowel **u** preceding **ü**. Syllables are arranged in order of tone, that is, Tone One, Tone Two, Tone Three, and Tone Four followed by neutral tone.

A

a 啊 (pause filler) (2-1); (softens sentence) (12-1R)

āiya 哎呀 "gosh" (18-1)

ài 唉 (indicates strong sentiment) (11-1)

ài 爱 love, like (12-1R)

àihào 爱好 interest, hobby (19-1)

àiqíng 爱情 love (16-1R)

àiren 爱人 spouse, husband, wife (12-1R)

ānjìng 安静 be quiet (14-1)

B

Bāxī 巴西 Brazil (22-1)

bǎ 把 (for things with handles); take (moves object before verb) (10-1, 10-1R)

bà 爸 dad, daddy (7-1R)

bàba 爸爸 dad, daddy (7-1R)

bái 白 be white; (surname) (4-1R)

Bái Shé Zhuàn 白蛇传 Chronicle of the White Snake (19-2)

báibái 拜拜 bye-bye (13-1)

báicài 白菜 cabbage (4-1, 4-1R)

báijiǔ 白酒 clear liquor or spirits; white wine (7-2R)

Báirén 白人 Caucasian (4-1R)

báisè 白色 the color white (6-1R)

báitiān 白天 during the day, daytime (4-1R)

bǎifēnzhī 百分之 percent (19-2)

Bǎishì Kělè 百事可乐 Pepsi-Cola® (12-2R)

bàifǎng 拜访 pay a formal call on someone (16-2)

bàituō 拜托 ask someone to do something (16-1)

bānguolai 搬过来 move over (6-2)

bānyùn 搬运 transport (22-2)

bàn 办 do, handle, take care of (3-1R)

bànfǎ 办法 way of handling something (3-1R)

bàngōngshì 办公室 office (21-1R)

bànjià 半价 half price (2-2R)

bànshì 办事 take care of matters (3-1R)

bāng 帮 help (6-1, 16-1R); gang, group (16-1R)

bāngmáng 帮忙 help (16-1, 16-1R)

bāngzhù 帮助 help (9-1)

bàngqiú 棒球 baseball (21-1)

bāo 包 wrap (4-2, 4-2R); (surname) (4-2R)

bāoguǒ 包裹 package, parcel (18-2)

bāoqilai 包起来 wrap up (4-2, 4-2R)

báo 薄 be thin (in dimensions) (10-1)

báobǐng 薄饼 pancake (10-1)

bǎo 饱 be full, satiated (12-2)

bǎo 保 protect; guarantee (4-1R)

bǎohù 保护 protect (23-2R)

bǎozhèng 保证 guarantee (4-1, 4-1R)

bào 报 newspaper (3-2R, 14-1)

bàogào 报告 report (17-2)

bàotíng 报亭 newspaper kiosk (3-2)

bàozhǐ 报纸 newspaper (3-2, 3-2R)

bēi 杯 glass, cup (for beverages) (9-1)

běibù 北部 northern part (20-2R)

Běijīng Túshūguǎn 北京图书馆 Beijing Library (20-2)

bèi 倍 time(s) (24-1)

bèi 被 quilt; by; (indicates passive) (23-2, 23-2R)

bèizi 被子 quilt (23-2R)

běn(r) 本 (for books, dictionaries) (3-2)

běnlái 本来 originally (6-2)

běnzi 本子 notebook (3-2)

bǐ 比 compare (22-1)

bǐ 笔 writing instrument (3-2)

bǐbushàng 比不上 not be able to compare (12-2)

bǐfang shuō 比方说 for example (21-1)

bǐqǐlái 比起来 compare (5-2)

bǐrú 比如 for example (21-1)

bǐrú shuō 比如说 for example (21-1)

bǐsài 比赛 competition (22-1)

bìyè lùnwén 毕业论文 honors thesis (17-2)

biānhào 编号 serial number (2-2)

biàn 便 convenient (7-1R)

biàn 变 change; be transformed (23-1R)

biànchéng 变成 turn into, become (23-1R)

biàndāng 便当 box lunch (12-1)

biànfàn 便饭 simple meal (11-1)

biànhuà 变化 change (23-1, 23-1R)

biànxié 便鞋 slipper (7-1R)

biāozhǔn 标准 be standard, level (8-1, 18-1)

biǎo 表 watch (to tell time) (6-2)

biǎojiěfū 表姐夫 cousin's husband (10-1R)

bié kèqi 别客气 "don't be polite" (10-2)

biérén 别人 another person, others (14-2)

bīng 冰 ice (3-1)

bīnggùn(r) 冰棍 ice pop (3-1)

bǐng 饼 pancake, biscuit (10-1)

bìng 病 get sick; illness, disease (17-1, 17-1R)

bófù 伯父 uncle (15-1)

bómǔ 伯母 aunt (15-1)

bówùguǎn 博物馆 museum (19-1)

bú dà 不大 not very much (23-1)

bú kèqi 不客气 "you're welcome" (9-2R)

bú yàojǐn 不要紧 be unimportant; "never mind" (1-1, 12-1R)

bú yòng 不用 don't need to (7-1R)

bú yòng xiè 不用谢 "you needn't thank me" (7-1R)

bú yòng zhǎole 不用找了 "you needn't give change" (7-1R)

búdàn...érqiě 不但···而且 not only...but also (11-1R)

búduànde 不断地 unceasingly, continuously (22-2)

búyào kèqi 不要客气 "don't be polite" (12-1)

bǔkè 补课 make up a class (11-1)

bǔxíbān 补习班 cram school (11-1)

bù 步 step, pace (12-1, 12-1R)

bù 部 (measure for films) (20-1); part, section (20-2R)

bù gǎn dāng 不敢当 "don't dare accept" (11-2, 11-2R)

bù hǎo yìsi 不好意思 be embarrassing, embarrassed (1-2, 5-2R)

bù rú 不如 not be as good as (11-2)

bù zhīdào 不知道 (I) wonder (6-1)

bùfen 部分 part, portion (20-2, 20-2R)

C

cái 才 not until, then, just (4-1, 4-1R)

cáiliào(r) 材料 material (22-2)

Cài 蔡 Cai (surname) (16-1)

cài 菜 vegetable (4-1, 4-1R); dish of food (7-1)

càichǎng 菜场 market (4-1, 4-1R)

càidān(r) 菜单 menu (7-1, 9-1R)

càihuā 菜花 cauliflower (14-2R)

càishìchǎng 菜市场 marketplace (4-1R)

cān 参 participate (8-1R)

cānguān 参观 visit (19-1, 19-1R)

cānjiā 参加 take part in, participate (8-1, 8-1R)

cāntīng 餐厅 dining room; restaurant (12-2)

cānzhuō 餐桌 dining table (14-2)

Cáo 曹 Cao (surname) (22-1)

cǎo 草 grass (14-2, 14-2R)

chāzi 叉子 fork (7-1)

chá 茶 tea (12-2, 12-2R)

chá 查 examine, check (24-1R)

cháguǎn(r) 茶馆 teahouse (12-2R)

cháhàotái 查号台 information, directory assistance (24-1R)

cháshù 茶树 tea tree, tea plant (14-2R)

cházì 查字 look up characters (24-1R)

chàbuduō 差不多 be about the same (5-1)

chǎn 产 produce (18-1R)

chǎnpǐn 产品 product (18-1R)

cháng 常 often; common (surname) (9-1R)

cháng 尝 taste (9-2)

Chángbái Shān 长白山 Changbai Mountains (4-1R)

chángcháng 常常 often (9-1R)

chángkù 长裤 long pants (6-2)

chǎng 场 (for movies) (20-1)

chàng 唱 sing (19-1, 19-1R)

chànggē(r) 唱歌 sing a song (19-1, 19-1R)

chāoshì 超市 supermarket (5-2)

chǎo 吵 be noisy (14-1)

chǎofàn 炒饭 fried rice (8-2)

chǎomiàn 炒面 fried noodles (8-2)

chēhuò 车祸 car accident (24-2)

chénpǎo 晨跑 jog in the morning (21-1)

chènshān 衬衫 shirt (6-2)

chēng 称 weigh, weigh out (5-1)

chéng 成 become, turn into (24-2)

chénggōng 成功 succeed (21-1, 21-1R)

chéngjī 成绩 grade; results, achievements (17-2, 17-2R)

chéngjīdān(r) 成绩单 transcript (17-2R)

chībǎo 吃饱 eat one's fill (12-2)

chībuxià 吃不下 can't eat (10-1)

chīchēng 吃撑 eat until one bursts (12-2)

chīdào 吃到 succeed in eating (12-1)

chīdelái 吃得来 can or like to eat (9-2)

chīguàn 吃惯 be used to eating (9-2, 9-2R)

chīsù 吃素 eat vegetarian food (5-1)

chōu 抽 take out, draw out (16-1R)

chōukòng 抽空 find time (16-1, 16-1R)

chōuyān 抽烟 smoke (16-1, 16-1R)

chūchǎn 出产 produce, manufacture (18-1R)

chūkǒu 出口 export (4-1); exit (5-2)

chú 除 remove (10-2R)

chúfáng 厨房 kitchen (14-1)

chúle...yǐwài 除了···以外 besides; except for (10-2, 10-2R)

chúle...zhīwài 除了···之外 besides; except for (10-2, 10-2R)

chúzhípiào 储值票 stored-value ticket (1-2)

chuān 穿 put on, wear (6-1, 6-1R)

Chuāncài guǎnzi 川菜馆子 Sichuan-style restaurant (12-2R)

chuán 传 transmit (13-2R)

chuán 船 boat, ship (17-1R)

chuánhuà 传话 pass on a message (13-2R)

chuánzhēn 传真 facsimile, fax (13-2, 13-2R)

chuánzhēnjī 传真机 FAX machine (13-2R)

chuānghu 窗户 window (14-1)

chuáng 床 bed (14-2, 14-2R)

chūn 春 spring (21-2R)

chūnjià 春假 spring vacation (21-2, 21-2R)

Chūnjié 春节 Chinese New Year (21-2R)

chūntiān 春天 spring (21-2R)

cíhuì 词汇 vocabulary (18-1)

cì 刺 fish bone (11-1)

cōng 葱 scallion (10-1)

cóng...qǐ 从···起 starting from (2-2)

cónglái 从来 all along, always (20-2)

cónglái méi...-guo 从来没···过 have never ever...before (20-2)

cuì 脆 be crisp (4-1)

cuò 错 error, mistake (24-1)

cuòguo 错过 miss (2-1)

D

dáfù 答复 answer, reply (16-2)

dǎ 打 play (a sport) (21-1)

dǎ duìzhé 打对折 give a 50% discount (6-2)

dǎ tàijíquán 打太极拳 practice taiji (21-1)

dǎ Zhōngguo jié 打中国结 tie Chinese-style knots (24-2R)

dǎjié 打结 tie a knot (24-2R)

dǎpò 打破 break, smash (24-2R)

dǎqiú 打球 play a ball game (21-1, 21-1R)

dǎrǎo 打扰 disturb (16-2)

dǎsuan 打算 plan (8-1)

dǎtīng 打听 inquire (16-2)

dǎtīngdào 打听到 inquire and find out (16-2)

dǎzhé 打折 give a discount (6-2)

dà bìng 大病 major illness (17-1R)

dà bùfen 大部分 greater part, majority (20-2, 20-2R)

dà duōshù 大多数 great majority (12-1R)

dà shēng 大声 in a loud voice (14-1, 14-1R)

dàbiàn 大便 defecate; feces (7-1R)

dàjiā 大家 everybody, everyone (9-1)

dàkǎo 大考 final examination (17-1R)

Dàlián 大连 Dalian (city in Liaoning Province) (18-1R)

dàlù 大陆 mainland (1-1)

dà-pái-cháng-lóng 大排长龙 form a long line (2-2)

dàsǎo 大嫂 wife of oldest brother (12-1)

dàshǐ 大使 ambassador (15-2, 15-2R)

dàshǐguǎn 大使馆 embassy (15-2R)

dàxiǎo 大小 size (6-1)

dàyī 大衣 overcoat (6-2R)

dāi 待 stay (15-1)

dāibuzhù 待不住 not be able to stay (15-1)

dài 戴 put on, wear (6-2)

dài 代 take the place of; generation (12-2, 12-2R); for, on behalf of (18-2)

dàifu 大夫 doctor (23-1)

dàikè 代课 teach in place of someone (12-2, 12-2R)

dàikè lǎoshī 代课老师 substitute teacher (12-2R)

dàitì 代替 replace, substitute (12-2R)

dān 单 single; odd-numbered; list (9-1R)

dānhào 单号 odd number (9-1R)

dānrénchuáng 单人床 single bed (14-2R)

dānrénfáng 单人房 single room (9-1R)

dānwèi 单位 work unit; organization (9-1R)

dānwu 耽误 delay, get held up (24-2)

dānzi 单子 list (9-1R)

dàn 蛋 egg (7-1)

dàn 但 but (9-2)

dāng 当 should (10-2R); serve as, work as (20-1)

dāngrán 当然 of course (10-2R)

dāozi 刀子 knife (7-1)

dǎoméi 倒霉 be out of luck (24-2)

dǎoyǎn 导演 director (20-2)

dào 道 (for courses of food) (8-2)

dào 倒 on the contrary, and yet (21-1R, 24-2)

dàodǐ 到底 after all, really (22-2, 22-2R)

dàoshi 倒是 actually, to the contrary (21-1, 21-1R)

-de 地 (adverbial marker) (9-1)

déle 得了 and that will do (24-2)

dēng 登 climb (22-2)

dēngshang 登上 climb onto (22-2)

děng 等 as soon as, once (13-2)

děng huǐr 等会儿 in a little while (15-2)

Dèng 邓 Deng (surname) (14-2)

dǐ 底 bottom, base; ground (22-2R)

dǐxia 底下 underneath (22-2R)

Dì'èrcì Shìjiè Dàzhàn 第二次世界大战 World War II (22-2R)

dì'èrshēng 第二声 second tone (14-1R)

dìlǐ 地理 geography (20-2R)

dìqū 地区 area, district, region, zone (16-1R)

dìsānshēng 第三声 third tone (14-1R)

dìsìshēng 第四声 fourth tone (14-1R)

dìtiě 地铁 subway (1-2)

dìtú 地图 map (3-2, 14-1R)

dìxiàshì 地下室 basement (21-1R)

Dì'yīcì Shìjiè Dàzhàn 第一次世界大战 World War I (22-2R)

dìyīshēng 第一声 first tone (14-1R)

diǎn 点 (pattern for decimals) (19-2)

diǎn 点 count, check (4-2)

diǎn 点 order, choose (7-1)

diǎncài 点菜 order dishes of food (7-1)

diàn 店 shop, store (2-1)

diàn 电 electricity (14-2)

diànfèi 电费 electricity fee (14-2, 24-2R)

diànshì 电视 television (22-1, 22-1R)

diànshì jìzhě 电视记者 television reporter (22-1R)

diànshì jiémù 电视节目 television program (22-1, 22-1R)

diànshìjī 电视机 television set, TV set (22-1R)

diànshìtái 电视台 television station (22-1, 22-1R)

diànyǐng(r) 电影 movie (20-1, 20-1R)

diànyǐng míngxīng 电影明星 movie star (20-2)

diànyǐngyuàn 电影院 movie theater (20-1, 23-1R)

diào 掉 fall, drop; lose, misplace (24-1, 24-1R)

diàozi 调子 tune, melody (19-1)

Dīng 丁 Ding (surname) (18-1)

dìng 定 reserve, book (8-1); settle, decide (13-1)

diū 丢 lose (24-1)

Dōngběi 东北 the Northeast, Manchuria (8-2)

dōngbù 东部 eastern part (20-2R)

dǒng 懂 understand (19-2R)

dòng 栋 (measure for buildings (2-1)

dòng 洞 hole (24-2)

dòufu 豆腐 tofu (7-1)

dú 读 read aloud; study (3-1, 23-2R)

dúshū 读书 study (3-1, 23-2R)

dúzhě 读者 reader (23-2R)

duǎn 短 be short (not long) (6-2)

duǎnkù 短裤 short pants (6-2)

duì 对 to, toward (8-2); pair off against (22-1)

duì 队 team, group (21-1, 21-1R)

duì...gǎn xìngqu 对···感兴趣 be interested in (13-1, 13-1R)

duì...lái shuō 对···来说 as regards, for, to (21-2)

duì...shúxi 对···熟悉 be familiar with (8-2)

duì...yǒu xìngqu 对···有兴趣 be interested in (13-1R)

duì...yǒu yánjiū 对···有研究 have expertise in (19-2R)

duì-dá-rú-liú 对答如流 reply to questions fluently (18-1)

duìmiàn 对面 across (1-2)

duìzhé 对折 50% discount (6-2)

dùn 顿 (for meals) (11-1)

duō jiǔ 多久 for how long? (1-2R)

duō kuī 多亏 be thanks to (18-1)

duō xiè 多谢 "many thanks" (4-1)

duōshù 多数 majority (12-1R)

duǒ 躲 dodge, avoid (24-2)

E

ěxin 恶心 be nauseous, feel like vomiting (23-1)

è 饿 be hungry (10-2)

èi 欸 yeah (2-2)

ér 而 also, and, yet, but, moreover (11-1R)

érqiě 而且 moreover, and, also (11-1R)

éryǐ 而已 only, and that is all (11-1R)

F

fā 发 put forth, issue, distribute (24-2R)

fāmíng 发明 invent; invention (24-2R)

fāpiào 发票 itemized bill; receipt (6-2, 24-2R)

fāshāo 发烧 have a fever (23-1)

fāshēng 发生 happen (24-2, 24-2R)

fāxiàn 发现 discover; discovery (24-2R)

fāyīn 发音 pronunciation (18-1, 24-2R)

fázi 法子 way, method (3-1R)

fǎ 法 way, method (3-1R)

Fǎguo 法国 France (3-1R)

Fǎguo rén 法国人 French person (3-1R)

Fǎwén 法文 written French (3-1R)

Fǎyǔ 法语 French (language) (4-2R)

fānqié 蕃茄 tomato (4-1)

fànguǎn(r) 饭馆 restaurant (7-1, 12-2R)

fànwǎn 饭碗 rice bowl (7-1)

fāngbian 方便 be convenient (14-2)

fāngyán 方言 dialect (4-2R)

fáng 房 house; room; (surname) (2-1R)

fángjiān 房间 room (2-1R)

fàng 放 put; let go, set free (1-1R, 7-2)

fàngjià 放假 take a vacation (21-2, 21-2R)

fàngxīn 放心 be at ease, relax (1-1, 1-1R)

fángzi 房子 house (2-1, 2-1R)

fángzū 房租 rent (14-2)

fēi 非 not; Africa (9-1R)

fēi 飞 fly (17-1R)

fēi...bù kě 非···不可 must (23-2)

fēicháng 非常 extremely (9-1, 9-1R)

fēijī 飞机 airplane (17-1R)

fēijīchǎng 飞机场 airport (17-1R)

fēixīyān qū 非吸烟区 non-smoking section (16-1, 16-1R)

féi 肥 be fatty (of food) (5-1)

Fèichéng 费城 Philadelphia (24-2R)

fèi 肺 lung (23-1)

fèi 费 spend; expense; (surname) (24-2R)

fèiyán 肺炎 pneumonia (23-1)

fèiyòng 费用 expenses, cost, fee (24-2R)

fēn 分 divide, separate (8-1); part, fraction (19-2)

fēnchéng 分成 divide into (8-1)

fēnjī 分机 extension (13-2)

fēnzhī 分之 (for fractions) (19-2)

fèn(r) 份 (for newspapers, magazines) (3-2)

fēng 风 wind (8-2R)

fēngfù 丰富 be abundant (10-1)

fēngshèng 丰盛 be sumptuous (12-2)

fēngwèi(r) 风味 local taste; special flavor (8-2, 8-2R)

fū 夫 man; husband (10-1R)

fūren 夫人 madam, lady; another's wife (9-1, 10-1R)

fú 服 clothing (6-2R)

fúwù 服务 serve (11-1R)

fúwù shè 服务社 service club (21-2R)

fúwùyuán 服务员 attendant, waiter, waitress (11-1, 11-1R)

fù 付 pay (11-1)

fù 父 father (18-2R)

fùjìn 附近 in the vicinity (5-1)

fùmǔ 父母 parents (18-2R)

fùmǔqīn 父母亲 parents (19-2R)

fùqián 付钱 pay money (11-1)

fùqīn 父亲 father (19-2R)

G

gāi 该 should, ought (6-2R)

gǎi 改 change; correct (11-1, 11-1R)

gǎicuò 改错 correct mistakes (11-1R)

gǎiháng 改行 change one's line of work (11-1R)

gǎitiān 改天 on some other day (11-1, 11-1R)

gānbēi 干杯 drink a toast; "Bottoms up" (9-2)

gǎn 感 respond; feel (10-1R, 13-1); touch, move (20-2)

gǎn 敢 dare (11-2, 11-2R)

gǎn 赶 rush, make a dash for (23-2R)

gǎndào 赶到 rush to a place (23-2R)

gǎnkuài 赶快 quickly (23-2, 23-2R)

gǎnmào 感冒 catch cold (23-1)

gǎnxiè 感谢 thank (9-1, 10-1R)

gàn 干 do (20-1)

gāngcái 刚才 just now, just (11-1)

gānghǎo 刚好 just, as it happens (6-2)

gāngqín 钢琴 piano (19-1)

gāngqínjiā 钢琴家 pianist (20-1)

gāogēn(r)xié 高跟鞋 high-heel shoes (6-1, 6-1R)

gāojí 高级 be high-class (8-1)

gào 告 tell (13-2R)

gàobié 告别 bid farewell (18-1)

gàocí 告辞 take leave (16-2)

gàosu 告诉 tell (2-1, 13-2R)

gē(r) 歌 song (19-1, 19-1R)

gébì 隔壁 next door (3-2)

gè- 各 each, every (9-2, 9-2R)

gèguó 各国 each country; various countries (9-2R)

gèwèi 各位 each person (polite) (9-2R)

gèzi 个子 height, stature, build (21-1)

gēn 跟 with, and; heel (2-1R)

gēn(r) 根 (for long, thin things) (3-1, 3-1R)

gēn...jiǎng 跟⋯讲 tell (2-1, 2-1R)

gēn...shuō 跟⋯说 tell; repeat (2-1, 2-1R)

gēnběn 根本 basically, fundamentally (3-1R)

gèng 更 even more, more (10-1R)

gōng 功 merit; achievement (21-1R)

gōngchē 公车 public bus (1-2)

gōngchǐ 公尺 meter (2-1)

gōngfū 功夫 kung fu (21-1, 21-1R)

gōngfu 工夫 time (17-1)

gōngjīn 公斤 kilogram (4-1R)

gōngjìng bù rú cóng mìng 恭敬不如从命 show respect is not as good as follow orders (11-2)

gōngkè 功课 homework; schoolwork (21-1R)

gōnglǐ 公里 kilometer (22-2)

gōngshēng 公升 liter (2-2)

gōngshìbāo 公事包 briefcase, attaché case (4-2R)

gōngyòng 公用 public (2-1, 7-1R)

gōngyòng cèsuǒ 公用厕所 public toilet (2-1)

gōngyòng diànhuà 公用电话 public telephone (2-1, 7-1R)

gōngyù 公寓 apartment (14-1)

gōngyuán 公园 park (21-1)

Gòngchǎn Zhǔyì 共产主义 Communism (18-1R)

gònghéguó 共和国 republic (19-2)

gòu 够 be enough (7-1, 7-1R); reach (12-1)

gòu...-de 够⋯的 quite, rather (22-2)

gòubuzháo 够不着 be unable to reach (12-1)

gòudezháo 够得着 be able to reach (12-1)

gūjì 估计 reckon, estimate (8-1)

gù 故 cause, reason; therefore (20-1R)

gùshi 故事 story (20-1, 20-1R)

guā 刮 scrape (15-1)

guā húzi 刮胡子 shave (15-1)

guà 挂 hang, hang up (13-2, 13-2R)

guà diànhuà 挂电话 hang up phone; make phone call (13-2R)

guài 怪 blame; be strange (19-1R)

guài...-de 怪⋯的 quite, rather (24-2)

guàibudé 怪不得 no wonder (19-1, 19-1R)

guān 观 look at (19-1R)

guānxi 关系 relationship, connection (7-2R, 16-1)

guānyú 关于 about, concerning (17-2, 17-2R)

guǎn 管 control, manage; (surname) (15-1R)

guǎn 馆 establishment; hotel; restaurant (12-2R)

guǎnzi 馆子 restaurant (12-2, 12-2R)

guàn 惯 be used to, accustomed to (9-2R)

guǎnggào 广告 advertisement (14-1)

guìtái 柜台 counter (5-2)

guóhuà(r) 国画 Chinese painting (19-1, 19-1R)

guójì 国际 international (13-1, 13-1R)

guójì guānxi 国际关系 international relations (13-1R)

guójì hépíng 国际和平 international peace (13-1R)

Guójì Jùlèbù 国际俱乐部 International Club (13-1)

guójì xuéxiào 国际学校 international school (13-1R)

guójiā 国家 country (24-1)

Guóyǔ 国语 Mandarin (1-1, 4-2R)

Guóyǔ Zhōngxīn 国语中心 Mandarin Center (23-2)

Guóyuè shè 国乐社 Chinese music club (21-2R)

guǒ 果 fruit (4-2R)

guǒzhī 果汁 juice (12-2)

guò mǎlù 过马路 cross the road (24-2)

guòlai 过来 come over (6-2)

guòqu 过去 go over, pass by (6-2)

-guo 过 (expresses completed action) (11-1)

H

hái 孩 child (15-1R)

hái bú shi 还不是 if it isn't (17-1)

háishi 还是 or (3-1)

háizi 孩子 child (15-1R)

hǎi 海 ocean, sea (11-2)

hǎiliàng 海量 great capacity to drink liquor (11-2, 11-2R)

hài 嗨 "hi" (11-1); (indicates exasperation) (13-1)

hánjià 寒假 winter vacation (21-2)

hàn 和 with (5-2); and (21-1)

Hàn-Yīng 汉英 Chinese-English (3-2)

hǎo 好 very (1-2)

hǎo jiǔ 好久 for a very long time (1-2R)

hǎo jiǔ bú jiàn 好久不见 "long time no see" (1-2R)

hǎo lei 好嘞 "all right," "O.K." (7-2)

hǎohàn 好汉 brave man (22-2)

hǎotīng 好听 be nice-sounding, pretty (19-1)

hàomǎ(r) 号码 number (6-1)

hē 喝 drink (7-2, 7-2R)

hēchá 喝茶 drink tea (12-2R)

hēzuì 喝醉 get drunk (9-2)

hé 合 be in accord with (24-2R)

hé 河 river (11-2)

héliú 河流 rivers (16-2R)

héshēn 合身 be well-fitting (of clothes) (24-2R)

héshì 合适 be the right size, fit (6-2)

hésuàn 合算 be worthwhile, reasonable (in price) (24-2, 24-2R)

hézuò 合作 cooperate; cooperation (24-2R)

hēi 黑 black (6-1R)

Hēirén 黑人 Black (person) (6-1R)

hēisè 黑色 the color black (6-1R)

hēng 哼 hum (19-1)

hóng 红 be red (14-1R)

hóngjiǔ 红酒 red wine (14-1R)

hóngsè 红色 the color red (14-1R)

hòu 厚 be thick (10-1)

hòu 后 after (18-2)

hú 湖 lake (11-2)

hútòng(r) 胡同 small street, alley (5-1)

húzi 胡子 beard, moustache (15-1)

hù 护 protect, guard (23-2R)

hùzhào 护照 passport (23-2, 23-2R)

huā 花 spend (17-1)

huā(r) 花 flower (14-2, 14-2R)

huācǎo 花草 flowers and grass (14-2R)

huāqián 花钱 spend money (17-1)

huá 华 China (19-2R)

Huárén 华人 Chinese person; Chinese people (19-2R)

huà 划 plan (20-1R)

huà 化 change; melt (16-2R)

Huà 华 Hua (surname) (19-2R)

huà 画 paint (19-1, 19-1R)

huà(r) 画 painting (19-1)

huàhuà(r) 画画 paint (19-1)

huàhuà(r) 画画 paint (19-1R)

huàjiā 画家 painter (artist) (20-1)

huàxué 化学 chemistry (16-2R)

huài 坏 be bad (13-1, 13-1R)

huānyíng guānglín 欢迎光临 welcome (polite) (2-2)

huáng 黄 be yellow; (surname) (14-1R)

Huáng Hǎi 黄海 Yellow Sea (14-1R)

Huáng Hé 黄河 Yellow River (14-1R)

huángsè 黄色 the color yellow (14-1R)

huídào 回到 come back to (11-2)

huílai 回来 come back (11-2)

huíqu 回去 go back (11-2)

huíxìn 回信 respond with a letter (18-2R)

huì 会 gathering, meeting (13-1)

huì...-de 会…的 be likely to, would, will (5-2)

húnshēn 浑身 entire body (23-1)

huó 活 to live; alive (9-1R)

huǒ 火 fire (24-1R)

huǒchē 火车 train (24-1R)

huǒshān 火山 volcano (24-1R)

huǒshānkǒu 火山口 crater of a volcano (24-1R)

huò 或 or (1-2, 1-2R)

huòshi 或是 or (1-2, 1-2R)

huòzhě 或者 or (1-2R)

J

jī 绩 achievement, accomplishment (17-2R)

jī 鸡 chicken (5-1)

jīdàn 鸡蛋 chicken egg (7-1)

jīdàn tāng 鸡蛋汤 egg soup (7-1)

jīròu 鸡肉 chicken meat (5-1)

jí 急 be in a hurry; be worried, nervous, excited (7-2R, 15-1, 23-2)

jí 及 and; reach (10-1R)

jí 极 utmost, very, extremely (5-1R)

-jíle 极了 extremely (5-1, 5-1R)

jíshì 急事 urgent matter (7-2, 7-2R)

jǐ 己 self (8-2R)

jì 既 since (15-2R)

jì 寄 send (18-2)

jì 记 record (13-2)

jì 际 border, boundary, edge (13-1R)

jì 计 calculate; plan; (surname) (20-1R)

jìchéngchē 计程车 taxi (1-1)

jìhua 计划 plan (20-1, 20-1R)

jìrán 既然 since (15-2, 15-2R)

jìrán...jiù 既然···就 since (15-2, 15-2R)

jìsuànjī 计算机 computer; calculator (20-1R)

jìxialai 记下来 write down, note down (13-2)

jìzhě 记者 reporter, journalist (1-2R)

jìzhě tuán 记者团 reporters group (21-2R)

jiā 加 add (2-2R)

jiā 夹 pick up (with chopsticks) (10-1)

jiācài 夹菜 pick up food (with chopsticks) (10-1)

jiācháng cài 家常菜 home-style cooking (12-2)

jiājù 家具 furniture (2-1, 2-1R)

jiājù diàn 家具店 furniture store (2-1, 2-1R)

jiāmǎn 加满 fill up (2-2, 2-2R)

Jiā'nádà 加拿大 Canada (3-1R)

Jiā'nádà rén 加拿大人 Canadian person (3-1R)

jiārù 加入 join (21-2)

jiāyóu 加油 add gasoline, refuel; "Hang in there!" (2-2, 2-2R)

jiāyóuzhàn 加油站 gas station (2-2, 2-2R)

Jiāzhōu 加州 California (2-2R)

jiǎ 假 false; if (21-2R)

jiǎrú 假如 if (6-2, 21-2R)

jiǎrú...-de huà 假如···的话 if (6-2, 21-2R)

jià 假 vacation, leave (21-2, 21-2R)

jià 价 price (2-2R)

jiàmùbiǎo 价目表 price list (22-1R)

jiàqián 价钱 price (2-2, 2-2R)

jiàrì 假日 holiday, day off (21-2, 21-2R)

jiān 间 (for rooms) (14-1)

jiǎn 检 examine (24-1R)

jiǎn 简 simple; (surname) (9-1R)

jiǎn 剪 cut (14-2)

jiǎncǎo 剪草 mow the lawn (14-2)

jiǎnchá 检查 inspect, examine; inspection (24-1, 24-1R)

jiǎndān 简单 be simple (9-1, 9-1R)

jiǎndào 捡到 pick up (24-1)

jiǎntǐzì 简体字 simplified character (17-2R)

jiàn 见 see (1-2, 1-2R)

jiàn 建 build, establish (22-2, 22-2R)

jiànchéng 建成 build to completion, construct (22-2R)

jiànkāng 健康 health (9-2)

jiāng 姜 ginger (10-2)

jiāng 将 will, be about to; take (20-1R)

jiānglái 将来 in the future (20-1, 20-1R)

jiǎng 讲 speak, say, explain; tell the story of (2-1R, 20-1)

jiǎng jiàqián 讲价钱 discuss price, bargain (2-2R)

jiǎng xiàohua 讲笑话 tell a joke (10-1R)

jiǎnghuà 讲话 speak (2-1R)

jiǎngjià 讲价 discuss price, bargain (2-2R)

jiàng 酱 thick sauce (10-1)

jiàngyóu 酱油 soy sauce (10-2)

jiāo 教 teach (18-2R)

jiāoliú 交流 exchange; interaction (16-2R)

jiāoshū 教书 teach (18-2R)

jiāowài 郊外 countryside around a city (21-2)

jiǎozi 饺子 dumpling (10-2)

jiào 教 teach; teaching; religion (18-2R)

jiàoshì 教室 classroom (14-2, 21-1R)

jiào-xué-yǒu-fāng 教学有方 have an effective method in teaching (18-2, 18-2R)

jiàoyù 教育 education (21-2, 21-2R)

jiàoyuán 教员 instructor (18-2R)

jiē 街 street (15-2)

jiē 接 receive, meet, welcome (11-2R)

jiē diànhuà 接电话 take a phone call (11-2R)

jiēfēng 接风 give a welcome dinner (11-2, 11-2R)

jié 结 tie; knot (24-2R)

jié 节 restrict, control; economize (5-2R)

jiéguǒ 结果 as a result, in the end; result (18-2, 24-2, 24-2R)

jiémù 节目 program (22-1, 22-1R)

jiéshěng 节省 be frugal, thrifty; save (5-2, 5-2R)

jiéyùn 捷运 mass rapid transit, MRT (1-2)

jiě 解 loosen (1-1R)

jiějué 解决 solve, resolve (1-1, 1-1R)

jiè 界 boundary; circles (22-1R)

jiè 借 borrow; lend (24-1)

jièshūzhèng 借书证 library card (24-1)

jīn 斤 catty (about 1⅓ lbs.) (4-1, 4-1R)

jīnyú 金鱼 goldfish (11-1R)

jǐn 仅 only (10-1)

jǐn 紧 be tight, tense (12-1R)

jǐnzhāng 紧张 be nervous, intense (12-1R)

jìn 尽 to the very limit, exhaust; carry out (16-2R, 18-2)

jìn kě'néng 尽可能 exert maximum effort (16-2R)

jìn(r) 劲 energy (23-1)

jìn zérèn 尽责任 fulfill a responsibility (18-2R)

jìnbù 进步 progress (18-2)

jìnkǒu 进口 import (4-1)

jìnkuài 尽快 as fast as possible (16-2R)

jìnlì 尽力 do one's best (16-2, 16-2R)

jìnliàng 尽量 to the best of one's ability (16-2, 16-2R)

jìnrù 进入 enter, come in (5-2R)

Jīngjù 京剧 Peking opera (19-2)

jīnglǐ 经理 manager (20-2R)

jǐngchájú 警察局 police station (23-2)

jìng 敬 drink to (9-1)

jiū 究 study (19-2R)

jiǔ 久 be long (of time) (1-2R)

jiǔ 酒 liquor, wine, spirits (7-2, 7-2R)

jiǔliàng 酒量 capacity for drinking alcohol (11-2R)

jiù shì 就是 just, simply (16-2)

jiùmìng 救命 "help!" (24-1)

jiǔxí 酒席 banquet, feat (8-1, 8-1R)

júzi 橘子 orange (4-2)

jù 具 implement, tool (2-1R)

jù 句 phrase; sentence (9-1, 9-1R)

jùcān 聚餐 get together for meal (9-1)

jùchǎng 剧场 theater (19-2)

jùlèbù 俱乐部 club (13-1)

jùzi 句子 sentence (9-1, 9-1R)

juǎnqilai 卷起来 roll up (10-1)

juǎn 卷 roll up (10-1)

jué 决 decide (1-1R)

juédìng 决定 decide, determine; decision (1-1R)

K

kāfēi 咖啡 coffee (5-2)

kāi 开 turn on (22-1)

kāihuì 开会 hold or attend a meeting (13-2)

kāiyǎn 开演 begin to be shown (of a film) (20-2)

kàn 看 think, consider (2-2); call on, visit (16-1)

kànbào 看报 read a newspaper (3-2R)

kànbìng 看病 see a doctor (23-1)

kàndào 看到 see (2-1)

kàndǒng 看懂 understand by reading (19-2R)

kànjian 看见 see (4-2)

kànshū 看书 read (3-2R, 19-1)

kǎo 烤 bake, roast (9-2)

kǎo 考 take a test (17-1, 17-1R)

kǎoshì 考试 test, examination; take a test (17-1, 17-1R)

kǎoyā 烤鸭 roast duck (9-2)

kǎoyūn 考晕 become dizzy from testing (17-1)

kào 靠 depend on, lean on (22-2, 22-2R)

kě 渴 be thirsty (10-2)

kě'ài 可爱 be loveable, cute (12-1R)

kě bú shì 可不是 "that's for sure" (22-2)

kěkào 可靠 be reliable, dependable (22-2R)

Kěkǒu Kělè 可口可乐 Coca-Cola® (12-2R)

kělè 可乐 cola (12-2, 12-2R)

kěpà 可怕 be frightful, terrible, horrible (14-2R)

kěxiào 可笑 be laughable, funny (10-1R)

kè 课 lesson; class (12-2R)

kè 客 visitor, guest (9-2R)

Kèjiā huà 客家话 Hakka (language) (9-2R)

Kèjiā rén 客家人 Hakka (person) (9-2R)

kèqi 客气 be polite (10-2)

kèrén 客人 guest (9-2R)

kètīng 客厅 living room (12-2)

kōng 空 empty; air (13-1R)

kōngqì 空气 air, atmosphere (13-1R)

kōngtiáo 空调 air conditioning (14-1)

kòng(r) 空 free time (13-1, 13-1R)

kǒushuǐ 口水 saliva (4-2R)

kūlong 窟窿 hole (24-2)

kǔ 苦 be bitter (7-2)

kùzi 裤子 pants (6-2)

kuài 快 be fast, quick; soon, quickly (1-1R)

kuàilè 快乐 be happy (9-1, 12-2R)

kuàizi 筷子 chopsticks (7-1)

kuān 宽 be wide (22-2)

kuòjiàn 扩建 expand (22-2)

L

là 辣 be peppery hot (7-2)

làjiāo 辣椒 hot pepper (7-2)

la 啦 (combined form of le and a) (1-1)

lái 来 bring, give (4-2); (about to do something) (9-1); (verb substitute) (9-2)

lái diànhuà 来电话 call on the telephone (17-2)

-lái...-qù 来⋯去 back and forth, all over the place (2-1)

láibují 来不及 not have enough time (10-1R)

láidejí 来得及 have enough time (10-1R)

láiwǎn 来晚 come late (16-1)

láixìn 来信 send a letter (18-2; 18-2R)

lánqiú 篮球 basketball (21-1)

lǎo 老 be tough (of food) (11-1)

lǎo 老 very (12-2)

lǎonián 老年 old age (21-2)

lǎonián rén 老年人 old people (21-2)

lè 乐 cheerful, happy, joyful (12-2R)

le 了 (indicates action continuing up to the present) (1-1)

lèi 类 kind, type, category (20-2, 20-2R)

lei 嘞 (sentence final particle) (7-2)

lěngpán(r) 冷盘 cold dish (8-2)

lí(r) 梨 pear (4-1)

Lí Shān 梨山 Pear Mountain (4-1)

lǐ 理 pay attention to (20-2R)

lǐjiě 理解 understand; understanding (20-2, 20-2R)

lì 利 sharp; benefit (18-1R)

lì 力 strength; force (16-2R)

lì 立 stand; establish (14-1R)

lìdài 历代 successive dynasties (22-2)

lìkè 立刻 immediately (14-1, 14-1R)

lìliang 力量 strength, force (16-2R)

lìqi 力氣 strength, effort (16-2R)

lián 连 even; link, connect; (surname) (18-1, 18-1R)

lián...dōu 连⋯都 even (18-1, 18-1R)

lián...yě 连⋯也 even (18-1R)

liánxì 联系 contact (8-2)

liánxùjù 连续剧 soap opera, serial (22-1)

liǎng 两 ounce (50 grams) (7-2)

liàng 量 capacity, amount (11-2R)

liàng qiǎn 量浅 "capacity is shallow" (11-2)

liào 料 material (10-2R)

liàozi 料子 fabric (10-2R)

línqū 林区 forest region (16-1R)

línshí 临时 at the last minute (16-1)

lǐng 领 lead; head (14-1R)

lǐngshì 领事 consul (14-1R)

lǐngshìguǎn 领事馆 consulate (14-1R)

lìng 另 in addition; another (14-2R)

lìngwài 另外 in addition; another (14-2, 14-2R)

liú 流 flow (16-2R)

liú 留 keep; leave behind (8-2R); ask someone to stay (18-2)

Liú 刘 Liu (surname) (13-1)

liú húzi 留胡子 grow a beard or moustache (15-1)

liúbù 留步 "don't see me out" (16-2)

liúhuà(r) 留话 leave a message (13-2)

liúlì 流利 be fluent (18-1, 18-1R)

liúxià 留下 leave behind (8-2, 8-2R)

liúxué 留学 study abroad (8-2R)

liúxuéshēng 留学生 study abroad student (8-2R)

lóu 楼 building; floor (20-2R)

lóushàng 楼上 upstairs (20-2, 20-2R)

lóuxià 楼下 downstairs (20-2, 20-2R)

lǚxíng 旅行 travel; trip (13-2)

lǚxíngshè 旅行社 travel agency (13-2)

lùn 论 discuss, debate (17-2R)

lùnwén 论文 thesis, dissertation (17-2, 17-2R)

M

mā 妈 mom, mommy (7-1R)

māma 妈妈 mom, mommy (7-1R)

máfan 麻烦 be troublesome (15-2); trouble (18-1)

Málà Zábànr 辣杂拌儿 Sesame Hot Spicy Medley (12-1)

mámahūhū 马马虎虎 so-so; not too bad (17-2)

Mápó Dòufu 麻婆豆腐 Pockmarked Old Woman's Tofu (7-1)

mǎ 马 horse; (surname) (15-1R, 24-2)

mǎlù 马路 road (24-2)

mǎshàng 马上 immediately, right away (15-1R)

mǎyǐ 蚂蚁 ant (7-1)

Mǎyǐ Shàngshù 蚂蚁上树 Ants Climbing a Tree (7-1)

mà 骂 scold, curse (23-2)

mǎidān 买单 pay the check (11-1)

màidiào 卖掉 sell off (24-1R)

màiwán 卖完 finish selling, be sold out (1-2)

mán...de 蛮⋯的 quite (11-1)

mántou 馒头 steamed bun (7-2)

mǎn 满 be full; fill (2-2, 2-2R)

Mǎnrén 满人 Manchu (2-2R)

màn 慢 be slow (1-1, 1-1R)

màn yòng 慢用 "take your time eating" (12-1)

màn zǒu 慢走 "take care" (1-1R)

mànmān lái 慢慢来 take one's time (5-2)

mànpǎo 慢跑 jog; jogging (17-1R)

máng 忙 be busy with (15-1)

mánghuài 忙坏 extremely busy (13-1, 13-1R)

máo 毛 feather, hair, fur (21-1)

máoyī 毛衣 sweater (6-2R)

Méi 梅 Mei (surname) (22-2)

méi cuò 没错 that's right (24-1)

méi guānxi 没关系 "it doesn't matter" (7-2R)

méi shémme 没什么 you're welcome (24-1)

méi wèntí 没问题 there is no problem (1-1, 1-1R)

méi yìsi 没意思 be uninteresting (5-2R)

méiyou yòng 没有用 not have any use (19-2)

měi 每 every, each (8-1R)

Měiyǔ 美语 American English (4-2R)

Měiyuán 美元 U.S. dollar (8-1R)

mén 门 (for courses) (17-2)

ménqiánqīng 门前清 finish alcohol before leaving (12-2)

mèng 梦 dream (1-2)

mǐ 米 meter (7-2R)

mǐ 米 uncooked rice; (surname) (7-2, 7-2R)

mǐfàn 米饭 cooked rice (7-2, 7-2R)

mǐjiǔ 米酒 rice wine (7-2)

miǎnqiǎng 勉强 do with great effort, force (16-2)

miàn 面 flour; noodles (10-1)

miànbāo 面包 bread (5-1)

miànbāo diàn 面包店 bakery (5-1)

miào 庙 temple, shrine (2-1)

mín 民 people (19-2R)

Mínguó...nián 民国⋯年 year of the Republic (19-2R)

míng-bù-xū-chuán 名不虚传 have well deserved reputation (22-2)

míng jiào 名叫 be named (20-1)

míngbai 明白 understand (20-2)

Míngcháo 明朝 Ming Dynasty (22-2)

míngdān 名单 name list, list of names (9-1R)

míngtiān jiàn 明天见 "see you tomorrow" (1-2R)

míngxìnpiàn 明信片 postcard (18-2, 18-2R)

mótuōchē 摩托车 motorcycle (2-2)

Mò 莫 Mo (surname) (9-1)

mǔ 母 mother; female (18-2R)

mǔqīn 母亲 mother (19-2R)

mù 目 eye (22-1R)

Mùzhà 木栅 Muzha (1-2)

N

ná 拿 hold, take (3-1, 3-1R)

náguoqu 拿过去 take over (6-2)

náhǎo 拿好 hold well, hold firmly (3-1, 3-1R)

nálai 拿来 bring here (6-2)

náqu 拿去 take away (6-2)

náshànglái 拿上来 take up (13-2)

náshàngqu 拿上去 take up (13-2)

náxiaqu 拿下去 take down (13-2)

nǎiyóu 奶油 cream (3-1)

nánbù 南部 southern part (20-2R)

nándào...ma 难道⋯吗 don't tell me that (21-2)

Nánfēi 南非 South Africa (9-1R)

nánguài 难怪 no wonder (19-1R)

nánháir 男孩儿 boy (15-1R)

nánháizi 男孩子 boy (15-1R)

nào 闹 suffer (from an illness) (23-1)

nàobuhǎo 闹不好 suffer from an illness and not get better (23-1)

nǎrde huà 哪儿的话 "not at all" (18-2)

nèi 内 inside, within (6-2R)

nèirén 内人 one's wife (polite) (12-1)

nèiróng 内容 content (20-2)

nèixiàng 内向 be introverted (18-1R)

něixiē 哪些 which ones?, which? (3-2R, 21-1)

nèixiē 那些 those (3-2R, 23-2)

nèiyī 内衣 underwear (6-2R)

nèn 嫩 be tender (11-1)

nénglì 能力 ability, capability (16-2R)

niándài 年代 decade (20-1)

niándǐ 年底 end of the year (22-2R)

niánqīng rén 年轻人 young people (21-2)

niànshū 念书 study (3-1)

niú 牛 cow, ox; (surname) (5-1, 5-1R, 15-1)

niúròu 牛肉 beef (5-1, 5-1R)

niúyóu 牛油 butter (5-1R)

nòng 弄 do, make (15-2)

nònghǎo 弄好 fix, prepare, finish (15-2)

nǚháir 女孩儿 girl (15-1R)

nǚháizi 女孩子 girl (15-1R)

O

ó 哦 (indicates interest or excitement) (1-1)

ǒu'ěr 偶尔 once in a while, occasionally (21-1)

P

pà 怕 fear, be afraid of (7-2, 14-2R)

pái 排 row, line (20-2, 20-2R)

páiháng 排行 rank in a family (20-2R)

páiqiú 排球 volleyball (21-1R)

pánzi 盘子 dish, plate (8-2)

pǎo 跑 run (17-1, 17-1R)

pǎobù 跑步 run paces, run (17-1, 17-1R)

pǎodào 跑到 run to (23-2)

pǎodiào 跑掉 run away (23-2, 24-1R)

pǎolai 跑来 run over here, come over (17-1, 17-1R)

pǎolái pǎoqù 跑来跑去 run all over the place (17-1R)

pǎoqu 跑去 run over there (17-1, 17-1R)

pàochá 泡茶 steep tea, make tea (16-1)

péi 赔 compensate (24-2)

pèi 配 coordinate, arrange (8-2)

pèngmiàn 碰面 meet (21-2)

pí 皮 skin; leather (23-2R)

píbāo 皮包 purse (23-2, 23-2R)

pídài 皮带 belt (23-2R)

píjiǔ 啤酒 beer (7-2)

píxié 皮鞋 leather shoes (23-2R)

píxié chǎng 皮鞋厂 leather shoe factory (23-2R)

piān 篇 (for theses, reports, essays) (17-2)

piānzi 片子 film, movie (20-1)

piàn 骗 trick, deceive (23-2)

piàoliang 漂亮 be pretty, look nice (4-1)

píndào 频道 channel (22-1)

pǐn 品 goods, product (5-1R)

pīngpāngqiú 乒乓球 Ping-Pong (21-1)

píng 坪 (unit of area, 36 sq. ft.) (14-1)

píng 平 be flat, even; tied (22-1)

píng 瓶 bottle (7-2)

píngcháng 平常 usually, ordinarily (9-1R)

píngguǒ 苹果 apple (4-2)

píngzi 瓶子 bottle (7-2)

pò 破 break, tear, split (24-2, 24-2R)

pòfèi 破费 go to great expense (11-1, 24-2R)

pòhuài 破坏 destroy, damage (24-2R)

pútao 葡萄 grape (4-2)

pǔbiàn 普遍 be widespread, common (5-2)

Q

qīmò kǎoshì 期末考试 final examination (17-1)

qīzhōng kǎoshì 期中考试 mid-term examination (17-1, 17-1R)

qīzhōngkǎo 期中考 mid-term examination (17-1R)

qí 骑 ride, straddle (2-2)

qíguài 奇怪 be strange (1-2)

qǐchuáng 起床 get up from bed (14-2R)

qǐlái 起来 get up (21-2)

qìshuǐ(r) 汽水 soda (12-2)

qìwēn 气温 temperature (23-1)

qìyóu 汽油 gasoline (2-2, 2-2R)

qiānbǐ 铅笔 pencil (3-2)

qiānmíng 签名 sign one's name (24-1)

qiānyuē 签约 sign a lease (14-2)

qiánbāo 钱包 wallet (23-2)

qiǎn 浅 be shallow (11-2)

qiáng 墙 wall (14-2)

qiáng 强 be strong, powerful (surname) (22-1, 22-1R)

qiáo 瞧 look (24-2)

qiē 切 cut, slice (5-1, 5-1R)

qiě 且 moreover, and, also (11-1R)

qīn 亲 parent, relative; to kiss (19-2R)

qīnrén 亲人 family member (19-2R)

qíncài 芹菜 Chinese celery (4-1)

qīngcài 青菜 green vegetable (4-1)

qīngshēng 轻声 neutral tone (14-1R)

qíng 情 sentiment; situation, condition (16-1R)

qǐng shāo hòu 请稍候 "please wait briefly" (6-2)

qǐngjià 请假 request leave (21-2, 21-2R)

qǐngkè 请客 treat (11-1)

qióng 穷 be poor (4-2)

qiú 球 ball, globe (21-1, 21-1R)

qiúduì 球队 ball-playing team (21-1R)

qiúxié 球鞋 athletic shoes (21-1R)

qū 区 area, district, region (16-1, 16-1R)

qù 趣 interest; interesting (13-1R)

qúnzi 裙子 skirt (6-2)

R

ràng 让 let; make; cause (10-2R)

ràng nǐ jiǔ děngle 让你久等了 "made you wait long" (10-2R)

Rén 任 (surname) (18-2R)

réngōng 人工 manual labor (22-2)

rénlèi 人类 mankind, humanity (20-2R)

rénlèixué 人类学 anthropology (20-2R)

rèn 任 duty; bear (18-2R)

rèn 认 recognize; know; admit (9-2R)

rénmín 人民 people (19-2, 19-2R)

Rénmín Jùchǎng 人民剧场 People's Theater (19-2)

Rénmín Rìbào 人民日报 *People's Daily* (19-2R)

Rénmínbì 人民币 RMB (PRC currency) (24-1)

rènshi 认识 recognize; know (9-2R)

Rìyǔ 日语 Japanese (language) (4-2R)

róng 容 allow; appearance; contain; (surname) (16-2R)

róngyi 容易 be easy (16-2R)

ròu 肉 meat (5-1, 5-1R)

ròusī(r) 肉丝 meat shred (7-1)

rú 如 if; be like, equal (6-2R)

rúguǒ 如果 if (6-2R)

rúguǒ...de huà 如果⋯的话 if (6-2R)

rù 入 enter (5-2R)

rùkǒu 入口 entrance (5-2, 5-2R)

ruò 弱 be weak (22-1)

S

Sān Mín Zhǔyì 三民主义 Three Principles of the People (19-2R)

sè 色 color (6-1R)

sè xiāng wèir jùquán 色香味儿俱全 color, aroma, taste all complete (12-2)

shāfā 沙发 sofa (14-2)

shālā 沙拉 salad (4-1)

shālācài 沙拉菜 lettuce (4-1)

shānqū 山区 mountain region (16-1R)

shānshuǐ huà(r) 山水画 landscape painting (19-1R)

shāng 伤 wound, injury; injure, hurt (24-2R)

shàngcài 上菜 bring food to a table (7-2)

shàngjiē 上街 go out on the street (15-2)

shàngkè 上课 have class (12-2R)

shànglái 上来 come up (13-2)

shànglóu 上楼 go upstairs (16-2, 20-2R)

shàngqu 上去 go up (13-2)

shàngshì 上市 come on the market (6-1)

shàngyǎn 上演 begin to play (of a film) (20-1)

shāowēi 稍微 somewhat, slightly (2-1)

sháozi 勺子 spoon (7-1)

shé 蛇 snake (19-2)

shè 社 society, organization (21-2R)

shèhuì 社会 society (21-2, 21-2R)

shèhuì zhǔyì 社会主义 socialism (21-2R)

shèhuìxué 社会学 sociology (21-2R)

shètuán 社团 organization, club (21-2, 21-2R)

shemmede 什么的 and so on (5-2)

shēn 深 be deep; dark (of colors) (11-2, 11-2R)

shēn 身 body; oneself (17-2R)

shēnsè 深色 dark in color, dark-colored (11-2R)

shēntǐ 身体 body; health (17-2R)

shēng 声 sound; tone (14-1R)

shēngbìng 生病 become sick (17-1R, 23-1)

shēngcài 生菜 lettuce (4-1R)

shēngchǎn 生产 produce, manufacture (18-1, 18-1R)

shēngdiào 声调 one (14-1R)

shēnghuó 生活 life (9-1, 9-1R)

shēngrì kuàilè 生日快乐 happy birthday (12-2R)

shēngyīn 声音 sound; voice (14-1, 14-1R)

shèngxia 剩下 be left over (1-2)

Shīdà 师大 National Taiwan Normal University (23-2)

shīhuǒ 失火 fire breaks out (24-1)

shīmǔ 师母 wife of one's teacher (18-2, 18-2R)

shīpéi 失陪 "sorry to have to leave" (12-1)

shí 识 know; recognize (9-2R)

shí 食 eat (5-1R)

shí 石 rock, stone; (surname) (11-2R)

Shí 石 Shi (surname) (11-2)

shídài 时代 period (22-2)

shípǐn 食品 food product, groceries (5-1, 5-1R)

shípǐn diàn 食品店 grocery store (5-1, 5-1R)

shítou 石头 stone (11-2, 11-2R)

shǐ 使 send; envoy; use (15-2R)

shǐyòng 使用 use, employ (15-2R)

shì 室 room (21-1R)

shì 世 generation; world (22-1R)

shì 市 city, municipality (3-2)

shì 视 look at, regard, inspect (22-1R)

shì 试 try; test (3-2, 17-1R)

shì ma 是吗 "really?" (19-1)

shìde 是的 yes (14-1)

shìhào 嗜好 hobby; addiction (19-1)

shìjiè 世界 world (22-1, 22-1R)

Shìjiè Bēi 世界杯 World Cup (22-1)

shìjiè hépíng 世界和平 world peace (22-1R)

shìjiè yǒumíng 世界有名 be world-famous (22-1R)

shìnèi diànhuà 市内电话 local telephone call (13-1)

shìqing 事情 thing, matter (16-1, 16-1R)

shìshi kàn 试试看 try and see (17-1R)

shìyǒu 室友 roommate, dorm mate (21-1, 21-1R)

shōu 收 accept (6-2)

shǒu 手 hand (2-1, 2-1R)

shǒubiǎo 手表 wristwatch (6-2)

shǒuqiú shè 手球社 handball club (21-2R)

shòu 受 stand, endure; receive (7-2, 7-2R)

shòubuliǎo 受不了 can't stand, can't endure (7-2, 7-2R)

shòushāng 受伤 suffer injury, be hurt (24-2, 24-2R)

shū 书 book (3-2, 3-2R)

shū 赢 lose (not win) (22-1)

shūcài 蔬菜 vegetable (4-1)

shūdiàn 书店 book store (3-2, 3-2R)

shūfáng 书房 study (3-2R)

shūzhuō(r) 书桌 desk (14-2)

shúxi 熟悉 be familiar (8-2)

shǔjià 暑假 summer vacation (21-2)

shù 数 number, figure; several (12-1R)

shù 树 tree (7-1, 14-2R)

shùlín 树林 woods, forest (14-2R)

shùxué 数学 mathematics (12-1R)

shuākǎ 刷卡 imprint a credit card (6-2)

shuāng 双 pair (6-1, 6-1R)

shuānghào 双号 even number (6-1R)

shuāngrénchuáng 双人床 double bed (14-2R)

shuāngrénfáng 双人房 double room (6-1R)

shuǐ 水 water (4-2R, 12-2)

shuǐdiànfèi 水电费 water and electricity fee (14-2, 24-2R)

shuǐfèi 水费 water fee (14-2, 24-2R)

shuǐguǒ 水果 fruit (4-2, 4-2R)

shùnbiàn 顺便 conveniently, in passing (1-2)

shùnlì 顺利 be smooth (9-1)

shuō shízàide 说实在的 to tell the truth (18-2)

shuō xiàohua 说笑话 tell a joke (10-1R)

shuōbudìng 说不定 can't say for sure (24-2)

sī 思 think (5-2R)

sīliǎo 私了 settle privately (24-2)

Sīmǎ 司马 Sima (surname) (15-1R)

sǐdiào 死掉 die (24-1R)

Sìrénbāng 四人帮 Gang of Four (16-1R)

sìshēng 四声 the four tones (14-1R)

Sòng 宋 Song (surname) (16-1)

sòng 送 give; deliver; see someone off or out (15-2, 15-2R)

sònggěi 送给 give as a present (15-2R)

sù 诉 tell (13-2R)

suān 酸 be sour (7-2)

suàn 算 figure, calculate; consider as (6-1, 6-1R, 12-2)

suànle 算了 "forget about it" (24-2)

suànqián 算钱 calculate money, figure a price (6-1R)

suànshang 算上 include, count (22-2)

suànshù 算数 count (12-1R)

suī 虽 though, although (12-2R)

suīrán 虽然 although, though (12-2, 12-2R)

suīrán...dànshi 虽然···但是 although, though (12-2R)

suīrán...kěshi 虽然···可是 although, though (12-2R)

suí 随 follow; (surname) (7-1R)

suíbiàn 随便 as you wish; be casual (7-1, 7-1R)

suíyì 随意 "as you like" (11-2)

suìshu 岁数 age (12-1R)

T

tā 它 it (20-2R)

Táibì 台币 NT (Taiwan currency) (24-1)

Táiwān Yínháng 台湾银行 Bank of Taiwan (1-1)

tàijíquán 太极拳 taiji (21-1)

tán 谈 chat, talk (15-2, 15-2R)

tánhuà 谈话 talk, speak; conversation; statement (15-2, 15-2R)

tāng 汤 soup (7-1)

táng 堂 (for classes) (11-1)

Táng 唐 Tang (surname) (13-1)

Tángcù Lǐjī 糖醋里脊 Sweet and Sour Pork (12-1)

tǎng 躺 lie down (17-1)

táozi 桃子 peach (4-2)

tè 特 especially (2-2, 2-2R)

tèbié 特别 especially (2-2, 2-2R)

tèdì 特地 especially (12-1)

tèzhēng 特征 special characteristic (24-1)

téng 疼 be painful, hurt (23-1)

tí 提 mention (13-1, 13-1R)

tí 题 topic; problem (1-1R)

tíqián 提前 move up (a time or date) (13-1, 13-1R)

tíyì 提议 propose (9-2)

tǐ 体 body (17-2R)

tǐjiǎn 体检 physical examination (24-1R)

tǐyù 体育 physical education (21-2, 21-2R)

tǐyùguǎn 体育馆 gymnasium (21-2, 21-2R)

tì 替 for (11-2, 11-2R)

tì...jiēfēng 替···接风 give welcome dinner for (11-2R)

tì...zhàn yíge wèizi 替···占一个位子 hold a seat for (13-2R)

tiān 添 add (18-1)

tiānqi yùbào 天气预报 weather forecast (12-1R)

tián 甜 be sweet (7-2)

tiánmiànjiàng 甜面酱 sweet flour sauce (10-1)

tiánshí 甜食 dessert (8-2)

tiāo 挑 pick out, select (4-2)

tiáo 调 adjust; blend (10-2R)

tiáoliào 调料 condiment, seasoning (10-2, 10-2R)

tiáozhěng 调整 adjust (2-2, 21-2R)

Tiàoqí 跳棋 Chinese checkers (19-1)

tiàowǔ 跳舞 dance (21-2)

tiē 贴 stick (18-2)

tīngbutàimíngbai 听不太明白 can't understand very well (20-2)

tīngdào 听到 hear (4-2)

tīngdǒng 听懂 understand by hearing (19-2R)

tīngjian 听见 hear (4-2)

tīngqīngchu 听清楚 hear clearly (14-1)

tíng 停 stop (2-2R)

tíngchē 停车 stop a car; park a car (2-2, 2-2R)

tíngchēchǎng 停车场 parking lot (2-2, 2-2R)

tóng 同 with (8-2)

tóng...liánxì 同···联系 contact (8-2)

tóngshí 同时 at the same time (9-1)

tóngzhì 同志 comrade; gay person (23-1R)

Tǒngyī 统一 7-Eleven® (name of store) (1-2)

tǒngyī 统一 unite, unify (2-2)

tǒngyī biānhào 统一编号 unified serial number (2-2)

tōu 偷 steal; stealthily (23-2, 23-2R)

tōukàn 偷看 steal a glance at (23-2R)

tóu 头 head (23-1)

tūrán 突然 suddenly (16-2)

tú 图 drawing, map, chart (14-1R)

tú 涂 smear, daub (10-1)

túshūguǎn 图书馆 library (14-1R)

tǔ 土 earth (5-2R)

tǔdì 土地 soil, earth, land, territory (5-2R)

tǔsī 土司 white bread (5-2, 5-2R)

tù 吐 spit, throw up (23-1)

tuán 团 group; organization (21-2R)

tuántǐ 团体 group (21-2, 21-2R)

tuō 脱 take off (16-1)

tuōxié 脱鞋 take off shoes (16-1)

W

wà 哇 "wow" (10-2)

wàzi 袜子 sock (6-1)

wàigōng 外公 grandfather (15-1)

wàiguoyǔ 外国语 foreign language (4-2R)

Wàijiāo Bù 外交部 Foreign Ministry (20-2R)

wàipó 外婆 grandmother (15-1)

wàisūn 外孙 grandson (15-1)

wàisūnnǚ(r) 外孙女 granddaughter (15-1)

wàixiàng 外向 be extroverted (18-1R)

wán 完 finish, complete (1-2, 1-2R)

wánquán 完全 completely (6-1)

wǎn 碗 bowl (7-1)

wǎnhuì 晚会 evening party (22-1)

wǎnliú 挽留 urge someone to stay (15-2)

wànyī 万一 if by chance, in case (16-2)

wǎng 网 net (21-1)

wǎngqiú 网球 tennis (21-1)

wàng 望 hope; watch (15-2R)

wàngdiào 忘掉 forget (24-1R)

wēi 危 danger; (surname) (24-1R)

wēixiǎn 危险 be dangerous; danger (24-1R, 24-2)

Wéiqí 围棋 Go (19-1)

wèi 为 for (12-1)

Wèi 魏 Wei (surname) (11-2)

wèi 味 taste; smell; flavor (8-2R)

wèidao 味道 taste (9-2)

wèile 为了 in order to, for (5-2)

wèir 味儿 smell, aroma (12-1)

wén 闻 smell something (10-2)

wénhuà 文化 culture (16-2R)

wénhuà jiāoliú 文化交流 cultural exchange (16-2R)

wényì 文艺 literature and art (22-1)

wényì wǎnhuì 文艺晚会 variety show (22-1)

wèntí 问题 question; problem (1-1, 1-1R)

wòfáng 卧房 bedroom (17-1)

wòshì 卧室 bedroom (14-1)

wūzi 屋子 room (15-1)

wǔshù 武术 martial art (21-1)

wù 务 do; matter; (surname) (11-1R)

wùlǐ 物理 physics (20-2R)

X

xī 吸 inhale, breathe in (16-1, 16-1R)

xī 希 hope (15-2R)

xībù 西部 western part (20-2R)

Xīcān 西餐 Western-style food (8-1)

xīwàng 希望 hope (15-2R)

xīyān 吸烟 smoke (16-1, 16-1R)

xīyān qū 吸烟区 smoking section (16-1, 16-1R)

Xīyī 西医 Western medicine; Western doctor (23-1R)

xí 席 feast, banquet; (surname) (8-1R)

xí 习 practice; (surname) (9-2R)

xíguàn 习惯 be accustomed to; custom, habit (9-2R, 16-1)

xǐ 洗 wash (7-1)

xǐjù 喜剧 comedy (22-1)

xǐshǒujiān 洗手间 bathroom (7-1)

xì 系 department (3-1, 7-2R)

xiā 虾 shrimp (5-1)

xià 下 play (chess or checkers) (19-1)

xià 吓 frighten (1-1)

xiàkè 下课 end class (12-2R)

xiàlai 下来 come down (13-2)

xiàlóu 下楼 go downstairs (16-2, 20-2R)

xiàqí 下棋 play chess (19-1)

xiàqu 下去 go down (13-2)

xiàsǐ 吓死 frighten to death (1-1)

xiān-gān-wéi-jìng 先干为敬 drink bottoms up to show respect (11-2)

xiān...zài 先···再 first...then (10-1)

xiān zǒu yíbù 先走一步 "take one step first" (12-1, 12-1R)

xián 咸 be salty (7-2)

xiǎn 险 danger (24-1R)

xiàn 线 wire, line, thread (13-2R)

xiàn(r) 馅 filling (10-2)

xiànjīn 现金 cash (6-2)

xiāng 相 mutually (15-1R)

xiāngdāng 相当 rather, quite (15-1R)

xiāngjiāo 香蕉 banana (4-2)

xiāngshuǐ(r) 香水 perfume (4-2R)

xiāngxìn 相信 believe, believe in (18-2R)

xiāngyān 香烟 cigarette (16-1R)

xiāngyóu 香油 sesame oil (10-2)

xiángqilai 想起来 think of (16-2)

xiángxiang kàn 想想看 try and think (3-2R)

xiǎng 想 think; want to (3-2R)

xiǎngfǎ 想法 way of thinking, opinion (3-1R)

xiǎngyào 想要 want to, would like to (3-2R)

xiàng 像 resemble, be like (5-2)

xiàng 向 toward, to (18-1, 18-1R)

xiàng...gàobié 向···告别 bid farewell to (18-1R)

xiàng...wènhǎo 向...问好 convey regards to (18-2)

Xiàngqí 象棋 Chinese chess (19-1)

xiàngzi 巷子 lane (2-1)

xiǎo bìng 小病 minor illness (17-1R)

xiǎo háizi 小孩子 small child (9-1, 15-1R)

xiǎo nánshēng 小男生 young male student, little boy (6-2)

xiǎo nǚshēng 小女生 little girl (6-2)

xiǎo péngyou 小朋友 little friend, child (15-1)

xiǎo shēng 小声 in a low voice; quietly (14-1, 14-1R)

xiǎobiàn 小便 urinate; urine (7-1R)

xiǎochī 小吃 snack (12-1)

xiǎode 晓得 know (1-2)

xiǎodòu 小豆 red bean (3-1)

xiǎofèi 小费 tip, gratuity (24-2R)

xiǎohái(r) 小孩 child (15-1R)

xiǎokǎo 小考 quiz (17-1R)

xiǎoshuō(r) 小说 novel (book) (19-1)

xiǎoshuōjiā 小说家 novelist (20-1)

xiǎotōu 小偷 thief (23-2, 23-2R)

xiào 笑 laugh, laugh at (10-1R)

xiàoduì 校队 school team (21-1, 21-1R)

xiàohua 笑话 joke; laugh at, ridicule (10-1R)

xiē 些 some (3-2, 3-2R)

xié 鞋 shoe (6-1R)

xiéchǎng 鞋厂 shoe factory (6-1R)

xiédiàn 鞋店 shoe store (6-1R)

xīn 新 be new, fresh (20-1R)

xīn nián 新年 New Year (20-1R)

Xīn nián kuàilè 新年快乐 "Happy New Year!" (20-1R)

xīnkǔ 辛苦 endure hardship (12-2)

xīnlǐxué 心理学 psychology (20-2R)

xīnlǐxuéjiā 心理学家 psychologist (20-2R)

xīnqíng 心情 mood, state of mind (16-1R)

xīnwén 新闻 news (22-1)

xīnxiān 新鲜 be fresh (4-1)

xìn 信 letter; have faith in, believe; (surname) (18-2, 18-2R)

xìnyòng 信用 credit; trustworthiness (18-2R)

xìnyòngkǎ 信用卡 credit card (6-2)

xìngqu 兴趣 interest (13-1, 13-1R)

xiū 修 build, repair; study, take (a course) (17-2, 22-2, 22-2R, 24-2)

xiūchē 修车 repair a vehicle (24-2)

xiūchēfèi 修车费 cost of repairing a vehicle (24-2, 24-2R)

xiūjiàn 修建 build, construct (22-2R)

xiūqilai 修起来 in the building of something (22-2R)

xūyào 需要 need (6-1)

xǔ 许 permit; (surname) (23-1R)

xuǎn 选 choose, select (17-2)

xuéfēn 学分 credit hour (17-2)

xuéqī 学期 semester, term (17-2)

xuéqī bàogào 学期报告 term paper (17-2)

xuéshēngzhèng 学生证 student I.D. (24-1)

xuéxí 学习 learn, study; study, studies (9-2R)

xuéyuán 学员 student (11-1R)

Y

yā zhēn'gān(r) 鸭胗肝 duck gizzard and liver (9-2)

yājīn 押金 deposit (14-2)

Yālí(r) 鸭梨 Ya pear (4-2)

yāròu 鸭肉 duck meat (5-1)

yāzi 鸭子 duck (5-1)

yān 烟 tobacco, cigarette; smoke (16-1, 16-1R)

yán 严 be stern, severe ; (surname) (15-1R)

yán 盐 salt (10-2)

yán 研 grind; study (19-2R)

yán 言 speech, word (4-2R)

yánjiū 研究 study, research (19-2R)

yánjiūshēng 研究生 graduate student (19-2R)

yánjiūsuǒ 研究所 graduate school (19-2R)

yánjiūyuàn 研究院 research institute; graduate school (23-1R)

yánzhòng 严重 be serious, grave (15-1R)

yǎn 眼 eye (18-1R)

yǎnyuán 演员 actor (20-2)

yáng 羊 sheep (5-1)

yángròu 羊肉 mutton (5-1)

yàng 样 kind, variety (3-1)

yàngr 样儿 appearance, shape (24-2)

yāo 约 weigh out (4-2)

yào bú shi 要不是 if not, if it weren't for (18-2)

yàoburán 要不然 otherwise, or (1-2)

yàojǐn 要紧 be important (1-1, 12-1R)

yěxǔ 也许 perhaps, maybe (23-1, 23-1R)

yè 业 business, industry, study (3-1R)

Yè 叶 Ye (surname) (24-1)

yī 医 medical doctor; heal (23-1R)

yī 衣 clothing; (surname) (6-2R)

yī...bǐ yī 一···比一 one...compared with the next (5-2)

yī...jiù 一···就 as soon as (13-2)

yīfu 衣服 clothes (6-2, 6-2R)

yīguì 衣柜 clothes closet (14-2)

yīshēng 医生 medical doctor (20-1, 23-1R)

yīxué 医学 medicine, medical science (23-1R)

yīxuéyuàn 医学院 medical school (23-1R)

yīyuàn 医院 hospital (23-1, 23-1R)

yíkuài(r) 一块 together (11-1)

yílù píng'ān 一路平安 "have a good trip" (24-2)

yíyàng 一样 one kind; the same (6-1)

yǐ 以 take (12-2)

yǐ A dài B 以A代B substitute A for B (12-2, 12-2R)

yǐbiàn 以便 so that, in order to (8-2)

yǐjí 以及 and (10-1, 10-1R)

yǐnèi 以内 within (6-2, 6-2R)

yì 义 righteousness (18-1R)

yì 意 meaning, intention (5-2R)

yì 易 change; easy (surname) (16-2R)

yì-yán-wéi-dìng 一言为定 be agreed with one word (13-1)

yìbiān(r) 一边 on the one hand (15-2)

yìbiān(r) A yìbiān(r) B 一边A一边B do B while doing A (15-2)

Yìdàlì 意大利 Italy (18-1R)

Yìdàlìyǔ 意大利语 Italian language (18-1R)

yìdiǎn(r) xiǎo yìsi 一点小意思 gift (16-1)

yìdiǎn(r) yě bù 一点也不 not the least bit (5-1)

yìhuǐr jiàn 一会儿见 "see you in a little while" (2-1)

yìsi 意思 meaning (5-2R); intention (16-1)

yìxiē 一些 some (3-2R, 14-2)

yìzhí 一直 always, all along (9-2)

yīn 音 sound (13-1R)

yīnyuè 音乐 music (13-1, 13-1R)

yīnyuèhuì 音乐会 concert (13-1, 13-1R)

yīnyuèjiā 音乐家 musician (20-1)

yínháng 银行 bank (1-1)

yínhángjiā 银行家 banker (20-1)

yīng 应 should, ought (6-2R, 18-2)

yīng 英 hero; England, English; (surname) (23-1R)

yīngdāng 应当 should, ought (10-2R)

yīnggāi 应该 should, ought (6-2R)

yīnggāide 应该的 something one ought to do (24-1)

Yīnggélán 英格兰 England (22-1)

Yīngguo 英国 Britain, England (23-1R)

Yīngguo rén 英国人 citizen of England (23-1R)

yīnglǐ 英里 mile (22-2, 23-1R)

Yīngwén 英文 English language (23-1R)

Yīngyǔ 英语 English language (23-1R)

yíng 赢 win (22-1)

yǐng 影 shadow; image; film (20-1R)

yòng 用 use; with; need to (7-1, 7-1R)

yòngbuzháo 用不着 not need to (23-1)

yònggōng 用功 be hardworking, studious (21-1R)

yóu 油 oil; gasoline (2-2, 2-2R)

yóu 由 by; from (8-2, 8-2R)

yóujià 油价 price of gasoline (2-2, 2-2R)

yóujú 邮局 post office (2-1)

yóupiào 邮票 stamp (18-2)

yóuyǒng 游泳 swimming; swim (21-1)

yǒu yìdiǎn(r) 有一点 be a little (17-1)

yǒu yìsi 有意思 be interesting (5-2R)

yǒukòng(r) 有空 have free time (13-1, 13-1R)

yǒumíng 有名 be famous (22-1)

yǒuqián 有钱 be rich (4-2)

yǒuyòng 有用 be useful (19-2)

yòushǒu 右手 right hand (2-1, 2-1R)

yòushǒubiān 右手边 right-hand side (2-1, 2-1R)

yòuyǎn 右眼 right eye (18-1R)

yú 于 be located at, in, on; (surname) (17-2R)

yú 鱼 fish (11-1R)

yúkuài 愉快 be happy (9-1)

yúròu 鱼肉 the flesh of a fish (11-1R)

Yúxiāng Ròusī 鱼香肉丝 Fish Fragrant Meat Shreds (7-1)

yǔ 语 language (4-2R)

yǔfǎ 语法 grammar (18-1)

yǔliàng 雨量 rainfall (11-2, 11-2R)

yǔmáo 羽毛 feather, plumage (21-1)

yǔmáoqiú 羽毛球 badminton (21-1)

yǔxié 雨鞋 rain shoes (6-1R)

yǔyán 语言 language (4-2R)

yǔyánxué 语言学 linguistics (4-2R)

yǔyī 雨衣 raincoat (6-2R)

yù 育 education (21-2R)

yù 预 prepare; in advance (12-1R)

yùbào 预报 forecast (12-1R)

yùbei 预备 prepare (12-1, 12-1R)

yùbei zhōngxué 预备中学 prep school (12-1R)

yùshì 浴室 bathroom (14-1)

yuán 元 yuan, dollar; (surname; name of a dynasty) (2-2, 8-1R)

yuán 员 member (11-1R)

yuánlái 原来 actually, so (21-2)

yuánzhūbǐ 圆珠笔 ball-point pen (3-2)

yuánzhùmín 原住民 native people (19-2R)

yuàn 院 courtyard; institute (23-1R)

yuàn 愿 wish, want (10-2R)

yuàn 怨 blame (24-2)

yuànyi 愿意 be willing to, like to (10-2, 10-2R)

yuànzi 院子 courtyard, yard (14-2, 23-1R)

yuè 月 moon (20-1)

yuè...yuè 越⋯越 the more...the more (9-2)

yuèdǐ 月底 end of the month (22-2R)

yuèkǎo 月考 monthly test (17-1R)

Yuènányǔ 越南语 Vietnamese (language) (4-2R)

yūn 晕 be dizzy (17-1)

yùn 运 move, transport (21-1R)

yùndòng 运动 sport, athletics, exercise (21-1, 21-1R)

yùndòng xié 运动鞋 athletic shoes (21-1R)

yùnqi 运气 luck (21-1R)

Z

záyīn 杂音 noise, static (14-1)

zázhì 杂志 magazine (3-2)

zài 再 again, further, more (1-2R)

zàijiàn 再见 "good bye" (1-2R)

zàizuò 在座 be present (at banquet or meeting) (9-2)

zámliǎ 咱俩 the two of us (24-2)

zámmen 咱们 we (you and I) (7-1)

zǎo jiù 早就 long ago (9-2)

zǎowǎn 早晚 morning and evening (23-1)

zé 责 duty, responsibility (18-2R)

zérèn 责任 responsibility (18-2, 18-2R)

zěmme huí shì(r) 怎么回事 "what's the matter?" (23-2)

zěmme zhèmme 怎么这么 how come so (4-1)

zěnme bàn 怎么办 "what should be done?" (3-1R)

Zhā 查 Zha (surname) (24-1R)

zhàn 占 occupy (13-2R)

zhàn 战 battle, war (22-2R)

Zhànguó Shídài 战国时代 Warring States Period (22-2, 22-2R)

zhànxiàn 占线 be busy (of a telephone line) (13-2, 13-2R)

zhànzhēng 战争 war (22-2, 22-2R)

zhànzhēngpiàn 战争片 war film (22-2R)

zhǎng 涨 rise, go up (2-2)

zháojí 着急 worry, get excited (7-2R)

zháoliáng 着凉 catch cold (23-1)

zhǎohuílai 找回来 find and get back (23-2)

zhào 照 shine; illuminate; take (photos) (19-1, 19-1R)

zhàogu 照顾 care; take care of (9-1)

zhàoxiàng 照相 take a photograph (19-1, 19-1R)

zhàoxiàngguǎn 照相馆 photo studio, photo shop (19-1R)

zhàoxiàngjī 照相机 camera (19-1R)

-zhě 者 person who does something (1-2R)

zhè 这 right away (15-1)

zhèixiē 这些 these (3-2, 3-2R)

zheige 这个 (pause filler) (16-1)

zhēng 争 compete; fight (22-2R)

zhěng 整 exact, sharp (of clock times) (21-2, 21-2R)

zhèng 证 evidence; proof (4-1R)

zhèng zài 正在 just be in the midst of (13-2)

zhènghǎo(r) 正好 just, as it happens (19-2)

zhèngjiàn 证件 identification paper (23-2)

zhī 支 (for pens, pencils) (3-2)

zhīnèi 之内 within (6-2, 6-2R)

zhí 直 be straightforward, frank (16-1)

zhí dào 直到 straight up to, until (17-1)

zhí shuō 直说 speak frankly (16-1)

zhǐ 纸 paper (3-2, 3-2R)

zhì 志 aspiration; ideal (23-1R)

zhōngbù 中部 central part (20-2R)

Zhōngcān 中餐 Chinese-style food (8-1)

Zhōngguo cài 中国菜 Chinese food (4-1R)

Zhōnghuá 中华 China (19-2)

Zhōnghuá Mínguó 中华民国 Republic of China (19-2, 19-2R)

Zhōnghuá Rénmín Gònghéguó 中华人民共和国 People's Republic of China (19-2, 19-2R)

zhōngjiān 中间 in the middle (10-1)

zhōngnián 中年 middle age (21-2)

zhōngnián rén 中年人 middle-aged people (21-2)

Zhōngyī 中医 Chinese medicine; Chinese doctor (23-1R)

zhōngyú 终于 finally, at last (22-2)

zhǒng 种 kind (3-2, 3-2R)

zhòng 种 plant (14-2)

zhòng 重 be heavy (15-1R)

Zhōu 周 Zhou (surname) (2-1)

zhōumò 周末 weekend (10-2)

zhū 猪 pig (5-1)

zhūròu 猪肉 pork (5-1)

zhǔ 煮 boil (10-2)

zhǔ 主 master, host, lord; main (5-2R)

zhǔkè 主客 main guest (9-2R)

zhǔrén 主人 host (9-2)

zhǔshí 主食 staple food, main food (7-2)

zhǔxí 主席 chairperson (8-1, 8-1R)

zhǔxiū 主修 major in; major (3-1, 22-2R)

zhǔyào 主要 mainly; essential, main (10-2; 20-2)

zhǔyì 主义 doctrine (18-1R)

zhǔyì 主意 idea, plan (5-2, 5-2R)

zhǔzhāng 主张 advocate (5-2R)

zhù 注 concentrate on (17-2R)

zhù 祝 wish (9-1)

zhùjiě 注解 annotation, explanatory note (17-2R)

zhùmíng 著名 be famous, well-known (20-1)

zhùyì 注意 pay attention to (2-1, 17-2R)

zhùyuàn 住院 be in a hospital, be hospitalized (23-1R)

zhuāzhù 抓住 catch hold of (23-2)

zhuān 专 special; expert (3-1R)

zhuānjiā lóu 专家楼 foreign experts building (20-2R)

zhuānyè 专业 major (in college) (3-1, 3-1R)

zhuānyuán 专员 specialist (11-1R)

zhuǎn 转 transfer (13-2)

zhuǎnchéng 转成 turn into (23-1)

zhuǎnjinlai 转进来 turn in (2-1, 2-1R)

zhuǎnxì 转系 transfer to another department (7-2R)

zhuǎnyǎn 转眼 glance; blink eyes; in the blink of an eye (18-1, 18-1R)

zhuǎn/zhuàn 转 turn, go around, revolve (2-1, 2-1R)

zhuàn 传 chronicle, biography (19-2)

zhuàn 赚 earn (17-1)

zhuànlái 转来 come turning around (2-1)

zhuànlái zhuànqù 转来转去 turn back and forth (2-1R)

zhuànqián 赚钱 earn money (17-1)

zhuànqù 转去 go turning around (2-1)

zhuàng 撞 bump into (24-2)

zhuō 桌 table; (for banquets) (8-1, 8-1R)

zhuōzi 桌子 table (8-1R)

zì 自 self; from (8-2R)

zìdiǎn 字典 dictionary (3-2)

zìjǐ 自己 oneself (8-2, 8-2R)

zìxíngchē 自行车 bicycle (24-2)

zìyóu 自由 freedom; be free (8-2R)

zǒng 总 collect, sum up; always (4-2R)

zǒnggòng 总共 altogether, in all (4-2, 4-2R)

zǒngjīnglǐ 总经理 general manager (20-2R)

zǒnglǐngshì 总领事 consul general (14-1R)

zǒnglǐngshìguǎn 总领事馆 consulate general (14-1R)

zǒngshi 总是 always (15-1)

zū 租 rent (14-1)

zūchuqu 租出去 rent out (14-1)

zú 足 foot; enough (22-1R)

zúqiú 足球 soccer (22-1, 22-1R)

zúqiú duì 足球队 soccer team (22-1R)

zúqiú shè 足球社 soccer club (22-1R)

zúqiúsài 足球赛 soccer competition (22-1)

zuì 醉 become drunk (9-2)

zuì'ài 最爱 favorite (12-1R)

zuìhǎo 最好 it would be best (14-1)

zuǒshǒu 左手 left hand (2-1, 2-1R)

zuǒshǒubiān 左手边 left-hand side (2-1), 2-1R)

zuǒyǎn 左眼 left eye (18-1R)

zuò 做 do; make (8-1R)

zuò 坐 sit in/on; take; by (1-1)

zuò mǎimài 做买卖 do business (8-1R)

zuòcài 做菜 cook, make food (8-1R)

zuòdōng 做东 serve as host (11-1)

zuòfǎ 做法 way of doing something (3-1R)

zuòfàn 做饭 cook, make food (8-1, 8-1R)

zuòmèng 做梦 have a dream (1-2)

zuòshì 做事 do things, work (8-1R)

zuòyè 作业 homework (3-1R)

zuòzhě 作者 author, writer (1-2R)